The publisher gratefully acknowledges the
generous contributions to this book provided by
the Simpson Humanities Endowment Fund of the
University of California Press Foundation
and by Yoko Ono Lennon.

Thing of
Beauty

Jackson Mac Low

Thing of Beauty

New and Selected Works

Edited by Anne Tardos

University of California Press

Berkeley Los Angeles London

University of California Press, one of the most distinguished
university presses in the United States, enriches lives around
the world by advancing scholarship in the humanities, social
sciences, and natural sciences. Its activities are supported by
the UC Press Foundation and by philanthropic contributions
from individuals and institutions. For more information, visit
www.ucpress.edu.

University of California Press
Berkeley and Los Angeles, California

University of California Press, Ltd.
London, England

For acknowledgments of permission for previously published
poems, please see credits, p. 449.

Library of Congress Cataloging-in-Publication Data

Mac Low, Jackson.
    Thing of beauty : new and selected works / Jackson Mac
Low ; edited by Anne Tardos.
        p.   cm.
    Includes bibliographical references and index.
    ISBN 978-0-520-24936-3 (alk. paper)
    1. Experimental poetry.   2. Performance art—Texts.
    I. Tardos, Anne.   II. Title.

PS3563.A31875T45   2008
811'.54—dc22   2007026357

Manufactured in the United States of America
16   15   14   13   12   11   10   09   08
10   9   8   7   6   5   4   3   2   1

This book is printed on New Leaf EcoBook 50, a 100% recycled
fiber of which 50% is de-inked post-consumer waste, processed
chlorine-free. EcoBook 50 is acid-free and meets the minimum
requirements of ANSI/ASTM D5634-01 *(Permanence of Paper)*.

Contents

* Previously unpublished.

Selections from *Asymmetries 1–260* and Later Asymmetries
(1960–61)

Selections from HSC and HSCH

Waldoboro Poems*

Foreword

I met Jackson in 1975, when mutual friends introduced us. Jackson had just moved from the Bronx to a loft in Washington Market, the part of lower Manhattan now known as Tribeca, the same loft from which I write these words, a few months after his death. This is where Jackson and I spent 26 years together: writing, creating paintings and collages, traveling, participating in festivals, recording radio plays, and performing in our own, each other's, and our joint works. Jackson was a major influence on my work and on my life, and even during his painful last years, our life was cheerful and happy.

I call this book *Thing of Beauty* after Jackson's first antiwar poem and because I consider his work exactly that—a thing of beauty. While the poem of that title he wrote at 15 made clear a reference to Keats, I am not doing so directly, nor am I saying that the most outstanding feature of Jackson's work was lyrical beauty. I am pointing to his distinct concern with the value of beauty in art, and though he rarely wrote about it, we had innumerable conversations on the subject. It was not until late in his life that he finally spelled out his preoccupation with beauty in art, in the instructions he wrote for the musicians interpreting one of his compositions:

> I intend that pieces such as this one should give full scope to the imagination, initiative, and sense of beauty of each of the performers. I ask them to be co-composers with me in making use of the musical materials I give, within the loosely defined limits I propose, to make a complexly beautiful object existing in time.
>
> The beauty of it is "complex" in that it will incorporate the results of decisions that may often be "imperfect." The many forces at work within the individuals and the community of performers and the environment in which they make and implement their decisions will only flickeringly bring about moments of beauty.

For beauty is not the only value embodied in these acts of communal composition. The senses of beauty of the composer-performers will inevitably differ, even sometimes conflict, and will be expressed differently. The decisions made by others than the "instigating composer" are not controlled by him. He asks only for certain qualities of good will and intense mutual attention to all the sounds audible as well as to all the composer-performers.

He values freedom—everybody's freedom within this composer-performer community. He is neither the dictator nor (when he participates in the ensemble) the primary soloist. He is willing to risk that moments will occur in performances that he will not perceive as beautiful.

Often such moments will embody other values than beauty, such as energetic initiative or imaginativeness, but the consequences of freedom— as vaguely as it may be defined—are sure not to accord at times with the senses of beauty of all members of any particular community of composer-performers, much less those of every member of its community of hearers. This is a risk I am deliberately taking.[1]

In many other performance instructions Jackson asked for this "good will" on the part of the performers, and only late in life did he get as specific as asking for beauty. He had an uncanny ability to see beauty in virtually everything that was not vulgar. Some perceive Jackson's work as being about consciously disregarding aesthetic values, at least during the periods when he was working with systematic chance operations; however, this is a simplistic take on what he was doing, and it overlooks both the constants and the fundamental changes in his attitudes and ways of working over the years. One constant during his life was his love of, and striving for, beauty. His intermittent work with nonintentional and indeterminate methods, such as chance operations, never precluded or interfered with his attention to beauty, even when he was looking to free himself from allowing individual taste and other artistic value judgments to interfere with the results. In his work, beauty was always present.

1. From Instructions for "Music for Gathas in Memory of Armand Schwerner" (1999), part of a work entitled "Four Vocabulary Gathas *in Memoriam* Armand Schwerner," a piece we wrote collaboratively, but to which Jackson later added a musical score. I did not include the piece in this book, since it is featured prominently in a recent book of Jackson's performance works, *Doings: Assorted Performance Pieces, 1955–2002* (New York: Granary Books, 2005), wherein an excerpt of the music notation also appears, albeit without these instructions from which I quote.

In the following outline of the history of Jackson's work I rely not only on reconstructing my own experiences with Jackson and our many conversations, but also on quoting and adapting talks he gave and papers he wrote toward the end of his life, in which he continually reformulated his view of the progression of his life's work. In writing the introductions to individual poems and groups of poems in this book, I have also relied heavily on Jackson's own descriptions and terminology. In addition, I've included his essay "Poetry and Pleasure" as the "author's introduction" to this book. Jackson worked on this essay from 1999 to 2002, and I think it helps open up the world revealed in this book.

From 1937 to 1954, Jackson wrote many poems, most of which were written in ways then generally considered "traditional." At first he wrote free verse, but in 1939 he began writing metrical verse, both rhymed and unrhymed, as well as prose. Until 1954 and occasionally thereafter, until his death in December 2004, Jackson continued to write both free and metrical verse. Late in 1954 he began devising and using "systematic" methods in composing both verbal works and musical and performance works. His first such methods involved various kinds of chance operations, and the first work he wrote this way was "5 biblical poems" (the "2nd biblical poem" is included in this book).

In using chance operations, Jackson was not concerned (at that time or later) with getting results that would be "interesting" or "about" anything specific; rather, he used them to make works that were (to the greatest extent possible) free of his own individual taste, memories, and psychology, including any artistic and literary traditions that might otherwise have influenced his process of composition.

Jackson's motivation for writing verbal works and composing music in these more "impersonal" ways came from an interpretation of Zen Buddhism that led him and various other artists of the 1950s and 1960s and later to try making artworks that were minimally egoic. In a talk he gave in Tucson in 2001, he said that he and these other writers and composers

tried to make artworks with as little intervention as possible from the individual ego. We considered the ego a formation that stood in the way of one's perceiving "reality as such." The use of chance operations seemed at the time a good way to minimize egoic motivations. The definition of the term "ego" implicit in this case was that of Zen Buddhism, not that of Freudian psychology. It included all the Freudian "institutions of the psyche"—id, ego, and superego—all "layers of the mind," conscious, liminal, and unconscious. To use a Zen Buddhist term, I was attempting to write and to make other kinds of audible and visible artworks "from the No-Mind."

It was only later, after years of studying and irregularly practicing Buddhism, as well as years of utilizing such artmaking methods, that I realized that using those methods is as egoic as other ways of making artworks—that, in short, there are no shortcuts to "enlightenment."

Moreover, while Buddhism enjoins us to lessen the hegemony of the ego in its most widely accepted sense—the dominance of what one experiences as her individual will—it more importantly calls us to realize that the self is ultimately illusory. As the 18th-century Scottish philosopher David Hume observed, we never experience the self but only perceptions. "When I enter most intimately into what I call myself, I always stumble on some particular perception or other," Hume wrote. "I never can catch myself at any time without a perception, and never can observe anything but the perception." But an understanding of the self—even though the term is ultimately meaningless—is only attained by working *through* what each of us thinks of as "my self," not by attempting to evade or abolish it.

However, by the time I realized that the artmaking methods that I'd mistakenly thought were "nonegoic" are not, I had come to value them for their own sake. As often happens, what were conceived and devised as means toward a highly elevated end came to be valued, if not as ends in themselves, as means toward less exalted ends: I liked the kinds of poems and other verbal works and the music that I could make with those methods. So I continued to employ them (though not exclusively) and came eventually to combine them with other artmakingways. Buddhism had led me to them but no longer provided me with justifications or motivations for utilizing them.[2]

Jackson used systematic methods exclusively, including chance operations and "translation methods"—that is, systematically translating the notation of musical works into words and vice versa—from December 1954 until May 1960, when he began devising the two main groups of methods he called "deterministic" (the acrostic and diastic methods, which I describe

2. "A Talk about My Writingways, University of Arizona, Tucson, 24 January 2001." Written in New York, early December 2000–24 January 2001. [unpublished manuscript]

below). Each of these deterministic methods uses two texts—a source text and a seed text—to produce a raw output, which Jackson might then work on in various ways.

In the 1960s, when he first devised deterministic methods, he thought of them as kinds of chance operations. It was only in the early 1990s that he realized that such methods were fundamentally different from chance operations, because deterministic methods do not involve what could rightly be called "chance," unless one makes a mistake. That is, if one applies a deterministic text-selection method multiple times to the same source text and seed text, making no mistakes, the method's output will always be exactly the same. Chance operations are likely to produce a different output each time. Nevertheless, even though deterministic methods don't involve chance, you cannot predict their output.

Jackson offered this explanation of the reasons behind his use of deterministic methods:

> I felt these ways of working allowed me to lessen dependence on the illusory ego and let "the rest of the world" enter into the works. Especially, I wanted to allow linguistic units "to speak for themselves," that is, without having to express an ego—its likes, opinions, transitory emotions, and so on. In short, I tried "to evade the ego"—let reality speak rather than this illusory person.[3]

Later, he came to realize that neither chance operations nor deterministic methods are truly nonegoic. We often talked about the fact that even when he used a nonegoic system, he was still consciously choosing the verbal materials (e.g., the source and seed texts used in some deterministic methods); thus, his conscious mind and personal tastes were inevitably involved in the compositional process, as when his pacifist anarchism and other political convictions become evident even in works made using systematic methods.

Despite the realization that neither chance operations nor deterministic methods used in artmaking are nonegoic, the *illusion* that they were

3. "Person, Personae, Look on the Page, Orality and 'Voice,' or, Living as a Verbal Artist as a Person." Talk written for presentation at Naropa Institute, Boulder, Colorado, in July 1994, and subsequently revised. [unpublished manuscript]

motivated him and justified their continued use. (Actually, he rarely employed chance operations alone after April 1960, though he did continue to use them as auxiliary methods.)

As we can see in the selections from *Stanzas for Iris Lezak* and *Asymmetries,* his first deterministic text-selection method was an "acrostic reading-through text selection," which was the principal method he used when making poems and other verbal works from May 1960 to January 1963. In using this and related methods, he would read through a source text to find, successively, words and/or other verbal units—word fragments, phrases, other sentence parts, or even whole sentences—that have the successive letters of the words of a seed text as their first letters. For example, he might have spelled the word *cats* acrostically by finding, as he read through the poem's source text, the words "Castrated Animals Tire Soon." The verbal units he selected were chosen deliberately or by chance operations or by some other impersonal method at the beginning of each poem's composition. He often used the title of the source text as the seed text for the poem that was being written.

In early January 1963, Jackson devised and began using the deterministic methods that he called "diastic reading-through text-selection methods." Here, as with acrostic methods, he used a seed text to select from a source text the words (or other linguistic units) that became the method's raw output. However, in using diastic methods, he would spell *through* the seed text in words (or other linguistic units) that he would come across as he read through the source text. That is, he would select words or other linguistic units with the letters of the seed text in the positions that they occupy in the seed text. For example, he might have spelled through the word *word* by selecting "White gOats agReeably heeD." (After 1989, he employed a computer program—written for him by the poet and critic Charles O. Hartman—that automated this diastic method.)

Jackson didn't always use diastic methods in completely straightforward ways. For instance, the poems in *The Pronouns* (1964) were made by a modified diastic method that involved selecting words or phrases with an "ing" (e.g., "being" or "making something") that he had written on index cards, which then functioned as the source text. Each card had one to five such words or phrases written on it, and Jackson would incorporate each word or phrase into a sentence, along with adverbs of time. Each of the forty poems in *The Pronouns* comprises a connected group of instructions for dancers or other performance artists.

He wrote *Words nd Ends from Ez* (1981–83) by reading through Ezra Pound's *Cantos* and finding words and ends of words (ranging from all except the first letter of a word to only its last letter) by means of a diastic method in which the name "Ezra Pound" was the seed text.

Most of his verbal works from the 1980s were written either by diastic methods or by methods involving "liminal decisions"—selecting thoughts on the threshold between consciousness and the unconscious or not quite conscious, what he often termed "direct writing" or "intuitive composition." From 1981 to 1989 he alternated between these two methods.

The 100 poems in *Twenties* (1989–90) were made by gathering words, phrases, and other linguistic material from his inner and outer environments—he frequently wrote original drafts while traveling, at concerts, and otherwise away from home, which he would later revise at home. He would put this environmental material into a simple verse form, each poem consisting of five unrhymed quatrains with lines of varying lengths. He termed such loose constraints on form "fuzzy verse."

From November 1990 through early 1995, he wrote the first drafts of his 154 Forties using the same method he used to write the *Twenties:* gathering words, phrases, and sometimes whole sentences that he saw, heard, or thought of as he wrote. He used no other method in making these "fuzzy verse" poems, each of which consists of eight five-line stanzas where the first three lines are rather long, the fourth line is very long, and the last line is short.

In April 1998, he began writing his Stein series, poems based on texts by Gertrude Stein, which he finished (except for some later revisions) on Christmas Day 2000. The series includes 161 poems, most of them two to four pages long, but some much longer (the longest is 55 pages). Of these poems, Jackson says:

> The way I wrote making the Steinpoems permitted me to use all of my writingways, or just a few of them, as I preferred. It also allowed me to intervene in the makingprocess more flexibly than when I only selected source and seed texts (personally or methodically) and ran them through the diastic word-selection process without altering its output in any significant way.

Though the whole makingprocess starts out with someone else's work and a deterministic method (which may be preceded by auxiliary chance operations), this combination of writingways allows me "to engage with contingency" rather than simply "to accept the results of contingency"—as I did before and during the 1980s at those times when I composed verbal and musical works by means of chance operations and/or deterministic methods.[4]

In 2001, Jackson began making poems using combinations of ways similar to those he had used to write the Stein series, but using sources and seeds by authors in addition to Gertrude Stein. In the HSC and HSCH series, for example, as in the Stein series, Jackson used a text-selection method to gather a vocabulary of words and phrases that he then worked into their final shape.

The three parts of this book reflect Jackson's three major "writingways." Part I includes work from 1937 to 1954 and is the shortest section of the book, not because I consider the works from that period less important than his later works, but because that was Jackson's own preference—he was actively involved in the planning of this book up until his final days. As he says in his introduction to *Representative Works: 1938–1985,* which also emphasizes work created after 1954:

> Readers will quickly discover [that] the years since 1954 are much better represented than those before. This isn't because I think badly of my earlier work. I can imagine a fairly substantial *Selected Earlier Works*. But with the "5 biblical poems," begun in December 1954, I started producing poems and performance pieces markedly different from both my own previous works and those of other verbal artists.
>
> Why did I begin at that time composing poems, musical works, group performance works ("simultaneities"), and plays by means of chance operations? Why did I begin to *view performance* as central and texts as primarily notations for performance (if only by a silent reader)? Why did my work begin to include silences longer than those occasioned by punctuation marks (sometimes *much* longer) as well as indeterminate features (ones realized differently at each performance)?
>
> Certainly, no one—least of all [John] Cage—tried *to persuade* me to

4. "A Talk about My Writingways."

change my ways. And when I first encountered aleatoric methods, I felt strong reservations about them, which I openly expressed. Nevertheless, not much later, I found myself employing systematic-chance methods of my own—and composing both determinate and indeterminate works with them—with great pleasure and gusto. The explanation, if any, must be sought not only in the realm of my artistic activities, but in the wider sphere of my life in general.[5]

Part II, covering the period from December 1954 to March 1979, begins with one of the "5 biblical poems" and includes selections from published volumes and from such previously uncollected works as the later asymmetries and miscellaneous pieces that were not part of any series. The works in this part, as in the book as a whole, appear in roughly chronological order, except for the selection of Light Poems, which were written intermittently over several decades but are presented here as a group.

As we've already seen, there were never any hard-edged transitions in Jackson's ways of working. Even as he wrote poetry by means of wholly or partially nonintentional methods involving chance operations and deterministic methods, he also continued to write traditional verse, as in the Odes for Iris (1971), a book-length series of highly personal poems. I've included many lesser-known poems in the deliberately large selection from this work.

Jackson was also a prolific visual artist, and I have included a few drawings and photographs, but I've kept these to a minimum because the emphasis here is on his poetry. (Many of his visual performance scores were recently published in *Doings: Assorted Performance Pieces, 1955–2002.*)

Part III covers the period from September 1979, when he created the room-sized poetry environment "A Vocabulary for Annie Brigitte Gilles Tardos," to September 2004. The early 1980s marked another turning point in Jackson's work, one that, like the turning point in late 1954, is undoubtedly associated with the wider sphere of his life in general. During this period, as I've already mentioned, he moved away from nonintentional and systematic writing and returned to free writing and intuitive composition. (Even though the French Sonnets were written mainly in the early 1980s, I placed them in Part II, because they were composed entirely us-

5. Jackson Mac Low, *Representative Works: 1938–1985* (New York: Roof Books, 1986), xv.

ing systematic methods.) In his 1985 introduction to *Representative Works,* Jackson wrote:

> I feel sympathy for my self of the middle 1950s, since in the 1980s other changes have been happening in and to me. I find myself questioning all my beliefs and ways of working—*questioning though not rejecting* [emphasis added]. Some beliefs, such as my opposition to warfare, interpersonal and interspecific violence, exploitation, and authority depending on violence, are stronger than ever. About others I have reservations of varying intensity.
>
> Without rejecting compositional methods followed over a quarter century, I am exploring new ways as well as reexamining older ones. I am, for instance, much more interested in texts per se—works primarily for readers, though they can also be read aloud or performed—and in works written or composed directly (sometimes spontaneously), rather than by means of chance operations.[6]

In 2002, Jackson wrote in an unsent letter to a friend: "The first thing you (& everyone else) should know about me, my works, and my ways, & how I think about them now is that all of them are always changing. But, also, that I've never repudiated any work I've written, composed, or painted (or otherwise made for visual reception)."

A year earlier, he said on the subject of not using nonintentional methods exclusively:

> I didn't feel there was "anything wrong" in expressing my opinions or emotions or perceptions. Merely that the attempt to produce determinate and indeterminate literary works by nonintentional methods was both worthwhile in itself and consonant with Buddhist insights about the world and the person.
>
> But I never stood in one place. In 1960 I began to allow performers' choices to determine significant features of performances of nonintentionally composed verbal and musical scores as well as of ones intentionally composed. In short, I allowed what some Buddhist teachers call "the conventional ego" to interact with what was determined nonintentionality.
>
> . . . I write and compose both "directly" and "indirectly," but I truly believe that the works I now write directly [e.g., the Forties] are less suffused and determined by the conventional ego than they would have been had I

6. Ibid., xvi.

not—for several decades—written and composed primarily by noninten-tional methods.[7]

In Part III, I have included a large number of poems from the 154 For-ties, previously collected only in small groups and many appearing here for the first time. The Forties were written freely and without the use of any system or method other than a predetermined verse format. They re-veal the inner workings of Jackson's mind and his encyclopedic knowledge as no other works do.

Selecting from the voluminous Forties and the even more voluminous Stein series was the greatest challenge in putting this book together. Nei-ther of these two book-length series has been collected, although many ap-peared in magazines. Their substantial representation here along with Jackson's other later works, such as selections from the books *Pieces o' Six* and *From Pearl Harbor Day to FDR's Birthday,* is intended to extend the momentum of *Representative Works,* the last "new & selected," which was published in 1986.

Many of Jackson's introductions, endnotes, and descriptions appear throughout this book, which makes for a certain amount of redundancy, but Jackson favored redundancy, and more importantly, the notes are in-trinsic to the poems—in some cases, they are longer than the poems them-selves. In a sense, some of these notes are themselves poetry.

As a lifelong Buddhist, who understood that in order to live life fully it's necessary to embrace one's death, Jackson was on intimate terms with his own death, as we can see from many poems, most notably the 1958 poem "Sonnet of My Death," which ends with the lines:

My death arises through the limbs like vine
and nuzzles silently the heart and tongue;
it rubs against the brain and through the eyes
it gazes like a wistful dog whose one
communication is to lick and touch
and claim the body I do not call mine.

7. "A Talk about My Writingways."

During the final months of his life, when we were both quite conscious of the upcoming and sadly inevitable event, I kept coming across one of his very last poems lying around the house, entitled "It Will Glow Unseen Until It Doesn't" (HSCH 1). It was one of his many ways of saying good-bye.

I have often thought of Jackson as an alchemist, who could, as if by magic, transmute simple verbal, musical, and visual elements into things precious and solid. I am grateful to him for all the beauty and strength he brought into my life and into the world we inhabit.

—Anne Tardos, 2006

Poetry and Pleasure

JACKSON MAC LOW

for Anne Tardos

It often seems to me that the whole point of art is pleasure—the pleasure of making artworks and the pleasure of experiencing them.

"Whole point" is both an overstatement and ambiguous. I wished to bring back to attention the fact that people make artworks both because doing so is pleasurable and in order to cause pleasure to others. There are also other notable reasons for doing so. The primary reason for making an artwork is to bring it into being. All others—even pleasure—are subsidiary to that.

There are many kinds of art—probably more kinds today than ever before. This may be because many more kinds of pleasure are admissible and admitted today than formerly. Some artists and art-experiencers gain simple pleasures from simple artworks. Others experience complex pleasures from complex artworks. But then, some obtain complex pleasures from simple artworks or simple pleasures from complex artworks. People are widely various. It follows that artworks are also. This variety is in itself one of the positive pleasure-giving aspects of living in a society where many kinds of people and many kinds of pleasure and many kinds of artworks are admissible and admitted.

It is probably a paradox that this can happen in a society in which many people and actions of people cause many kinds of pain—often kinds of pain that do not come about necessarily, as from diseases and injuries that cannot be avoided. The kinds of pain that people suffer in present-day societies are often due to clumsy social, economic, and political arrangements that simply need not be so clumsy, so slovenly. Some of them are the result of—and help to further the ends of—overweening impulses and desires. Many others are due to the infrastructures that bulwark present-

An earlier version of this essay was posted on the Internet in 1999.—A.T.

day political, economic, social, and psychological systems. Now, the most glaring of all of these are the current wars and their results. So now more than ever there is a pressing prevailing need to change these arrangements and to prevent warfare and other causes of unnecessary suffering.

So many artists and experiencers of art believe that the point of art is to change these slovenly, pain-causing—and boredom-causing—arrangements. I do not think this "point" is at odds with pleasure. Artworks that cause pleasure can also—just because they give pleasure and because of the kinds of pleasure they give—cause shifts in social and economic arrangements, sometimes subtle shifts that may be partially caused by changes in the ways the materials of the arts are used and shaped. However, this is seldom something that can be aimed at directly. It is of course untrue that artworks "make nothing happen." But what they may make happen is never really predictable. This is why most agitprop artworks are such dismal failures, both as art and as social sanitation.

I refer, of course, to W. H. Auden's saying, in the second part of his poem "In Memory of W. B. Yeats" (February 1939) that "poetry makes nothing happen: it survives / In the valley of its making where executives / Would never want to tamper; . . . / . . . it survives, / A way of happening, a mouth." This followed a period in the early 1930s when Auden, like a myriad of other idealistic people, was a "communist sympathizer" with no knowledge of the millions killed in the Soviet Union during the forced collectivization and murder of well-to-do peasants (1929–33) or of the Great Terror begun with the murder of Sergei Kirov, and the ensuing Moscow Trials (1936–38). (He was certainly no "Stalinist.") When he went to Spain, for seven weeks in early 1937 to become an ambulance driver for the Loyalists, but was put briefly to writing propaganda instead, he was shocked to find the churches in Barcelona closed. Though he had rejected the church, he found that the existence of churches and what happened in them were important to him. He supported the Loyalist government because he realized that if fascism spread worldwide, it would make life and work impossible for most artists and for everyone who cared for justice, liberty, and culture, but his poem "Spain" (April 1937) is much less committed than it seemed when he wrote it. By the end of that year he seems largely to have rejected political solutions to the current political, economic, and social horrors of which he was all too strongly aware.

However, artworks *do* make things happen, at the very least, pleasure and pain. And the kinds of pleasures and pains they may cause are hardly ever predictable. (Thus Horace's never-followed admonition against arguing about tastes has more than a little justification.) The politically aware artist can hope that what gives her pleasure and what gives her pain will give others the kinds of pleasures and pains that may help engender more positive social arrangements. The point is still ultimately pleasure.

The classic example is tragedy, which first causes pain by arousing pity and terror and then, by ridding one of those feelings, leads to kinds of pleasure that would not have been experienced otherwise. (Also, some works may first cause boredom but ultimately, for those who "stick with them," pleasure.)

Verbal art, of which poetry is considered the prime exemplar (why, I don't know), is often thought to have a worthier end than "mere pleasure." Both that and pleasure itself are thought to be caused by either the matter or the form of the work. In the latter case the writer may be castigated as "formalist." The "form" of the work is thought to be the "point" of it and nothing more. Traditionally, this castigation has pointed toward a lack in the work's "content." It may be damned as trivial or somehow wrong or absent, for instance.

What seems strange is that a poet is seldom condemned as "materialist." Seldom is she jumped on because she takes too much care with, or delights too much in, her words themselves—the materials of her art—or the way they relate with each other. But perhaps this does not happen all that seldom! Think of Emily Dickinson, Gertrude Stein, and James Joyce. Their "materialist" works have been endlessly condemned—usually for qualities extraneous to the nature of their materials (except possibly in the case of Joyce, whose very materials—his words and/or the situations they bring to mind—have often been condemned as pornographic or scatological). Often a concentration on the materials of artworks rather than on their "content" has itself been considered "formalist."

The kinds of pleasure that poems may bring about are as various as the kinds of pleasure that poets may take in making them. (This is of course true also of the kinds of pain they may cause.) The reason why some poets delight in making poems in other ways—otherwise—than others do could be that they feel a need for other pleasures than those they've experienced from poems hitherto. This doesn't at all mean that they need reject the poems of others—past writers or those writing presently but not "otherwise"—or the pleasures those poems may cause. (Unfortunately, many who write in more usual ways feel that "otherwise" works are attacks upon them and their own works. Those who strongly favor the coexistence of both usual and "otherwise" works get it from both sides.) It isn't even that some people "just delight in novelty." Some writers (and other artists) often delight in being surprised by what they make.

For more years than I care to remember I've often made verbal and other artworks by methods that insure that I will not always be in control of what comes into the works. (So what comes in may justly be said to be, to some significant degree, "unpredictable.") One group among many methods of this kind is what John Cage called "chance operations," which he first utilized in making music in the early '50s and began in the late '60s to use in making verbal works. Because of the fact that chance is associated with dice, works made by chance operations are often called "aleatory." This term may be appropriate for some kinds of chance-operational methods, such as the ones I devised and used most often between winter 1954 and spring 1960. However, it is quite inappropriate for other methods that also lead to unpredictable results that may surprise the artists as much as other experiencers.

A number of such methods that I've used since 1960 may justly be called "deterministic": what happens when they are utilized is not a matter of chance if one uses them without making mistakes. (I sometimes made some mistakes of this kind before my methods were automated as computer programs—and sometimes I still do so when I use unautomated methods—so chance may creep in willy-nilly.)

Two groups of deterministic methods that I've often utilized make use of two texts—a source text and a seed text. (Either text may have been written by the writer herself or by others.) Unlike chance operations, their outputs, when they're used correctly with the same source and seed texts, will always be the same. In one group the writer reads through a source text and finds successively words, phrases, sentence fragments, sentences, and/or other linguistic units that have the letters of the seed text as their initial letters. This group is called "*acrostic* reading-through text-selection methods." I devised and used some of these methods most often, but not exclusively, from May 1960 to January 1963, and occasionally since then.

The other group of deterministic methods that make use of both source and seed texts are called "*diastic* reading-through text-selection methods." I first devised and utilized some of these methods in 1963. In using them, the writer (or her digitized surrogate) reads through the source text and successively finds words or other linguistic units that have the letters of the seed text in positions that correspond to those they occupy in the seed text. (The neologism "diastic" was coined on analogy with "acrostic" from the Greek words *dia,* through, and *stichos,* line. The writer "spells through" the seed text when she "spells it out" in linguistic units successively drawn from the source text which have the letters of the seed text in corresponding positions.)

Another group of deterministic methods, which I began using while writing my first chance-operationally composed works, "5 biblical poems," at the end of 1954 and the beginning of 1955, are ones in using which the writer "translates" the notes, rests, and/or other features of the notation of a musical work "into" words from some source text by either the writer or others. (As a composer I've sometimes used the opposite method of "translating" the letters and spaces of a verbal text into musical notation.)

Often all such methods—chance operations, deterministic methods, and others—are spilled into an indiscriminate bin labeled "Methods." (I avoid this term because it is all too redolent of surgery.) And all of them—along with quite different kinds of works—are often dubbed "aleatory" or "aleatoric." (This is especially true in music, where works that involve various degrees and kinds of *choice* on the part of performers—including many kinds of improvisation—are nevertheless called "aleatoric" because the composer herself has not made all the choices!) Everything in the bin may be tainted with a contempt or dislike that may arise from the fact that the artwork is thought *not* to be entirely the work of the individual artist. Whatever may come into it may not be the result of choices—on whatever level—of the artist. The dislike may arise from a kind of despair or fear that the "self"—the "subject"—is being intrinsically denigrated.

Indeed, these methods and others first arose from an attempt to lessen (or even vainly to try to do away with) the hegemony of the ego of the artist in the making of the artwork. This attempt first sprang from Buddhist considerations. Ultimately, the ego in the largest sense (in Zen and other Buddhist psychologies the ego includes all of the parts of the individual psyche, including all three of the Freudian "institutions" of the psyche, the ego, the id, and the superego—and in fact, the entire individual self) is considered to be a kind of temporary illusion consisting of five continually changing "baskets" of sensations, impulses, perceptions, emotions, and thoughts—to simplify the matter grossly. They stand in the way of a perception of reality that is somehow selfless.

What happened to me in the course of using such methods for several decades was that I realized that these methods, too, and the actions of utilizing them, are products of the ego, that the ego is inescapable except possibly when one reaches a clear and egoless state of open perception of reality. It was always obvious that I had not reached such a state, and it seems all too probable that I'll never reach it. Nevertheless, I came to find these methods, and the works made with their help, valuable in themselves. Things happen while using the methods—valuable things—that probably could not have come about without them.

In making "simultaneities"—poems and other verbal, verbal-musical, and musical works (as well as some involving actions and/or visual components) for groups of two or more persons in which the performers make choices among the verbal materials and/or nonverbal sounds that are given as "parts of the pieces"—I came, I still think rightly, to believe that I was making works that have a directly political value. The community made up of the performers is a model of a society that has certain characteristics that I would like to see abound in the wider society: the individual performers exercise initiative and choice at all points during the piece but are also—by listening intensely and responding to all they hear, both other performers' and ambient sounds both within and outside of the performance space— constructing an aural situation that is not merely a mixture of results of egoic impulses, but an aural construction that has a being of its own.

Ultimately, artmaking, including the making of poems, seems to me to be primarily the making of "objects" that are valuable in themselves. One can supplement this "in themselves" in many directions with various "becauses." The most obvious one is what I started with: pleasure. Artworks are valuable both in themselves and because they cause pleasure—kinds of pleasure not usually available from other sources. And "otherwise" artworks are valuable because they bring about new kinds of pleasure.

Social "becauses" abound: new kinds of poems, for instance, may change the ways people use and perceive language. The late Paul Connolly, following Richard Rorty, said (as quoted in the flyer for the conference on poetry and pedagogy at Bard College in 1999) that speaking differently changes a culture and that different ways of speaking are most prevalent in poetry. This may well be true, but what guarantees that speaking differently will change our culture in ways we would find desirable?

Because I now find all writingways (and other artmakingways) valuable, I've pursued two main ways of writing during the 1990s and early 2000s. Both of them are deeply involved with contingency, but differently than my writings were before 1990.

From October 1990 to early 1995 I wrote the first drafts of the poem series 154 Forties, and before and since 1995 I've been revising them. I made the Forties by "gathering" words, phrases, etc., from my outer and inner environments, i.e., from whatever I happened to be hearing, seeing, *or thinking of* while writing their first drafts, and revising them afterwards. Each poem comprises eight five-line stanzas which have the "fuzzy verse form" of three moderately long lines followed by one very long line, and then a short line.

Although I revised the Forties' words in several ways, what I changed most were "caesural silences" and neologistic compounds. The former are notated as spaces of several different lengths within verse lines, which signify different durations of silence. Each of the latter link together two or more words and they are of two kinds, "normal" and "slowed-down" compounds, the former being read somewhat more rapidly than single words, the latter a little more slowly.

However, because I continue to find pleasure in being surprised by what I write, I've currently been pursuing a writingway involving both diastic reading-through text-selection, drawing sequences of single words from a source text, and careful revision of the output of this deterministic method. Prof. Charles O. Hartman of Connecticut College, New London, wrote the program DIASTEXT, a digitization of a form of diastic text selection that uses the whole source text as the seed text (a method that I had devised and discarded in 1963), and sent it to me in June 1989. Later, Prof. Hartman sent me several versions of his program that allow the use of separate source and seed texts.

With the help of DIASTEX5 (1994), I wrote Stein, a series of 161 poems, from April 1998 to the end of 2000 (frequently making revisions after that).

Since 2000 I've been I've been pursuing this writingway while using other sources, such as poems by Keats, Gerard Manley Hopkins, and Rosmarie and Keith Waldrop and prose by the philosopher Charles Hartshorne.

Recently I've realized that Charles Hartman, by sending me these programs, "gave me permission" (as Robert Duncan would have said) to combine a "deterministic" method of text selection, whose source and/or seed texts might be determined by "nonintentional" methods and whose output is unpredictable, with the free composition of poems, within specific constraints. This happened because reading through the source text to find the output words—the most labor-intensive part of reading-through text selection—had been automated and become almost instantaneous. Since I'd come to realize that so-called nonintentional methods of composition were no more Buddhist than other ways of making artworks (because they too are egoic), there was no reason not to combine all my writingways as I usually do now.

In writing Stein, I sometimes utilized random-digit chance operations, numerological operations, or other means to locate the page numbers of source texts and seed texts by Gertrude Stein in *A Stein Reader*, ed. Ulla E. Dydo (Evanston, IL: Northwestern University Press, 1993), a collection in making which the editor had recourse to the texts' earliest manuscripts and typescripts. In making later poems in Stein, I sometimes used such methods to locate "seed texts" in Stein's *Tender Buttons* to use with the whole book as source text. I usually revised the output of this automated "deterministic" method, but occasionally I chose to accept the minimally revised "raw output" of the program as a poem. I haven't yet done so when making poems by diastic text selection and revisionary composition of this output from other sources and seeds by other authors than Gertrude Stein.

To articulate the poems in strophes, I've often made use of a number sequence derived from an algebraic sequence that the French mathematician Edouard Lucas devised to test for Mersenne prime numbers and published in 1880.[1] This sequence—1, 3, 4, 7, 11, 18, 29, etc.—determines the numbers of verse lines (which are often normative sentences) or of typographical lines, in successive strophes of the poems. I've sometimes em-

---

1. A Mersenne prime is a specific type of prime number, named after its inventor, the French monk Marin Mersenne (1588–1648), which must be reducible to the form 2^n -1, where n is a prime number. The 44th Mersenne prime, $2^{32,582,657}$ -1, was found on September 11, 2006.—A.T.

ployed an extension of this sequence that ascends, then descends, then ascends, etc. (e.g., 1, 3, 4, 7, 11, 18, 29, 18, 11, 7, 4, 3, 1, 3, 4, 7, 11, 18, 29, 18, 11, 7, etc.). Alternately, I've sometimes used the sequence of whole numbers (1, 2, 3, 4, etc.) or that of prime numbers (2, 3, 5, 7, etc.), and sometimes I've found a plausible sequence of numbers of lines, etc., in the paragraphs of an unrevised output.

In short, I make poems such as those in Stein by using the outputs of a digitized method as raw materials for free composition within specific constraints. The most important constraint is to use the root morphemes of all the nouns, verbs, adjectives, and adverbs in the output to make the lines of the poems. "Helping words"—structure words such as prepositions and conjunctions, but also pronouns and forms of "to be," "to do," and "to make"— are freely modified, deleted, or added to. Although in many of these poems the lines are complete normative sentences, in others they're not. Often these verse lines are such that the reader or hearer must exercise initiative and imagination to find or make these sentence sequences meaningful. When I modify the output minimally, so that all or most of the words retain the forms that the author of the source text (e.g., Stein) gave them, the reader or hearer has to "mine" the individual "sentences" for meanings.

Often the poems I make in these ways surprise me in different ways. How I modify the result of an initial method is often a function of my reaction to it, which I can hardly ever predict. Most of my recent ways of working— which during the 1990s, until I began the Stein series in 1998, hardly ever involved either chance operations or deterministic methods—have several things in common: they are almost always ways in which I *engage with contingency.*

At first I'm in charge, to whatever extent I allow, of what happens when I select the method and source and seed text. In the moment when these are "run through" the digitized method I'm not in charge at all, but from then on I am free to compose the poems (utilizing the root morphemes of lexical words and other words as described above). I am as free to make use of my imagination and acoustic, semantic, and other skills as any poet who commits herself to work within limits such as those imposed by a verse form. Though I "engage with contingency," in doing so, I've determined in each case the boundaries of that contingency. The kinds of poetry made in these ways are hardly "found poetry."

Writing in ways that combine method, contingency, and free composition and the poetry and other work produced by doing so not only surprise me. They often give me pleasure. And I'm glad to say that people I can believe have said that the results of these writingways have also given *them* pleasure.

New York: March, June 1999; March–April 2002

Acknowledgments

Danielle Ben-Veniste has my deeply felt gratitude for her indefatigable assistance in putting this book together. Her understanding and passion for Jackson's work was surpassed only by her diligence and devotion to the project. This book would not be what it is without her contribution in making the final selections and in coordinating the book as a whole.

Lenny Neufeld's editorial contributions were indispensable. My thanks to Laura Cerruti, acquisitions editor of the University of California Press, who encouraged and graciously supported this project every step of the way. Many thanks to senior editor Rachel Berchten and copy editor Ellen F. Smith for their close attention to every detail in this complex book. Personal thanks to Mei-mei Berssenbrugge, Lyn Hejinian, and Joan Retallack for their constant and reliable friendship and support. I am grateful to Thomas Hummel for his selfless assistance. And most of all, thanks to Jerome Rothenberg, who was the primary force behind this book from the very beginning.

I know that Jackson would join me in thanking them all.

Anne Tardos

PART I

1937–1954

Thing of Beauty

It was a thing
Of Beauty;
Small, precious
Not strong nor large,
But beautiful.

She was a thing
Of Beauty;
Slender, graceful
Not strong nor tall,
But beautiful

He was a thing
Of Beauty;
Tall, Manly
Not small nor delicate
Like the other
Beautiful things,
But beautiful.

Came War
Came Slaughter
And Destruction;
Wrought for holy causes—
They said.

Both sides fought
For the Good
Of Mankind
By destroying
The things
Of Beauty

The Small and Precious,
The Slender and Graceful,
The Tall and Manly;
Destroyed,
Transformed by men;
It, to a meaningless
Powder
She, to a shapeless,
Jellylike Mass
Of Matter
He, to a festering,
Limbless,
Decapitated,
Corpse.

The good of Mankind
Was served—
They said.

October 1937

HUNGER STrikE whAt   doeS   lifemean

&

Water and water and water and water
Whater you thinking about
Or are you doing
what areyou doing
Fire in grates are greates
Ingrates in grate
great ingrates in great grate
great grate greasy great grate
grating
g r a v e r l o w
    GRATE
God and god and god and god
G r o d   an d grod in grate
in great ingrate in grate in great grate
Growl great grate
Grin g r o w l i n ggreat grate
Great grown ing grateS
Grod and grod and grod and grod

AND   GROD

G L O W

GLORY GLOW

g l o r y   and   g l or y and g lory andglory

GROUCH

Grow   grouc h
G r o w   and grow and grow andgrow

A n d　　　Grow　　　(grunt)
Great　gracious　grunt
G O　　and go a n D
go　　　go　　g o gogo go
go　　　go go go

Ǧ　　Ŏ　　Ď

Go god go god go
　god　gogoD
　　　　O　　G O D

g ain　g a m e s　gain
　　　　　g a m es
gain　gay　gam e S
g ame　gain games

G o L l Y　god agog agog
gog gog goggog　g o g　gog gog gog

G R O G

G R U C H　g r u c h　gruch
　g r a g　　gr ag　grag

g l u g

And the bathtub went down the drain
Ukraine
Cranium　U k r a i n i u m
　　　　(Uranium)
　You　c r a n i u m　crane
Crane yum you crane
You crane Ukraine
Krake and krake and krake and krake and cake (krake)

G a k e^{gage} cake   gag gag gaggag gaggaggaggag   gag

              g o n g

gog   gog   gawg   gawg   gawg

              goug goug

    <u>G O D</u>   (cod)

Gay cake gotta gay cake go gotta gay cake

gaga gotta gay cake

gong gong gonk

                  God in his mercy is good
                  God in his mercy is good
                  God in his mercy is good
                  God in his mercy is good
                  God in his mercy is good
                  God in his mercy is good
                  God in his mercy is good
                  God in his mercy is good
                  God in his mercy is good
                  God in his mercy is good
                  God in his mercy is good
                  God in his mercy is good
                  God in his mercy is good
                  God in his mercy is good
                  God in his mercy is good
                  God in his mercy is good
                  God in his mercy is good
                  God in his mercy is good
                  God in his mercy is good
                  God in his mercy is good
                  God in his mercy is good
                  God in his mercy is good

God in his mercy is good
God in his mercy is goog
Gog in his mersy iz goog
Gog im fis merky ib goog
Gog ig gis mergy ig goog
Gog ig gig gergy ig goog
Gog ig gig giggy ig goog
Gog gg ggg ggggy gg goog
Gog gg ggg ggggg gg gggg
ggg gg ggg ggggg gg gggg
ggggggggggggggggggggggg

ggggggggggggggggggggggggggggggggggggggggggggggggggggggggggggggggggggggg

ston ston tont tont ston stant stont stint stit
      Hi stonet stont stit
stit stlit stlod stlott stlit stlodstlott
  stloff stlow slow slow slowly
slow   slow   slowbly
    s l a b l y   s l o w ly
  s l o w b l y
    slob blob
blob blob blob
blob   blob blob blos blop
blob blob blobg blog
b r a g b r i m b r a g
b r a g brimming brrraag

      b l o o g l y   blagly

    blagly bloogly
bland   blagly bloogly
     bloogly blong

        Blong

                    Blong
                    Blong

g

G   L   O   S   T   E   rrrrrrrrrrrrrrrr

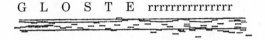

G l a b b e r   glabber glabber
glad to be of service
so glad to be of service
sinfully glad to be of service

              for   his   hit   surface
                    (surflakes)

good guy can't carry cash
              crash
good guy can't carry cash
cood cguy cgan't gary gpash

g la ss   g la ss   g l a ss   g la ss   g la ss
                                   .
                                         (gloss)

                         g   r   o   u   c   h

Can't go
Can't go carry nothing
scant   ko   scary   sluthing

                    s   l   o   p

slinguliar slop

         slaresly   slasely

slap   slap   slap
            slooker

                S

                S   L   A   P
                    SLANK

plap plaster plap psplap

                    prask

                            pony

November 1938
Kenilworth, Ill.

First three pages of original manuscript of "H U N G E R   ST r I kE   wh A t   doeS lifemean," 1938.

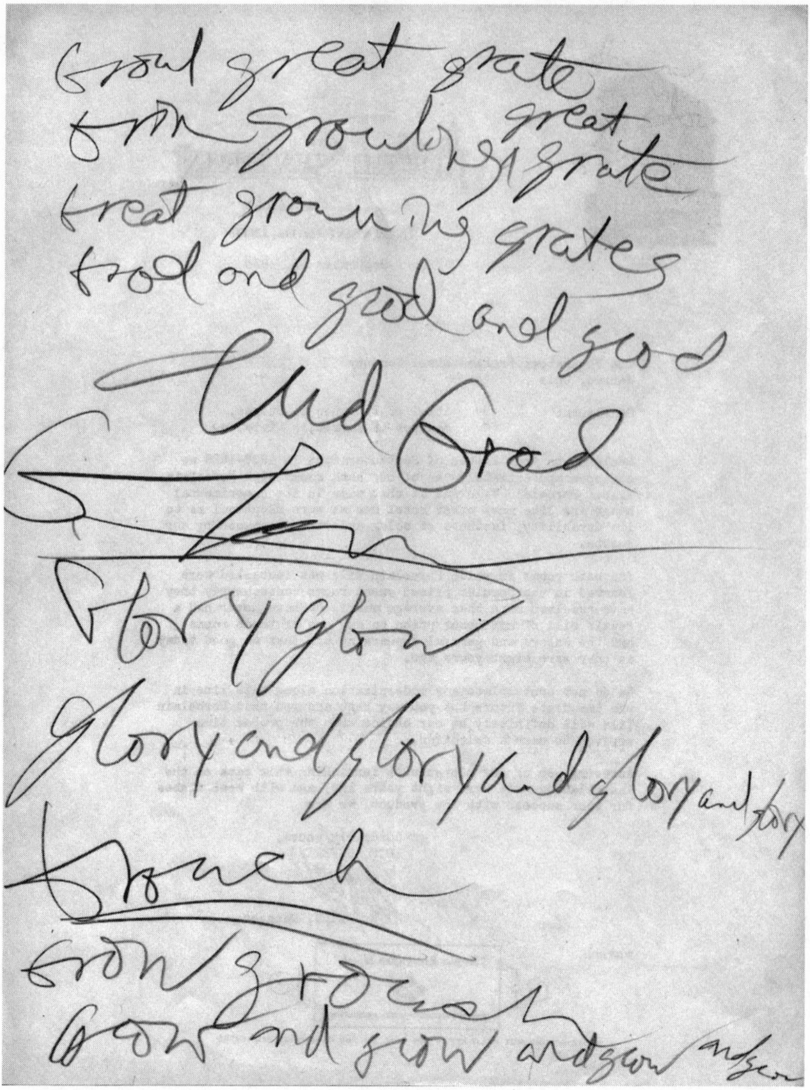

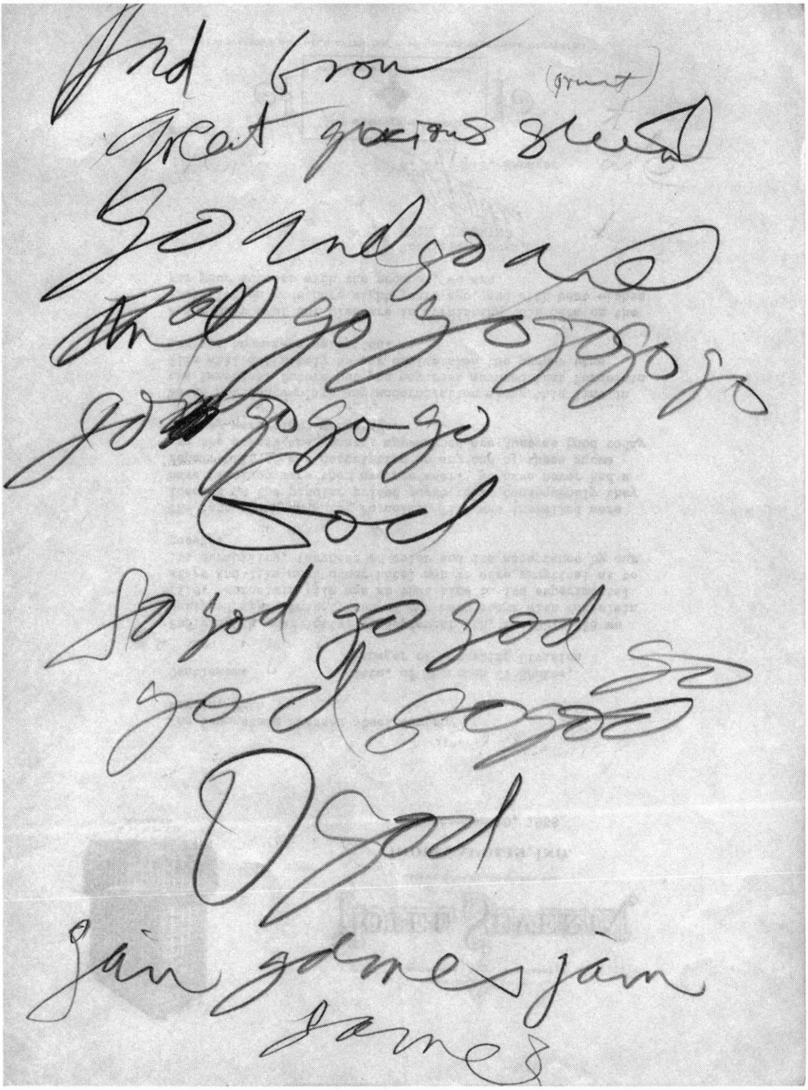

And brown
(grunt)
Great gracious sleed
Go and go a
And go go go go go
go go go go
God
So god go god
god go go
O God
jam games jam
james

Gone-II

They told him to go—
And he went
They told him to kill—
And he killed
They told him to die—
And he died
They don't tell him
Anything
Anymore

28 September 1938

Experiments in Surrealism

* * *

Triumph

Growings lavender specialists
Greatness are silken clavichord

* * *

Rachel

Clever are the asterisks
They do glow
Upon awnings rogent
Classless crumb-spoons

Gravitate fluctuatingly to crashover
        Mildly palpitate
        Crazed is the lounge

* * *

Rhododendron

What shall I do with myself
Shall I twist it to embers

* * *

Paradise

Rainings
Lots of high   gems

1938

Dirge in Days Minor

Days dark but death-pale
Sunlight mocks as cake to a beggar
        Men are short or tall with masks
        Things are short or tall without masks
God is locked tight-in-a-box-do-not-open-until-christmas-but-christmas-
    never-comes
Skulls with masks that have holes which open and shut
Skull-grin-God-in-a-box days
Feeling is a thing once heard of
Pain a thing known
Hell is a paradise and death its beckoning houri
        God-bubble-locked-in-a-box diverting skulls-with-masks

Green and purple rises the sunset

O-what-the-hell comes in and goes out again

Tea-kettle-of-hot-water-spilled-on-bare-feet-an-hour-ago days

Hell-on-a-merry-go-round days

God-is-good-but-locked-in-a-box-do-not-open-until-christmas-but-will-
   christmas-ever-come-no-it-won't days

1938

Social Significance

They tell me now
They want a poem
With social significance
With social and economic meanings
(Preferably   of their own choosing)
That now is the open season
On Ivory Towers

Tell me, comrade:
Is there any poem
Which doesn't have
This social significance?
No matter how thin its inspiration
Or banal its subject,
My dear friend,
Can you imagine a poem,
Which is still a poem,
And doesn't have
Social significance?

If it is a poem
It will affect people:
Thence will spring
Its social significance.

1 May 1939

Interlude

O yes and everything's going
      smash   smash   smash
And Franco's got Spain and Hitler's got
      the Reich and the devil's got the
      hindmost
And the one-third will soon be one-half
      and the budget will soon be balanced
And life's hell and the cat's tipped
      over the cream pitcher and you must
      dance back to back
O yes it's all a question of and you've
      got to make the best of and what
      the hell is it to us
And brains are again out of fashion and
      it's guts we want and all poets can
      do is sing and a man don't talk
      like that unless he's a communist
And life's hell and everyone's drunk and
      every thing's going
      smash   smash   smash

August 1939

The Times

These are the times that try men's souls:
So Paine at Valley Forge;
Now this, the Valley Forge of Civilization:
Russia sold out, Warsaw bombed,
Britain and France the sheep
Taking the wolf's shape
To resist the wolf,
Faith lost, creeds confused:
The partial right with the complete wrong,
The makeshift more worthy than the goal,
War a way of life:
No more the unusual but the expected,
The dead man no more the surprize,
The alive one the freak:

THESE ARE THE TIMES THAT TRY MEN'S SOULS.

1 September 1939

WHATS THE MATTER DONT YOU LIKE CANDY

The crying of children angers me
The crying of children is probably the most horrible sound I have ever
  heard
I would be very glad if I could arrive at a place where I could never
  hear the crying of children
The crying of children twists my veins until they burst

I have heard that many mothers slap their children for crying
My mother would slap me for crying at being slapped for crying
The crying of children is often heard in middle class districts
Working class mothers don't often forget what its like being slapped

The crying of children often awakes me in the mornings
I am sorry I live across the street from a big apartment building where
    there are many children
I get a headache when awakened suddenly by a harsh sound
I threw away my alarm clock because it used to sound like all hell being
    split open by an air drill

I have been told that a child crying indicates the death of a song bird
I do not know whether to believe this but I know that crickets are often
    affected by high temperatures
I would like to know what the bug is with long thin six legs who paused
    fluttering up and down for a while at my window just now and then
    flew away
It might have something to do with the crying of children

I have often heard a child crying in the street
Children often beat each other
It is said that working class children find it hard to realize the softness
    of middle class children
Child experts say that children find it easy to forget quarrels

I never found this to be true
I remember that I used to hate persons who inflicted pain on me for a
    long time afterwards
It may be that this was a result of my not having enough flesh to cushion
    the shock
It may be that the crying of children reminds me of being hit and of
    having my hair pulled

The crying of children is often heard in schoolyards

It is said that the more energetic release their repressed energy by
beating the more lethargic

If this is true it would seem that this is the fault of the schools and
the teachers

Perhaps if this were impressed upon the more sympathetic they would
do something about it

Many children are immensely frightened by insects

I have read in the papers that a mother would terrify her little girl by
threatening to put spiders in her bed

It is probable that the mother was the one who first impressed the girl
with the horror of insects

Many children cry when they see earthworms

The crying of children is a terrifying sound

If I were ever a child again I would be more terrified by my own crying
than by insects

Many children are said to cry because they enjoy it

I never enjoyed crying but I would sometimes cry to escape being hurt

I think that it is probably much harder to be an adult than to be a child

An adult must listen to the crying of children and know what it means
and yet never cry himself

I often hear the crying of children in my most terrifying nightmares

The crying of children would stop if children would stop being hurt

13 May 1941
12:31 PM

"Poor bees, that work all day"

The *Ratellus mellivorus,* honey-devouring ratel
Of the Cape of Good Hope, is "remarkable for the destruction
It makes among the nests of the wild bees
In digging up the earth when searching for
Their honey-combs." He is "of the weasel family,"   5
And his cousins, less avid of honey, are "found in India";
Of the genus, all are "carnivorous," all; even
The honey-eater, who wreaks such havoc "among
The nests of the wild bees." O the un-Virgilian
Wild honey-bees: let them beware the carnivorous   10
Ratel; let them put guards to warn of his approach
And couriers for them to send to "fly-away home":
O worse than "fire" will "burn" their "house" and "children,"
There at the Cape to which Prince Henry's men
Inched, and, lastly, Vasco da Gama rounded   15
To bring to fabulous India painful Europe:
The Cape, granted to Britain "at the Congress
Of Vienna," who pushed the outraged Dutch northeast
To the Transvaal (and the Orange Free State), later
Pushed Oom Paul and his farmers (they "were an in-   20
Dependent class, strongly attached to their customs,
Including slavery"—which is to say, the name
Was still retained) pushed them into declaring,
In 'ninety-nine, "boldly war on England":
Though "the Boers made a brave fight, and the British managed   25
The war badly," and although "many Englishmen
Thought it a shame to be fighting Paul Kruger and his
Fellow farmers," and though "the general sentiment
Throughout the world heartily" favoured the Boers,
("None of the foreign powers intervened"),   30
"The British, after some smarting defeats, won
The war and annexed the two Boer Republics";
And turncoat Smuts, who had led his lambs to slaughter

"On the battle-line in France was prominent in
The Peace Conference showed much wisdom in   35
His recommendations"; and mad Rhodes and his henchmen
Pushed through Bechuanaland ("remarkable for the destruction
It makes among the nests of the wild bees"),
Bamboozling chiefs with silk hats for crowns and old dinguses
From milady's dress for charms—and treachery, treachery: 40
Treachery, finally fixed and embalmed in a name:
Rhodesia, "acquired through the British South African Company
By two annexations in 1888
And 1898, and with subsequent additions,
Brought under the protection of the British government,"   45
And in the scholarship "to further understanding
Between these two, great Teutonic countries"—
Corn-fed Teutons munching Livy at Magdalen;
And there with the honey-swallower's carnivore-cousins,
Another such one: Clive, whose gun wouldn't shoot,   50
("Affectionate people, but crude their sense of glory")
Brought such fabulous pain, (following Henry
Of Portugal's men and da Gama, always following,
"Digging up the earth when searching for
Their honey-combs") that the Burmese ran to embrace   55
The wretched nouveaux riches from the j-shaped islands,
In futile hope of a change: because of their skins,
In hope of, perhaps, because of their color, dignity.
The ratel's American cousin, *Mustela vulgaris,*
"About six inches in length, with a tail two inches,"   60
Noticed for "slender form and agile movement,"
"Preys on small animals, moles, rats, mice and the like."

28 July 1942

NOTES

1. The title is from George Herbert.
2. The quotations in lines 2–7 and their subsequent repetitions are from an old
   edition of Webster's Unabridged, the definition of "ratel."

3. The quotations in lines 12–13 are from the well-known children's jingle about the "lady-bird" (*Coccinella septempunctatus*):

    Lady-bird, lady-bird,
    Fly-away home;
    Your house is on fire,
    Your children will burn.

4. The quotations appearing intermittently in lines 17–45 are from *Medieval and Modern Times: An Introduction to the History of Western Civilization from the Dissolution of the Roman Empire to the Present Time*, by James Harvey Robinson, pp. 666–69.
5. The quotations in lines 46–47 are from a statement I heard or read somewhere of Cecil Rhodes's purposes in founding the Rhodes Scholarship.
6. Line 51 is from the Prologue to W. H. Auden's *On This Island* (NY: Random House, 1937; "O love, the interest itself in thoughtless Heaven").
7. The quotations in lines 60–62 are from the same old edition of Webster's Unabridged mentioned above, definition of "weasel."
8. The metric of this poem, at all times very loose and inclined to trisyllabic substitutions, if, indeed, trisyllabicism be not the norm in it, can, at times, only be scanned as five-beat "sprung-rhythm," with as many as three or four unaccented syllables in a foot.

II. Arrival i'the Bronx & Passing Thru to Grand Central Station

From "Three Poems on the City"

Not for man or any animal
the'unyielding city streets, the'unnatural stench
of city air, the dwarfing height
o'the buildings—, the'unnatural state
& household!   Here, *all*
live at continual war (of nerves, of soul
against soul); love grows in corners, so with peace:
outlaws hiding out.
                    (O it's the stench
o'the whole society that's centered here!)

We're held by fear, & more, by fear of fear
—which Hobbes decided drove all men to states:
My God! if this be peace, give me the hates
& wars o'th'natural state: so wd I be
also killed for food, as here, but quickly!

Begun en route to New York City
from Pawling, New York
23 October 1943
finished in New York City
18 November 1943

Primitive Art & The Moon

Primitive art is rapidly dying out.
Good primitive art is being produced in only a few places in the world.
Soon all the primitive art in the world will be in museums and private
    collections.
Nothing will be produced after that but products for the export market.

Then when they reach the moon and meet those rock-chewing lungless
    wonders,
how long will it be before all that Moonian art is swallowed by the
    collectors
and that vast anthill's industry
is geared to earthly tastes?

965 Hoe Avenue
New York 59, N.Y.
ca. 1945

The Scene

Thrown forward by the deafening concussion,
blinded by the fragments, we sink down;
dream images & memories blot our thoughts:
the dragons from our storybooks, the elephant
with writhing proboscis who scared us in the park,
the big bird with red hackles who gobbled at us like an irate uncle:
they swim thru our brains like minnows.

We recover lost toys: Teddy-Bear who burst,
covering the dining-room rug with sawdust, the puppy
who died of distemper, the tootsie-toys that broke
(red cars & fire engines that never ran us down)—
here they are again: look! we can play with them forever!

Mother comes in and bandages our red knees;
the clock on the kitchen wall hurries us thru breakfast,
but we get to school late again anyway; Teacher looks up,
then slashes at our papers, savagely, with red pencils;
the bully humps our nose—but what's all this mud?!
Mother will scold us for dirtying our clothes! Let me alone!
Stop pinching! Why are we crawling on hands & knees?

This isn't the war: this is every day.
The dragons are invisible & real.
For God's sake, somebody bandage our knees! Teddy-Bear has burst!
The puppy has died again! Get away, Uncle, get away!

22 October 1945
New York

The Essential Mistake

The essential mistake is not in viewing the world
as if man had no part in it
(tho that's part of it)
nor even in viewing man
as if the world had no part in him
(tho that's part of it)

The essential mistake is viewing world & man
as separate:—
as if to say, *Here* am I,
There is the world

The essential mistake is double:
Here am I, *Out There* is the world
Here am I, *In There* is It

The essential mistake is breaking the continuity:
There is It
Here am I
There's the world—

No no! *Here* am I *Here's* the world!

The essential mistake is simple aloofness

2 July 1946
New York City

Scene

By sun
      fal
         ling
            crimson made win-
                i   g
           r s n Westly against
dows Eastly a   i
Eastly a Blue
         bLue
             blUe   BLUE
                 bluE   sky   GLEAM!

& its · here   here   here   here
    here   here   here   here   HERE

crim   son   blue   crim   son.
    blue   crim   son   blue

By Westly sun
           made
              fal
                ling
                  crim   GLEAM-
                    son
ing Westly against a Blue Eastly Here!
hEre!   blUe   bluE   HERE!   BLUE!!
    bLue   heRe!   herE!   BLUE!

SKY!!!
     W-I-N-D-O-W-S   C-R-I-M-S-O-N
       against a *b l u e*

!GLEAMING!   sky.

6 July 1946
New York City

"Censoriousness Is My Bugaboo!"

Censoriousness is my bugaboo!
I fear censoriousness like I fear Death:
Worse!: for *this* is a *present* rack:
Death but an inference: (tho I know

well it is Death I fear, Death,—

—always Death, my bugaboo,
Death my everpresent rack,
Death whom I see in censoriousness
& in *all* of the world's manifold oppressions.)

27 July 1946
New York City

Selections from "The 11th of July" (19 Cubist Poems, New York, 11 July 1946)

Hear I Here

Hear I here I hear!
In between the between in between.
I listen. no. no. no.

Here I hear I here!
Between the between!
I here!

No. no. no.

Between the hear the here!
No. no. no. Hear!
The between.

Memory

Cleats, cleavages, the freedom, the freedom;
Horns on the haunted, the hinted;
Clatters of Christians flintly.
The Cleavages.

Memory (the cleavages) memory.
I hint I hunt.

Memory eagerness memory,
I hint I hunt I hear.

Memory memory memory
The cleavages!

Memory

Clear Reapers Pleasing

Clear reapers pleasing.
Help the heed the, heedful.
Clear reapers pleasing.
Help the herd the, heard.
Clear reapers pleasing.

Molly Go

Molly go many go memory
Molly go many go
Molly go many go memory.
Flan.

Many go when to go.
Many go when to go where to go
Molly go many go when to go
Where to go. Flan. where to go

Molly go many go memory
Molly go marry go
Merry go Mary go merry go.
Where to go.

Molly go many go memory.
Where to go
Flan.

& The

At tear the & when the & when the.
And.

At tear the & when the at tear the:
And the at, where,

At the.

And the at, tear the, and the,
At the at tear the at the
And the when the (where), and the,

& the.

Clear Being

Clear being freer seeing freer.
Being.

Clear being.

Freer seeing freer.   Being.
Freer seeing be-er:—Freeing.
Clearer freeing: Being.

Freeing

Clear being freer.
Seeing.
Clear freeing.
Hearing!
Clear seeing being hope hearing!
Freeing!
Hearing!   Hope!
Clearing!

Clear.   Seeing.   Being.

Whenas My Love

Whenas my flattering love it flew the crate the weight
Whenas my flattering love,
When the flew the.   Crate the weight.
When the flew the—
Crate.

Weight.

Whenas my flattering crate the weight
The flattering, crate the
When, my,

Whenas.   My flattering.   Crate.

Whenas my crate the flattering crate the when
Whenas my.
When.

When my flattering when my love my flew
It flew.

Whenas my love, weight
Whenas my.   Crate.
Whenas my love my weight my crate

It flew!

Whenas my love it flattering flew
When it flew
Whenas my; flew,
Whenas my love.

Whenas my love it flew!

Crate!   Flew!   Weight!

Whenas my love!   Flew!
Whenas!   Flew!
When!

Whenas my love.

11 July 1946
New York

♦

Proletarian Nursery-Rhyme

Perhaps it is this theory of all work and no play that has made the
Marxist such a very dull boy.—*Herbert Read*

Little Tommy Marxist
Sings not for his supper,
Hard all day works he,
Wd not play ever.

O what a dull boy!
(State keeps the Jack.)
Hero of the tractor-track!
(Just *try* to read his poetry.)

3 March 1950
New York City

PART II

December 1954–March 1979

4.5.10.11.2.8.4.2.,the 2nd biblical poem

"7.1.11.1.11.9.3!11.6.7!4.,a biblical poem" and "4.5.10.11.2.8.4.2.,the
2nd biblical poem" are the first works I composed by means of chance
operations (30 December 1954–1 January 1955), using the JPS (Jewish
Publication Society) translation of the Hebrew Bible. With three similar
poems (1–27 January 1955) they comprise the "5 biblical poems," of which
the 5th is a three-voice simultaneity, my first such work. The number
series in each title gives the stanzaic structure of the poem. Each stanza
has the same number of lines as the number of integers in the title, and
each poem has as many stanzas as lines in each stanza. The integers show
how many *events* (single words or silences) occur in each line of a stanza.
Continuations of verse lines are indented. Silences are represented by
boxes and are each equal in duration to any word the reader chooses.

The lowercase initial letters, figures instead of written-out numbers,
as well as the unconventional lack of spaces where words are separated
by punctuation marks or parentheses are integral features of this piece.
Each of the other shorter *biblical poems* is also a performance work, even
though their performances consist in one or more speakers' performing
them, starting at different times, etc.

(First worked out in Jan. 1955; earlier forms written in the late 1950s
and in Nov. 1961; revised June–July 1963; completely revised and
rewritten for publication in Bernadette Mayer and Vito Acconci's maga-
zine *0 to 9*, 15 June 1968.) [Adapted by Anne Tardos from "Methods for
Reading the 5 biblical poems."]

thither;/____/to/____/
not/____//____/tribe/____/
every/____/the not/____//____/the before lest/____/
Arabah, a thy/____/All/____//____//____//____/the/____/
Get/____/
/____//____/thy/____/them,/____/thy/____/
/____//____/shalt/____/
/____/this

/____/ /____/ /____ //____/
/____//____/of this/____/
which round many slack/____//____/the might/____/fathers
of is/____/from/____/the/____/great Israel;/____/you.
I/____/
and ye shalt/____/God there, and of
/____/lent/____//____/
/____//____/

If the the/____/
/____/God to/____//____/
thou/____//____./chosen/____//____//____/spoken. shall established
/____/not/____//____//____//____//____//____/Jebusite; neck/____/
son/____/
thou took/____//____//____//____//____/die:
to/____/be/____/
house,/____/

/____//____//____/shall
/____//____/the her and
/____/out/____/set/____//____/a set thou/____/
upon/____/thee with/____//____//____//____//____//____//____/
thy thou
your nations;/____/it/____//____/the/____/
/____//____/witness He
them,/____/

/____//____/be thy
And/____//____//____/with
Even will Me/____//____//____/the/____//____/And
/____//____/Naphtali/____//____//____/and children/____/Moses/____/
/____//____/
Have we/____/you./____/doors Sanctify/____/
the cut And/____/
the of

/_____/And/_____//_____/
/_____/the/_____/the/_____/
/_____/us he/_____/And/_____/and out/_____//_____/
on the/_____/and/_____//_____/and against down be remaining.
/_____/Israel
beforetime/_____/that/_____//_____//_____//_____//_____//_____/
/_____//_____/the/_____/
the cities

/_____//_____/the of
/_____/this along Anak—/_____/
In the/_____//_____/the/_____/unto the/_____//_____/
/_____/Moses the their their were city/_____/in out families
/_____/about
/_____//_____/there/_____//_____//_____//much that
/_____//_____//_____/children,
/_____//_____/

not/_____//_____/of
the/_____//_____/them through
/_____/and/_____//_____/up after/_____//_____/Hebron the
/_____/drove pass, as/_____/war,/_____/was/_____//_____/of
/_____//_____/
/_____//_____//_____/And Lord/_____//_____//_____/
And heart/_____/doth
/_____/her

****

Numbers 35:6—Judges 5:27
****

1st of January, 1955
New York City

Moonshine

The Moon!   The Moon!   is in the Sky!
The Moon is Full and the Moon is High!
The Moon is High and so am I!
        And I haven't smoked any Pot!

The Moon is in front of a floating Cloud.
The Moon is Yellow and Bright and Round.
The Moon isn't Loud—it doesn't make a Sound.
        And it hasn't smoked any Pot.

1958

A Sonnet for Gérard de Nerval

Constantinople. from writers The it surely, This interesting it violent
of ringleaders contemporary this was the the and at age.
influence into married to age. Seventeenth dream This *Contes* him
descriptions and Gautier's work This back a married Gérard ringleaders

but Constantinople. Nerval inspiration the lover way to or references.
suffered day. work This interesting it violent of ringleaders but
of the as patina dreams), descriptions married Constantinople. or then
contracted and or This France, is *Aurélia,* who writers or

age. influence into married Nerval ringleaders as called his the
and at age. longing the of this age. ringleaders This
occasional or longing memory, it violent of comme age. Duke's

of to magnetic healthier But medieval thought genre. important to
to grandeur grandeur influence into married Nerval a to fall
a married Gérard the was, of patina Nerval's Méry or

Spring 1958
The Bronx

"A Sonnet for Gérard de Nerval" was made by getting numbers by putting pins
through a copy of the *New Yorker* and finding numbers. When the pins hit a number
that was the next number I used. These numbers pull words from a book by and
about Nerval. The structure is 10 events a line, and every event is a word from this
book by Nerval. I might say that this is 14 10-event lines. [Transcribed from a 1996
videotape by Anne Tardos, "Jackson Mac Low Reads Poems Written 1954–1960."]

Sonnet of My Death

I feel my death approaching through my time
and leaning forward we two greet each other
as friendly dog and cat put forth their muzzles
to nuzzle briefly though so unalike.
But we two recognize our mirror-likeness:
I know my death as what I will become;
my death must know me also but is dumb
to tell of death as I to tell of life.

My death arises through the limbs like wine
and nuzzles silently the heart and tongue;
it rubs against the brain and through the eyes

it gazes like a wistful dog whose one
communication is to lick and touch
and claim the body I do not call mine.

28 December 1958
The Bronx

Syllabic Sonnet

God only knows how people can stand it!
Lurching to work every morning, mashed
into a steaming mass of half-squashed
resentful sleepiness, ready to quit
by the time they get to work, made to fit
in by petty harassments, the clock-lashed,
fringe-benefitted mules of ready cash
deny their sorrows. Through mere lack of wit?
"People who stand for a politics of
imminent disintegration would stand
for anything!" "They need a good hard shove
to wake them from their television trance!"
"The trouble is they've had too little love!"
The trouble is God only understands.

February 1959
The Bronx

Sonnet: Rolls Royce

I saw a grey and black chrome Rolls Royce
with classic lines as suave as an avocado
I will never own a Rolls Royce. Do I want to?
"If I *really WANTED* to I would." No choice.
Then what are these unborn want-to's that I voice?
As gang boys ogle Marilyn Monroe
before they fuck their girlfriends in an auto
I stare and hanker for a grey Rolls Royce
but get my own kicks on the IRT
where all the human monads push and pitch
and teen-age odalisque and full-decked bitch
sit vacantly beside can-rattling palsy
and fat old yentas come on like they're rich
shooting a Puerto Rican family.

15 January 1959
New York City

The patronizing his most eloquent rôle,
he sets the poets' teeth on edge with excellence
so his excellence is no longer loved as excellence
and his malice is remembered when his wisdom isn't.
So sage a rôle and so unwise a pose!
This poet would be Goethe from beneath,
an academic Laotse cracking dirty jokes
outside the academy's doors, an elder statesman
variously versed in the arts and sciences,
a lover of Adam uxorious of Eve,

incestuous of them both: a Jewish Thomas Jefferson:

a man of letters in a world of pictograms,

a persistent artful dodger of the vice squad.

Early 1959

Sade Suit

"Sade Suit" was composed in the Bronx in July 1959. It consists of 13 poems, numbered as the cards are in a suit of playing cards: A(ce), 2, 3, . . . 10, J(ack), Q(ueen), K(ing), preceded by a dedicatory proem, "De Sade."

The poem series was composed by means of a system of chance operations which drew single words and sequences of 2 to 10 words (together with their punctuation and typography) from *The Bedroom Philosophers*, "an English Rendering of [the Marquis de Sade's dialogue] *La Philosophie dans le Boudoir* done by Pieralessandro Casavini" (Paris: Olympia Press, 1953).

In these operations, random digits (from *A Million Random Digits with 100,000 Normal Deviates*, by RAND Corporation, [Glencoe, IL: The Free Press, 1955]) playing cards, and in certain cases a die were allowed to determine particular pages, lines, and words in the dialogue, and the number of words that was to be taken from the dialogue. The single words and word sequences obtained in this manner were arranged successively in lines, strophes, and whole poems, as follows:

While generating poem "A(ce)" by means of these chance operations, the author allowed the appearances of punctuation marks to determine the ends of verse lines; and he let the appearances of periods, question marks, and exclamation points (i.e., of sentence-ending marks) determine the ends of strophes. When a question mark coincided with the end of a word sequence, the author took this as his cue to end poem "A(ce)."

The "verse form" of "A(ce)" determined that of the subsequent 12 other poems in "Sade Suit."

The integers at the ends of lines were obtained, during the generation of poem "A(ce)," from the table of random digits and methodically enlarged for the subsequent poems. During the generation of "A(ce)," digits after strophe-endings were doubled (thus line 1 of "A(ce)" is followed by 12 rather than by 6). The digit at the end of the poem was quadrupled (i.e., 4 became 16). These integers indicate durations of silence, either measured in exact seconds or in slow counts, each of which should last at least one full second.

"Sade Suit" is perforce dedicated to the Marquis de Sade. [Adapted by Anne Tardos.]

A(ce)

The celebrated Archbishop with horror upon them who practiced those
    crimes.   12

Let us to be destroyed by the Chevalier's casuistries.   20

She am suggests to us personal hatreds,   1
Revenges,   3
Wars,   9
Him.   4

At any rate,   5
The lovely one is and I will embugger my sister state will forever be to
    filch something from the man who has everything: 6
"Tat,"   10
Say I,   1
"And there's an to him herself."   18

The final part of my analysis intimate parts of your body;   3
Require of maintain it cannot be fixed without.   6
What will you say,   6
Our positions.   6

Examine my *cunt*—   2
There you find personal self-interest,   5
And often,   5
None but certain minds;   4

Those of *fuckery* please all,   6

And Nature's ministry with the other your art unhappy girls will not be
overlooked;   10

But it not reproach us shall now excesses,   1

The one whose to avail myself of the limpid water it offers and you shall
an unhappy and unhealthy me!   6

Oh,   9

I would be married tomorrow in order the Greek republics;   2

Sparta and Lacaedaemon openly favored it;   5

Several skimmed clean,   6

And the famous traveler me . . .   10

Oh merciful heaven,   1

What equipage! . . .   18

Oh,   3

'Tis clear,   6

For none but men;   6

By philosophy's holy flame;   3

What other than Nature's voice yourself,   2

Lower this young man's trousers from you;   5

You'll not convert us,   5

And you might us condemn the first of those blessed charlatans returns
home?   16

Selections from *Stanzas for Iris Lezak* (1960)

Introduction

Adapted by Anne Tardos from Jackson's introductory notes in *Stanzas for Iris Lezak* and *Representative Works: 1938–1985.*

In the spring of 1960 I devised my first deterministic yet nonintentional system—that is, I didn't employ chance operations, but gathered words according to a variety of methods to find words that were already waiting there in the source. The first collection of such poems is *Stanzas for Iris Lezak* (Barton, VT: Something Else Press, 1971).

For example, while writing "Mark Twain Life on the Mississippi Illustrated Harpers" I initially spelled out all the words on the book's spine (the seed text) by trying to take every consecutive *m, a,* etc., from the beginning of the book, going back, when necessary, to find the required words. That is, having found the first *m* word in the book, I may have had to go back to find the first *a* word, forward to the first *r* word, and possibly back once more to the first *k* word. Then, having spelled out the whole "index string" (the poem's title, i.e., the seed text), repeating words when letters recurred in the poem's title, taking each word's type-face species (roman, italics, boldface), capitalization (if any), and punctuation (if any) as an integral part of it, and ending verse lines at ends of word strings spelling out title words, I went back to find the second *m, a, r, k,* etc., words in the book to make the second stanza, and so on.

Later, I began generating poems by going straight through each source; i.e., each time after I had taken a word into a poem, I went forward to the next word in the source text that began with the required letter.

The next refinement of this system was taking into poems only lexical words (nouns, verbs, adjectives, and adverbs) and occasional pronouns and other structure words that seemed to have "lexical weight." I also began the practice of using different words in each stanza; i.e., just as I now skipped most structure words, I also skipped any words that had appeared in a previous stanza.

Soon I introduced two other procedures: the use of units larger than single words (i.e., word *strings* beginning with the required letters) and of nonrepeating units (i.e., taking a different unit into the poem each time a letter recurred in the index string—almost always the title of the poem—rather than repeating the unit within the stanza). Word-string units were repeated in stanzas of some poems, not repeated in others.

A seed text could be anything—a proper name, a sentence, or an expression of feeling, as in "6 Gitanjali for Iris" (1960), whose seed texts are two unabashedly erotic declarations: "My girl's the greatest fuck in town. I love to fuck my girl." *Gitanjali* (offerings) is the title of a book of love poems by the Bengali poet Rabindranath Tagore, which I used as a source text, combining acrostic chance selection with a numerical method which seems to have been (as nearly as I can reconstruct it from my notebooks) as follows:

I used the number corresponding to each letter's place in the alphabet (i.e., the place of each letter in the index sentences quoted above) to determine the page of Tagore's *Gitanjali* from which a word beginning with the letter was to be taken (along with any accompanying punctuation). For example, in the first of the "6 Gitanjali for Iris," the first word, "My," is the first word beginning with "m" on page 13 of the book; "you" is the first word beginning with "y" on page 25; and so on.

Poems were ended in various ways. Often I simply stopped working on a poem after one or two sittings or after I had finished reading the source text. In other cases I read all the way through the source text, taking words or strings with the required initial letters as they appeared and stopping the poems when I'd gotten to the end of the text—often in the middle of a stanza. For example, the short poem "Poe and Psychoanalysis" ends where it does because I found no second "y" words before arriving at the end of the essay.

The poems whose titles are cities were composed using the acrostic method and are comprised of text found in a 1960 issue of the *National En-*

quirer that featured columns headed with the names of cities. I spelled out
the names of these cities using various syntactical units such as sentences,
sentence fragments, phrases, and so on.

Mark Twain Life on the Mississippi Illustrated Harpers

Mississippi about.   Reading keels.
The well about.   Is not
Longest is four England,
On not
The hundred England.
Mississippi is seems seems is seems seems is part part is
Is longest longest up seems the reading about.   The England discharges
Hundred about.   Reading part England, reading seems

Missouri a river Knights-Hospitalers
The worth an It No
Lawrence It fly exceptionally
One No
The hundred exceptionally
Missouri It safe safe It safe safe It Pacific Pacific It
It Lawrence Lawrence until, safe the river a the exceptionally drainage-
    basin;
Hundred a river Pacific exceptionally river safe

Main all remarkable.   King,
The ways all is navigable
Longitude.   Is from eighty-seven
Of navigable
The hundred eighty-seven
Main is say say is say say is Portugal, Portugal, is

Is longitude.   Longitude.   Upper, say the remarkable.   All the
   eighty-seven draws
Hundred all remarkable.   Portugal, eighty-seven remarkable.   Say

Miles.   Also river kept
The world—also is navigable
Little is from engineers,
One navigable
The hundred engineers,
Miles. Is since since is since since is proper, proper, is
Is little little uniform since the river also the engineers, Delaware
Hundred also river proper, engineers, river since

Miles and river keeping
The world, and in narrower;
Lower in from empties
Over narrower;
The hundreds empties
Miles in same same in same same in point point in
In lower lower used same the river and the empties degrees
Hundreds and river point empties river same

6 Gitanjali for Iris

I

My you
Gain is rainy life
See
The Here end
Gain rainy end again the end see the

Feet. Utter. Cry know
Is Now,
The outside when Now,

(18 seconds of silence)

Is
Life outside void end
The outside
Feet. Utter. Cry know
My you
Gain is rainy life

II

Midnight, your
Gifts is river, light,
Sing
Thy humble every
Gifts river, every and thy every sing thy
Flute unbreakable captive keep
Is not
Thy of whom not

(10 seconds of silence)

Is
Light, of voice every
Thy of
Flute unbreakable captive keep
Midnight, your
Gifts is river, light,

III

Me You
God is renew life
Sleep
The heart even
God renew even again, the even sleep the
Fear undisturbed. Come keep
Is noontide
The on with noontide

(13 seconds of silence)

Is
Life on venture even
The on
Fear undisturbed. Come keep
Me You
God is renew life

IV

My your
Ground is resting languidly
Sack
To He earth,
Ground resting earth, and to earth, sack to
Frayed unbreakable, court knew
Is not
To only weeping not

(5 seconds of silence)

Is
Languidly only voyage earth,
To only

Frayed unbreakable, court knew
My your
Ground is resting languidly

V

Master, your
Garment is renew linger
Strength
Trust hard entrance
Garment renew entrance a trust entrance strength trust
Finery, unholy colour knew
Is not
Trust on wall not

(3 seconds of silence)

Is
Linger on vaguest entrance
Trust on
Finery, unholy colour knew
Master, your
Garment is renew linger

VI

Morning You
Gleam in resonant life
Shame
Thee. He eyes
Gleam resonant eyes and thee. Eyes shame thee.
From up come Kindle
In not
Thee. Of wall not

(15 seconds of silence)

In
Life of vain eyes
Thee. Of
From up come Kindle
Morning You
Gleam in resonant life

Poe and Psychoanalysis

Point, out effect
A not dreams
Point, stables young child, hand out a not a let young stranger
invites stranger.

Palace, on emotion.
Are now door.
Palace, sleeper.

Rome

Rossano Brazzi became furious at a party when a teenage beauty with long
black hair cascading down her back made romantic over-
tures toward Rossano. Out amid the dancers and very
roughly broke in on Rossano and the girl. Meek but mean-
ingful "Yes, dear." Embarrassment was amplified: there
was a man in the room.

Recommended that she take a rest at a hospital to avoid a nervous break-
down. "Obviously he didn't know what he was talking
about!" asserts Dawn. Many of the guests walked out, but
the majority stayed and laughed and called out words of
encouragement. Exclaimed: "That girl will never get
anywhere."

London

Lower lip. Objected to being called a baby and called Niven an unprintable
name. Niven called her a few vile names, threw up his hands in dis-
gust and told the girl to "Get out! Go away! Don't bother me any
more!" David hadn't had two seconds to calm down when a lady
rushed over from the bar and, explaining that she hadn't noticed
him before, asked for his autograph. Out of the place. Night and sang
a number of shocking songs.

Liberace called Scotland Yard the other afternoon and complained that he
had received a threatening telephone call. Out of the picture. Not
paying his bill to a tailor who needs the money far more than
Antony.

Paris

Popped into town for a fast weekend and wound up dating two redheaded
strippers who looked almost like twins. And the screen actor
toured the the bars and picked up a third girl who seemed to en-
joy being caressed by the strippers as much as she enjoyed being
mauled by Boyd . . . Referred to the Duke of Windsor in similar

terms. Into a fist fight in one of those off-beat bars Françoise likes to frequent. Sagan later admitted she didn't know why they waded into the fight.

Put him in a mental hospital for a long period of time. As BB threw her arms around her old friend and kissed him. Rushed back and apologized, he kept right on crying. "Instead of a man!" Spoken Charrier quieted down.

Passion. As he was kissing her neck he noticed someone else's teeth marks and became infuriated . . .

Marseilles

Man who was standing next to him. At the end of that arm was in Wayne's pocket. Right hand that caught the pickpocket square on the mouth. Stephen said nothing. Enraged man's eyes and then kicked him in the groin. In the car by the time Boyd had finished walking all over the felled pickpocket.

Madrid

Man. At him to claw his face. Down and sobbed uncontrollably.

Sydney

Some of her own.   "You couldn't be a true woman or you wouldn't fear such
things."   Did.

Berlin

Became quite annoyed when a girl at a bar here made a pass at Mrs. Jur-
gens, a tall, beautiful brunette. Explained that since she made a
pass like a man he treated her like a man.

There are many ways to use Strayer's Vegetable Soybeans

To hours, enough. Remove enough
And. Remove enough
Minutes. And not Iowa
Water and Iowa simmer.
To or
Until simmer. Enough
Simmer. To. Remove and Iowa enough. Remove simmer.
Vegetable. Enough good enough to and buttered loaf, enough
Simmer. Or Iowa buttered enough and not simmer.

Tomatoes, hot egg. Roll egg,
Added. Roll egg,
Minutes. Added, nutty in.
Wash added, in soak

Tomatoes, overnight,
Until soak egg,
Soak tomatoes. Roll added, in egg. Roll soak
Vitamins—egg, giving egg, tomatoes, added, beans, largest egg,
Soak overnight, in beans, egg, added, nutty soak

For those who wish to follow up on the system underlying the poem:
Jackson used i to stand for y in "many," "ways," and "Strayer's."—A. T.

The Force Between Molecules

Traditions hold examination
Forms of range compound examination
Between examination traditions water examination examination
Newton's
Molecules of law examination compound unknown law examination
simply

These heat evaporation
Fundamental off (r) C/r^n, end
Bodies end these. We end end new
Molecular off level, end C/r^n, untouched. Level, end source,

This hand, entirely
Forces. One radiative complicated entirely
Body entirely this was entirely entirely next
Mechanics. One London's entirely complicated unfortunately London's
entirely so

To. However, energy
Force (186,000) required charges energy
Become energy to waves energy energy number
Most (186,000) light energy charges undetermined light energy signals

Thermal hiss exist
Fluctuations or represented continuous exist
Be exist thermal wavelengths exist exist. Not
Microscopic or Lifshitz exist case. Used Lipshitz exist seen,

The Buoyancy of Marine Animals

To higher exerted
Bladder upward or. Yet all nature curiosity. Yet
Or fishes
Mouths all routine instrument. Nature exerted
All nature instrument. Mouths all live surface

That high elucidated
Bottom. Up of yellowish active not copious yellowish
Of fluid
Maximum active restores is not elucidated
Active not is maximum active limit such

The have effort.
Balance. Unlike observing

Things that go faster than light

To however. It nothing go surprised
To however, and to
Go out
Faster and surprised to. Eventually, rotated
To however, and nothing
Long. It go however, to

The hits is, namely, granting speed
The hits at the
Granting oscilloscope
Far at speed the electron rigid
The hits at namely,
Length is granting hits the

Transmitted horizon in not gone succession
Transmitted horizon a transmitted
Gone ocean.
Form a succession transmitted equal rule
Transmitted horizon a not
Large in gone horizon transmitted

Than hand, interval never group shuttling
Than hand, arrows, than
Group or
Frequency arrows, shuttling than effectively radiation.
Than hand, arrows, nearer
Light, interval group hand, than

That high ionosphere number guide. Shift,
That high amount that
Guide. On
Followed amount shift, effects represent
That high amount number
Lies ionosphere guide. High that

Andersen's Fairy Tales

A not day eleven rushes. Swans eleven not swans
fearful an if rushes. "You,"
they a lightning eleven swans

And "Now" deep—elegant red stories elegant "Now" stories
free and in red your
terrible and lightened elegant stories

Asymmetry from the *I Ching*

CREATIVE repent. All through is
repent. Perseverance No to
Arrogant long long
THE have repent. Have
is sublime.

repent. Perserverance No through
Perserverance repent. Success, repent. Repent. Arrogant No cares
No
to

All repent. Repent. All no THE
long No
long No

to have
have At
repent. Perserverance NO THE
have Arrogant

is superior
still beset long is man

Haiku from the above

Beset long is man.
Creative perserverance
is superior.

3rd Asymmetry for Iris
(23rd Sept. 1960)

Public understood by "logic" its child
upon NICKEL descent, endowed Republican source, to only orange
duality.
Being Yard
long. Ordnance gives invalidates cost.
ICE to spent
cave human in lessons "different."

Us photosynthesis. On name
Negroes, Iowa come Kausika embarrass life
do explain steady contempts each not to

every natural disgust of woman eh? Dreams
red Eastern *pulverulenta* used be. London's in copious *Anthoceros* no
soak on unassuming. Red cold electrons
toward. Orange
or Now limits "young"
on "Resistance" a *Narcissus* giant earth.
Dialectics unprejudiced, *Agaricus* latter *I* transformation year

be. Episode. Introduced not granting
you assent RIVALRY—De Quincey

less of number girl.
Of rocky, doubt nerve *Azotobacter* news Cereus *Echinocereus*
graduate it's vile experiencing synonym
interest no very annoyed land; in dignity as this effective seen
cause of stripped teeth

Iowa, Cuba Every
transmitted one
successive parents either never the

cases: at *versicolor* Ears
hunted union miles assasin "No"
is nutriment
leak enough *Sheet* several other night, simply
distortion. In 4th feel. Expression reply employed need trees?

An Asymmetry from Dhopeshwarkar on Krishnamurti

(29 Sept. 1960)

The taking aspects of Krishnamurti are not generalising
and investigating—the scientist's prejudice. An eye comes to life.
    Similarly,
opinions, for all their cogency, and even
knowing, are really ideas. So habits no less than action of the mind *are*
       concerned with urges, results to be attained, or ideals.
They are right. Each
need *branches* off there.
'Giving-me-satisfaction', etc., *is* not earlier. Reference and lining are
       sweet, and *of great* importance. *Each* is new
       to grasp.

Haiku from the above (29 Sept. 1960)

       An eye comes to life.
       Right. Each need branches off there.
       Each is new to grasp.

Zen and the Art of Tea

    Zen is thus necessarily shining with the tea. "Even the fully enlightened arhat may move proclaimed to be immediately harboring something of every three poisonous meditations, down comfortable to Bashō's sounds for by God himself—

    as every fallen leaf piling up on the swordplay, also the Mind you'll cherish—are altogether filled with Zen acquirements upon the foregoing or controlled enemies in the superior Mind and to conceive Hákuin's Oriental remains.

That made God particularly three; the leaf was secretly inclined to luxurious extravagances, even when the state was tinged,

are generally tinted along the provinces to the art monastery—generally altogether follow a mood for a studied bull, a man was making one out of the arhat into bamboo. The Onjōji is an historical Buddhist dictionary by Lake Biwa,

of the candidate, Hori Kintayū.

Thinking has learned the monk of many ways, known for Suruga but not Zen, at once beginning gold earlier as ultimately.

A Child's Garden of Verses Robert Louis Stevenson with Illustrations by Jessie Willcox Smith

The entire title serves as the seed, and the source is almost all of Robert Louis Stevenson's *A Child's Garden of Verses* (New York: Charles Scribner's Sons, 1928). It's possible to decode the method used, and although Jackson seems never to have written about this poem, it appears that the title is being spelled out acrostically, as in several other poems in *Stanzas,* using the first letter of the first word of a unit, each unit being a phrase, usually up to any punctuation. For example, the first line, "Afloat in the meadow by the swing," is the "A." The next paragraph, "Crow, hands, if two may read aright these rhymes of old delight and house and garden play, look kindly on. Days swing," spells "Child's," and so on. (For those who wish to follow up on the system underlying the poems: Jackson used c and s to stand for the x in Willcox, and sometimes used w to stand for v.)

In *Stanzas for Iris Lezak,* there were many typos in this poem, including missing text, which Jackson corrected by hand in his copy of the book. This is the first time the poem has been published in its correct form.—A. T.

Afloat in the meadow by the swing,

Crow, hands, if two may read aright these rhymes of old delight and house and garden play, look kindly on. Days swing,

green—afloat in the meadow by the swing, returns at last, double-quick; end Nod.

Off we go; for me:

very cool; end returns at last, swing, end swing,

returns at last, off we go; (battle been!)—end returns at last, travels the sun is not a-bed,

look kindly on. Off we go; upon my pillow lie; if two may read aright these rhymes of old delight and house and garden play, swing,

swing, travels the sun is not a-bed, end very cool; end Nod. Swing, off we go; Nod.

With lots of toys and things to eat, if two may read aright these rhymes of old delight and house and garden play, travels the sun is not a-bed, hands,

if two may read aright these rhymes of old delight and house and garden play, look kindly on. Look kindly on. Upon my pillow lie; swing, travels the sun is not a-bed, returns at last, afloat in the meadow by the swing, travels the sun is not a-bed, if two may read aright these rhymes of old delight and house and garden play, off we go; Nod. Swing,

(battle been!)—yet as I saw it,

just as if mother had blown out the light! End swing, swing, if two may read aright these rhymes of old delight and house and garden play, end

with lots of toys and things to eat, if two may read aright these rhymes of old delight and house and garden play, look kindly on. Look kindly on. Crow, off we go; crawls in the corners, system every night my prayers I say,

swing, marching by, if two may read aright these rhymes of old delight and house and garden play, travels the sun is not a-bed, hands,

as the blinding shadows fall as the rays diminish, under evening's cloak, they all roll away and vanish.

Children, you are very little, and your bones are very brittle; if you would grow great and stately, you must try to walk sedately. How do you like to go up in a swing, up in the air so blue? I love with all my heart: leaves double-quick. Sing a song of seasons!

Garden darkened, daisy shut, child in bed, they slumber—glow-worm in the highway rut, mice among the lumber. And now at last the sun is going down behind the wood, and I am very happy, for I know that I've been good. Reach down a hand, my dear, and take these rhymes for old acquaintance' sake! Down every path and every plot, every bush of roses, every blue forget-me-not where the dew reposes, "Up!" they cry, the day is come in the smiling valleys: we have beat the morning drum; playmate, join your allies!" Not a word will he disclose, not a word of all he knows.

Of farewell, O brother, sister, sire!

Vanish all things mortal. Every night my prayers I say, and get my dinner every day; and every day that I've been good, I get an orange after food. Reach down a hand, my dear, and take these rhymes for old acquaintance' sake! She wanders lowing here and there, and yet she cannot stray, all in the pleasant open air, the pleasant light of day; and blown by all the winds that pass and wet with all the showers, she walks among the meadow grass and eats the meadow flowers. Every Christian kind of place. Summer fading, winter comes—frosty mornings, tingling thumbs, window robins, window rooks, and the picture books.

Reach down a hand, my dear, and take these rhymes for old acquaintance' sake! On bee empty like a cup. Reach down a hand, my dear, and take these rhymes for old acquaintance' sake! Tiny woods below whose boughs

leads off until we reach the town of Sleep. It stares through the window-pane; sounds of the village grow stiller and stiller, stiller the note of the birds on the hill; dusty and dim are the eyes of the miller, deaf are his ears with the moil of the mill.

Such a life is very fine, but it's not so nice as mine: you must often, as you trod, have wearied *not* to be abroad. Through empty heaven without repose; each little Indian sleepy-head is being kissed and put to bed. Winds are in the air, they are blowing in the spring, everything! Now we behold the embers flee about the firelit hearth; and see our faces painted as we pass, like pictures on the window-glass.

Willie in all the town no spark of light. "Time was," the golden head irrevocably said; but time which none can find, while flowing fast away, leaves love behind. How do you like to go up in a swing, up in the air so blue?

In ships upon the seas. Last, love under grass alone he lies, so, when my nurse comes in for me, home I return across the sea, and go to bed with backward looks at my dear land of Story-books. That sits upon the pillow-hill, reach down a hand, my dear, and take these rhymes for old acquaintance' sake! All round the house is the jet-black night; it stares through the window-pane; it crawls in the corners, hiding from the light, and it moves with the moving flame. They trail behind her up the floor, I can wander, I can go; ocean, now, with my little gun, I crawl all in the dark along the wall, and follow round the forest track away behind the sofa back. So goes the old refrain.

Blinks. You too, my mother, read my rhymes for love of unforgotten times, and you may chance to hear once more the little feet along the floor.

Just as it was shut away, toy-like, in the even, here I see it glow with day under glowing heaven. Enough of fame and pillage, great commander Jane! So fine a show was never seen at the great circus on the green; for every kind of beast and man is marching in that caravan. Soon the frail eggs they shall chip, and upspringing make all the April woods merry with singing. I with your marble of Saturday last, empty heaven without repose; and in the blue and glowing days more thick than rain he showers his rays.

We into the laddered hay-loft smiles. Live laddered, children, you are very little and your bones are very brittle; if you would grow great and stately, you must try to walk sedately. Old carrying parcels with their feet such a life is very fine,

some are clad in armour green—(these have sure to battle been!)—some are pied with ev'ry hue, black and crimson, gold and blue; some have wings and swift are gone;—but they all look kindly on. My bed is waiting cool and fresh, with linen smooth and fair, and I must be off to sleepsin-by, and not forget my prayer. In the darkness houses shine, to keep me happy all the day. How do you like to go up in a swing, up in the air so blue?

And

clad hunting I called the little pool a sea; the little hills were big to me; for I am very small. Lies dew sin

great is the sun and wide he goes through empty heaven without repose; and in the blue and glowing days more thick than rain he showers his rays. And river, dew East and West are met, all the little letters did the

English printer set; while you thought of nothing, and were still too young to play, foreign people thought of you in places far away. Now Tom would be a driver and Maria go to sea, and my papa's a banker and as rich as he can be; but I, when I am stronger and can choose what I'm to do, O Leerie, I'll go round at night and light the lamps with you!

Of the world, flamingo

very proud and great, and tell the other girls and boys not to meddle with my toys. East and West are met, all the little letters did the English printer set; while you thought of nothing, and were still too young to play, foreign people thought of you in places far away. River sin East and West are met, all the little letters did the English printer set, while you thought of nothing and were still too young to play, foreign people thought of you in places far away. Sin

river, of the World, but East and West are met, all the little letters did the English printer set; while you thought of nothing, and were still too young to play, foreign people thought of you in places far away. River, try

lies of the world, under I called the little pool a sea; the little hills were big to me; for I am very small. Sin

sin try East and West are met, all the little letters did the English printer set; while you thought of nothing, and were still too young to play, foreign people thought of you in places far away. Very proud and great, and tell the other girls and boys not to meddle with my toys. East and West are met, all the little letters did the English printer set; while you thought of nothing, and were still too young to play, foreign people thought of you in places far away. Now Tom would be a driver and Maria go to sea, and my papa's a banker and as rich as he can be; but I, when I am stronger and can choose what I'm to do, O Leerie, I'll go round at night and light the lamps with you!

While here at home, in shining day, we round the sunny garden play, each little Indian sleepy-head is being kissed and put to bed. I called the little pool a sea; the little hills were big to me, for I am very small. Try hunting

I called the little pool a sea; the little hills were big to me for I am very small. Lies lies under sin try river, and try I called the little pool a sea; the little hills were big to me; for I am very small. Of the world, now Tom would be a driver and Maria go to sea, and my papa's a banker and as rich as he can be; but I, when I am stronger and can choose what I'm to do, O Leerie, I'll go round at night and light the lamps with you! Sin

but yawning

jolly fire I sit to warm my frozen bones a bit; East and West are met, all the little letters did the English printer set; while you thought of nothing, and were still too young to play, foreign people thought of you in places far away. Sin sin I called the little pool a sea; the little hills were big to me; for I am very small. East and West are met, all the little letters did the English printer set; while you thought of nothing, and were still too young to play, foreign people thought of you in places far away.

While here at home, in shining day, we round the sunny garden play, each little Indian sleepy-head is being kissed and put to bed. I called the little pool a sea; the little hills were big to me; for I am very small. Lies lies clad of the World, cloak, see.

Sin moored: I called the little pool a sea; the little hills were big to me; for I am very small. Try hunting

and home from the ocean,

coming down in an orderly way to where my toy vessels lie safe in the bay. Hi! I lie my fearful footsteps patter nigh, lawn alone, day, sun,

get back by day, *aunts*—round the house is the jet-black night; did for awhile together lie and, each little Indian sleepy-head is being kissed and put to bed. Now in the elders' seat we rest with quiet feet, orange after food. Forget-me-not where the dew reposes,

voice and drum, empty heaven without repose; red room with the giant bed where none but elders laid their head; sometimes things to bed I take, elders laid their head; see the people marching by,

repose; O the clean gravel! Bedroom handles. Every night my prayers I say, rhymes of old delight and house and garden play, the golden day is done,

lots of toys and things to eat, on either hand. Unforgotten times, is like a little boat; shine,

see the people marching by, through the keyhole, else but cook may go, vessel fast. Elders' seat we rest with quiet feet, night long and every night, sister, of Play; night my prayers I say,

whip, is the sun, the moon and stars are set, hay-loft smiles.

In the gloom of some dusty dining-room; ladybird, loud-humming, undaunted tread the long black passage up to bed. Smiles. The wintry sun a-bed, read my rhymes for love of unforgotten times, and every plot, the people marching by, in the blue and glowing days more thick than rain he showers his rays. O the smooth stream! Name was printed down by the English printers, sunless hours again begin;

but all your dozens of nurselings cry—you take your seat,

just to shut my eyes to go sailing through the skies—ere you could read it, side of the sea. Sound, is fairy bread to eat. Eyes,

we come! I could be a sailor on the rain-pool sea, look, little shadow that goes in and out with me, can at all, over the borders, cry, stray,

safe arrived, marching by, in the turf a hole I found, turning and churning that river to foam. Houses,

at the door at last;

crack goes the whip and off we go; the trees and houses smaller grow; last, round the woody turn we swing: good-bye, good-bye, to everything! Her dresses make a curious sound, in the darkness houses shine, parents move with candles; till on all, the night divine turns the bedroom handles. Leaves a-floating, drum, sand.

Golden day is done, a-bed, rocks. Drum, eggs the birdie sings and nests among the trees; the sailor sings of ropes and things in ships upon the seas. Now my little heart goes a-beating like a drum, with the breath of the Bogie in my hair; and all round the candle the crooked shadows come, and go marching along up the stair.

Orange after food. For I mean to grow as little as the dolly at the helm, and the dolly I intend to come alive; and with him beside to help me, it's a-sailing I shall go, it's a-sailing on the water, when the jolly breezes blow and the vessel goes a divie-divie-dive.

Very early, before the sun was up, I rose and found the shining dew on every buttercup; but my lazy little shadow, like an arrant sleepy-head, had stayed at home behind me and was fast asleep in bed. Eggs the birdie sings and nests among the trees; the sailor sings of ropes and things in ships upon the seas. Rocks. Sand. Eggs the birdie sings and nests among the trees; the sailor sings of ropes and things in ships upon the seas. Sand.

Rocks. Orange after food. Bright lamp is carried in, eggs the birdie sings and nests among the trees; the sailor sings of ropes and things in ships upon the sea. Rocks. The rain is raining all around, it falls on field and tree, it rains on the umbrellas here, and on the ships at sea.

Leaves a-floating, orange after food. Up into the cherry tree who should climb but little me? In the darkness houses shine, parents move with candles; till on all, the night divine turns the bedroom handles. Sand.

Sand. The rain is raining all around, it falls on field and tree, it rains on the umbrellas here, and on the ships at sea. Eggs the birdie sings and nests among the trees; the sailor sings of ropes and things in ships upon the seas. Very early, before the sun was up, I rose and found the shining dew on every buttercup; but my lazy little shadow, like an arrant sleepy-head, had stayed at home behind me and was fast asleep in bed. Eggs the birdie sings and nests among the trees; the sailor sings of ropes and things in ships upon the seas. Now my little heart goes a-beating like a drum, with the breath of the Bogie in my hair; and all round the candle the crooked shadows come, and go marching along up the stair. Sand. Orange after food. Now my little heart goes a-beating like a drum, with the breath of the Bogie in my hair; and all round the candle the crooked shadows come, and go marching along up the stair.

What's true and speak when he is spoken to, in the darkness houses shine, parents move with candles; till on all, the night divine turns the bedroom handles. The rain is raining all around, it falls on field and tree, it falls on the umbrellas here, and on the ships at sea. Her dresses make a curious sound,

in the darkness houses shine, parents move with candles, till on all, the night divine turns the bedroom handles. Leaves a-floating, leaves a-floating, upon it! Sand. The rain is raining all around, it falls on field and tree, it rains on the umbrellas here, and on the ships at sea. Rocks. And wall, the rain is raining all around, it falls on field and tree, it rains on the umbrellas here, and on the ships at sea. In the darkness houses shine, parents move with candles; till on all, the night divine turns the bedroom handles. Orange after food. Now my little heart goes a-beating like a drum, with the breath of the Bogie in my hair; and around the candle the crooked shadows come, and go marching along up the stair. Sand.

Bright lamp is carried in, you can see;

Japan, eggs the birdie sings and nests among the trees; the sailor sings of ropes and things in ships upon the seas. Sand. Sand. In the darkness houses shine, parents move with candles; till on all, the night divine turns the bedroom handles. Eggs the birdie sings and nests among the trees; the sailor sings of ropes and things in ships upon the seas.

What's true and speak when he is spoken to, in the darkness houses shine, parents move with candles, till on all the night divine turns the bedroom handles. Leaves a-floating, leaves a-floating, crack goes the whip and off we go; the trees and houses smaller grow, last, round the woody turn we swing: good-bye, good-bye to everything! Orange after food. Clearer grow; and sparrows' wings smooth it glides upon its travel,

sand. Me! In the darkness houses shine, parents move with candles, till on all, the night divine turns the bedroom handles. The rain is raining all around, it falls on field and tree, it rains on the umbrellas here, and on the ships at sea. Her dresses make a curious sound,

and when at eve I rise from tea, day dawns beyond the Atlantic Sea; and all the children in the West are getting up and being dressed.

Chief of our aunts—not only I, but all your dozen of nurselings cry— *What did the other children do?* Home from the Indies and home from the ocean, heroes and soldiers we all shall come home; still we shall find the old mill wheel in motion, turning and churning that river to foam. In the darkness shapes of things, houses, trees and hedges, clearer grow; and sparrows' wings beat on window ledges. Last, to the chamber where I lie my fearful footsteps patter nigh, and come from out the cold and gloom into my warm and cheerful room. Dear Uncle Jim, this garden grounds that now you smoke your pipe around, has seen immortal actions done and valiant battles lost and won. So, when my nurse comes in for me, home I return across the sea, and go to bed with backward looks at my dear land of Story-books.

Green leaves a-floating, castles of the foam, boats of mine a-boating— where will all come home? And all about was mine, I said, the little sparrow overhead, the little minnows too. Remember in your playing, as the sea-fog rolls to you, long ere you could read it, how I told you what to do; and that while you thought of no one, nearly half the world away some one thought of Louis on the beach of Monterey! Down by a shining water well

I found a very little dell, no higher than my head. Explore the colder countries round the door. Now in the elders' seat we rest with quiet feet, and from the window-bay we watch the children, our successors, play.

Of speckled eggs the birdie sings and nests among the trees; the sailor sings of ropes and things in ships upon the seas. From breakfast on through all the day at home among my friends I stay, but every night I go abroad afar into the land of Nod.

We can see our coloured faces floating on the shaken pool down in cool places, dim and very cool; till a wind or water wrinkle, dipping martens, plumping trout, spreads in a twinkle and blots all out. Escape them, they're as mad as they can be, the wicket is the harbour and the garden is the shore. Round the bright air with footing true, to please the child, to paint the rose, the gardener of the World he goes. Spring and daisies came apace; grasses hide my hiding place; grasses run like a green sea o'er the lawn up to my knee. Eskimo, little Turk or Japanee, Oh! don't you wish that you were me? Silly gardener! summer goes, and winter comes with pinching toes, when in the garden bare and brown you must lay your barrow down.

Rain may keep raining, and others go roam, but I can be happy and building at home. On goes the river and out past the mill, away down the valley, away down the hill. But yonder, see! apart and high, frozen Siberia lies; where I, with Robert Bruce and William Tell, was bound by an enchanter's spell. Every night at teatime and before you take your seat, with lantern and with ladder he comes posting up the street. Red room with the giant bed where none but elders laid their head; the little room where you and I did for awhile together lie and, simple suitor, I your hand in decent marriage did demand; the great day nursery, best of all with pictures pasted on the wall and leaves upon the blind—a pleasant room wherein to wake and hear the leafy garden shake and rustle in the wind—and pleasant there to lie in bed and see the pictures overhead—the wars about Sebastopol, the grinning guns along the wall, the daring escalade, the plunging ships, the bleating sheep, the happy children ankle-deep and laughing as they wade: all these are vanished clean away, and the old manse is changed to-day; it wears an altered face and shields a stranger race. The friendly cow all red and white, I love with all my heart: she gives me cream with all her might, to eat with apple-tart.

Let the sofa be mountains, the carpet be sea, there I'll establish a city for me: a kirk and a mill and a palace beside, and a harbour as well where my vessels may ride. Oh! don't you wish that you were me? Under grass alone he lies, scarlet coat and pointed gun, to the stars and to the sun. I saw the next door garden lie, adorned with flowers, before my eye, and many pleasant places more that I had never seen before. So goes the old refrain.

Slumber hold me tightly till I waken in the dawn, and hear the thrushes singing in the lilacs round the lawn. The gardener does not love to talk, he makes me keep the gravel walk; and when he puts his tools away, he locks the door and takes the key. Embers flee about the firelit hearth; and see our faces painted as we pass, like pictures, on the window-glass. Where shall we adventure, to-day that we're afloat, wary of the weather and steering by a star? Eastern cities, miles about, are with mosque and minaret among sandy gardens set, and the rich goods from near and far hang for sale in the bazaar:—where the Great Wall round China goes, and on one side the desert blows, and with bell and voice and drum, cities on the other hum;—where are forests, hot as fire, wide as England, tall as a spire, full of apes and cocoa-nuts and the negro hunters' huts;—where the knotty crocodile lies and blinks in the Nile, and the red flamingo flies hunting fish before his eyes;—where in jungles, near and far, man-devouring tigers are, lying close and giving ear lest the hunt be drawing near, or a comer-by be seen swinging in a palanquin; where among the desert sands some deserted city stands, all its children, sweep and prince, grown to manhood ages since, not a foot in street or house, not a stir of child or mouse, and when kindly falls the night, in all the town no spark of light. Nurse helps me in when I embark; she girds me in my sailor's coat and starts me in the dark. O how much wiser you would be to play at Indian wars with me! Now at last the sun is going down behind the wood, and I am very happy, for I know that I've been good.

When, to go out, my nurse doth wrap me in comforter and cap; the cold wind burns my face, and blows its frosty pepper up my nose. In winter I get up at night and dress by yellow candlelight. Though closer still the blinds we pull to keep the shady parlour cool, yet he will find a chink or two to slip his golden fingers through. He hasn't got a notion of how children ought to play, and can only make a fool of me in every sort of way.

I shall find him, never fear, I shall find my grenadier; but for all that's gone and come, I shall find my soldier dumb. Late lies the wintry sun a-bed, a frosty, fiery sleepy-head; blinks but an hour or two; and then, a blood-red orange, sets again. Lead onward into fairy land, where all the children dine at five, and all the play things come alive. "Up," they cry, "the day is come on the smiling valleys: we have beat the morning drum; playmate, join your allies!" Sometimes for an hour or so I watched my leaden soldiers go, with different uniforms and drills, among the bed-clothes, through the hills; and sometimes sent my ships and fleets all up and down among the sheets; or brought my trees and houses out, and planted cities all about. To you in distant India, these I send across the seas, nor count it far across. Round the house is the jet-black night; it stares through the window-pane; it crawls in the corners, hiding from the light, and it moves with the moving flame. Away down the river, a hundred miles or more, other little children shall bring my boats ashore. Though closer still the blinds we pull to keep the shady parlour cool, yet he will find a chink or two to slip his golden fingers through. I played there were no deeper seas, nor any wider plains than these, nor other kings than me. On goes the river and out past the mill, away down the valley, away down the hill. Nobody heard him and nobody saw, his a picture you never could draw, but he's sure to be present, abroad or at home, when children are happy and playing alone. So fine a show was never seen at the great circus on the green; for every kind of beast and man is marching in that caravan.

Black are my steps on silver sod; thick blows my frosty breath abroad; and tree and house, and hill and lake, are frosted like a wedding-cake. Years may go by, and the wheel in the river wheel as it wheels for us, children, today, wheel and keep roaring and foaming for ever long after all of the boys are away.

Johnnie beats the drum. Early, before the sun was up, I rose and found the shining dew on every buttercup; but my lazy little shadow, like an arrant sleepy-head, had stayed at home behind me and was fast asleep in bed. So you may see, if you will look through the windows of this book, another child, far, far away, and in another garden, play. She gives me cream with all her might to eat with apple-tart. In the silence he has heard talking bee and ladybird and the butterfly has flown o'er him as he lay alone. Evening when the lamp is lit, around the fire my parents sit; they sit at home and talk and sing, and do not play at anything.

When at eve I rise from tea, day dawns beyond the Atlantic Sea; and all the children in the West are getting up and being dressed. It is very nice to think the world is full of meat and drink, with little children saying grace in every Christian kind of place. Lamps now glitter down the street; faintly sound the falling feet; and the blue even slowly falls about the garden trees and walls. Leerie stops to light it as he lights so many more; and oh! before you hurry by with ladder and with light; O Leerie, see a little child and nod to him tonight! Children, mounting fast and kissing hands, in chorus sing: good-bye, good-bye, to everything! Oh, what a joy to clamber there, oh, what a place for play, with the sweet, the dim, the dusty air, the happy hills of hay! Cruel children, crying babies, all grow up as geese and gabies, hated, as their age increases, by their nephews and their nieces. Strangest things are there for me, both things to eat and things to see, and many frightening sights abroad till morning in the land of Nod.

Soon the frail eggs they shall chip, and upspringing make all the April woods merry with singing. Mary Jane commands the party, Peter leads the rear; feet in time, alert and hearty, each a Grenadier! In comes the playmate that never was seen. Try as I like to find the way, I never can get back by day, nor can remember plain and clear the curious music that I hear. Here we had best on tiptoe tread, while I for safety march ahead, for this is that enchanted ground where all who loiter slumber sound.

◆

Selections from *Asymmetries 1–260* and Later Asymmetries (1960–61)

Introduction

Adapted by Anne Tardos from "Methods for Reading and Performing Asymmetries 1–260"

Asymmetries are poems of which the words, punctuation, typography, and spacing of words on the page have been determined by certain kinds of deterministic but nonintentional operations. With a few exceptions, *Asymmetries 1–260,* like most of the 501 numbered Asymmetries (1960–61), were generated by an acrostic method. This involved drawing words, word strings, and in one case, syllables from current reading matter (or in a few poems, from the environment in which the poems were written). Usually an initial word was found in a text (or in the environment) and words (or strings) having its letters as their initial letters were then found by reading along in the text (or by careful perception of the environment). After the first line, the words or strings of which acrostically "spelled out" the first word, words beginning with the second and subsequent letters of the first word were found to begin the second and subsequent lines.

Asymmetries may be performed either by a single person or by a group including any number of people. Each performer follows either a Basic Method or one of nine other performance methods, while realizing successively each Asymmetry in a randomly selected or individually chosen series of the poems. The individual performers decide their own reading speeds and other performance parameters not specifically (or only partially) regulated by the methods followed. All individuals perform simultaneously.

Performers must become acutely conscious of both the sounds they themselves are producing and those arising from other performers, the audience, and/or the environment. It is essential to the realization of Asymmetries that all performers choose as many aspects and details as possible of their individual realizations within the context of as clear an awareness of the total aural situation at each moment as performance circumstances allow. In many circumstances—as when performers are *dispersed* within the space (e.g., around or in the midst of an audience or when performers and audience are identical), a procedure often followed in performances I've directed—each performer's impression of the total aural situation will necessarily differ from those of the others. What is asked for is concentrated attention to all sounds perceptible to the individual and an attitude of receptivity and responsiveness such that choices are made spontaneously, often seeming to arise from the whole situation.

Schematically, this "whole" can be represented by concentric spheres: the inmost is that of the individual performer; next, that of the whole performance group; next, that of the larger social group, including audience as well as performers; next, that of the performance space, including room acoustics, electronics, etc.; and finally, the larger spaces within which the performance space is situated: the rest of the building, the surrounding streets, neighborhood, city (or rural area), etc., all of which may affect significantly the aggregate of sounds heard by each individual at each moment. The spheres are best conceived as transparent and interpenetrating—not static shells but concentric ripples travelling simultaneously out from and in toward each center.

Asymmetry 1

Pain available ingredient.

news

ARTHRITIS rule through *hand* ritual
       impelling through.

                                        infinite
                    Three impending stretching
if fell

now,
            'office',
                        wasn't

Asymmetry 6

Dreams recent episodes awaken middle,
                                        such

results everyone sleep?

                        Used lasted,
                                        typical
        sleep
emotionally means:
                    objective thinking instructive.

            (Organs naturally.)

                            Activity
                    lower level young

aged greatly eye-
                    movements dreaming

move occur vocalize episodes.

Some observed Medical EEG

Asymmetry 7

Records eye-
                movements classified objective
        recounted.

                        Drops skin,

electric least eating contractions three
        related involve Chicago,

cardiac appeared related duration increase
        associates.

                        Cycle,

one no experiment

right illuminated glass happens two

determined enters trapped enough
                ray material,
                                internal
                natural ends
                                disadvantage.

See,
        emerging eight

Asymmetry 18

inspiring.

      name sins people instruction
        reverent "invoking"
    name
            [Goblins]

name
    Avalokitesvara
          magical
   enables

Asymmetry 94

Perhaps
     Every Rockefeller human asked,
             Perhaps
    Every
      seems

Every vivid,
     Every vivid,
         Every vivid,
             Every
   vivid,
     Every vivid,
         Every vivid,
             Every

vivid,
                    Rockefeller opposed Catholic
years

Rockefeller opposed Catholic kinds
                              Every vivid,
          Every vivid,
                    Every vivid,
                              footnote
          Every vivid,
                    life—
                              life—
          Every Rockefeller vivid,
                                        Every

human United States **Music** asked,
                              New

Asymmetry 137

Any kind of art has essentially such a
     background,
                    not have such a
     background,
                    can not youth,

Nature
          After having read Spinoza's
          "Ethica",
                    he was charmed by
          the doctrine,
                    and never gave it
          up throughout his life.

"und Unglück wird Gesang".

"rosa
        erred,
               and how I strived,"

"your goal:
      out,"
          "und was ich lebte,"
Raffael and classical antiquity,

Asymmetry 138

but his Italian voyage,
              "Under the sun"
   the same vigour of life:

"Unter der Sonn'"

Asymmetry 139

"Here sit I,
     enjoy,"
        "resignation"
    "enjoy,"

"enjoy,"
    nature,
       just in this coming

from nothingness and going
into nothingness there is
the gentle sound of humanity.

opposite of that of Spinoza.

yet has not passed
in the present.

reason why I say that the present
itself determines the present,
"enjoy,"
a moment of
time,
say,
opposite of that
of Spinoza.

nature,

"enjoy,"
nature,
just in this coming
from nothingness and going

Asymmetry 237

Chicago suburb.

He saw that Chicago suburb.

angel had
getting back on

                              Other
        surprises may develop,
                          for example,

He
        ear for Morse signals.

I saw that

Chicago suburb.

                  He
                      I saw that
                              Chicago suburb.

        Angel had
                  getting back on
                              Other

angel had
        name.

                  Collins was heading for
        Cushing,
                  negative,
                      getting back on
        ear for Morse signals.

                      Lake
                          Como,

Asymmetry 265

This
     is a large flag
          homes
              it glows
                 southwest
    city and

it glows
     This
         is a large flag

homes
    on the wall.

        Each band

Asymmetry 269

"in private—
      you can bury it"
            night McFadden
  had some disquieting news

night McFadden had some disquieting news
    "in private—
        you can bury it"
            grab
  the
    "(hate analo-
        gies . . .)

                                        you want
        the pitch..."
                        treas-
                                uries

Asymmetry 285

Today is a pussy
                ON
                        TELEVISION
                                TWO MINUTES
        AGO
                SAP!
                        delivers
                                —AMERICA
                                        "THE"
                                                Yet he
                found life without

ONE
        1939,
                ELVINA
                        IN AN INDIAN

detail
                throughout a
                        END HERE?

                                        HA!

                                                the European
                continent.

Perhaps sunlight

AN EYE

irrevocable

choice to

LOOK

AROUND ALL Y'LIKE!

Asymmetry 292

twinkle with delight at the persecution

WITH A

It is

NOW!

GOOD-

BY,

DEAR...

knew have

disappeared.

The objective conditions

LET'S SEE . . .

MAYBE SHE

ending.

Paradoxical as it may seem,

WHAT DO YOU MEAN?!

house will burn;

then I

AS

     YOU

         the

           stove.

               The house burns;

                         my

I STARTED

(nature)

         ANOTHER WAY!

               WHY SHOULD

                    I?

Asymmetry 372

THE INDICATOR HERE! !

               ELECTRICAL IMPULSES!

HERE! !

       ELECTRICAL IMPULSES!

               REMAIN HERE
     ELECTRICAL IMPULSES!

ELECTRICAL IMPULSES!

           LINGERED THERE TWO MONTHS!

Asymmetry 373

MISSION COMPLETED,
                    I BADE THEM GOOD-
                                        BY AND DEPARTED...
          SPACE AND TIME WARP...
                                        SPACE AND TIME WARP...
               I BADE THEM GOOD-
                              BY AND DEPARTED...
          ON THIS,
                         THE NEAREST PLANET!...

                                           NEAREST
          PLANET!...

I BADE THEM GOOD-
                       BY AND DEPARTED...

SPACE AND TIME WARP...
                             PLANET!

                                      AND TIME WARP...
          CAVES!

               EARTH...

Asymmetry 487

Key Largo,

surface tension Robert Schumann?

                                     "Sir Er- ([r] --------------------------------
[r] ------------------) nest Henry Shackleton."

                                           Wri- ([I] ---------------------------
[I] ------------------) t of right coloratura so- ([o] ---
[o] ------------------) prano;
                             "reductio ad absur- ([r] ----------------------------
[r] ------------------) dum" . . .
                           Great Commoner?

                           Stultify,

Smithsonian Institution!

                           Inscribable SWEE- ([i] ------------------------------
[i] -----------------------------)T TERRI SHORT PAUSE
                           ATROPOS pot- (-t-t-t-t-t-t-t-t-t-t-t-t-t-t-t-t-t-t
-t-t-t-t-t-t-t-t-t-t-t-t-t-t-t-t-t-t-t-t-t-t-t) wallo-([ə] --------------------------
[ə] -------------------------------) per?

                           Coloratura ([ə] -------------------------------
[ə] -------------------------------) soprano?

◆

Speech (9 August 1961)

Epigraph 1:
"When asked 'Is there not a difference between the killing that a revolutionist does and that which a policeman does?' Tolstoy answered: 'There is as much difference between cat-shit and dog-shit. But I don't like the smell of either one or the other.'" Simmons, *Tolstoy*, 651, quoted as Note 18, p. 754, of *The Icon and the Axe* by James H. Billington (New York, 1966).

Epigraph 2: "The Sea Gull" by Joseph Gould
[The "reader" climbs up onto a table or chair, flaps his arms wildly, like wings, & screams like a sea gull a good many times, as loudly & harshly & shrilly as possible.]

Directions for reading this poem aloud: Read the first epigraph & perform the second. Then read the poem slowly and deliberately. Where there are blank spaces, before or after words, horizontally or vertically, the reader must fall silent for larger or smaller durations of time corresponding relatively to the amounts of blank space on the page. Silences within "strophes" must all be longer than than those ordinarily occasioned by punctuation. Silences between strophes should range between a few seconds and several. Within these general guidelines the reader should proceed as he feels.

If I were to speak
it wd be in the voice of a gull
            not a sea gull
            but a pseudo gull
    like Joe Gould.

I wont do that now.

I might speak like a dog or a cat
        since one of each
    follows me around the house

all day
                    from room to room,
but their speech
                    is mostly silence.

I've been doing that for years.

Barking makes my throat sore
            meowing sounds silly
        silence is mis-
                    or un-
                        understood
and Joe Gould recited his poem "The Sea Gull"
            making like a sea gull
        to shake the sleepy Ravens up
                                years ago.

To speak.

"To have something to say"
            's the way they usually put it
        "if you have something to say"
                they say
        "you'll find a way to say it"
                            and so on.

Speaking.

I cd speak about murder
                having just read Camus
        the speech of a sane & reasonable man
                    gone too soon
        making the truly modest proposal
                that each of us
                        decide

to be murderers

        or accomplices of murderers

or not.

But negation

      is affirmation

          by denial

      of a repressed wish

            Freud

            1925.

That's the way with speech.

To say

     "I will not be a murderer

        or accomplice of murderers"

     voices my murderous heart.

Let it speak out.

Let the wish for murder

          or self-murder

     speak itself out.

"No"

    is the sign of the repressed

but knowing "No" 's the sign o' the repressed

    and saying "No" to murder

allows the murderous strength to side with life

        against murder.

Speak it.

I'll speak it.

No.

No murder is justifiable.

No one who murders
        or justifies murders
                for any reason at all
        is on the side of life.

I'll do nothing to aid him.*

The murderous strength of my heart
        will fight
                        to the
                                life
        against
                the murderers.

Too much of a speech.

But I've spoken.

---

*NOTE, 2:53 AM, Mon. 6 Feb. 1967: I meant, of course, that I wd not aid "him"
in his murdering or justifying of murder. I might very well aid him to escape being
murdered himself in the guise of "legal punishment"; or to escape being bombed
from the air for "terrorist" acts. JML

3 November Poems

1

Entropy announce
encyclopedic mushroom fertility
eagerness necessary
caries season in Orlando

tone focus

sliding meeting
concede necessary altitudes
Florentine excess sewer flute
fornication folk
far

furriers tropisms pusillanimous
personally puzzled
fleet tune finale

feature equation

critical hebetudes
creature fearless.

2

Monday Tuesday Wednesday Beacon Wax.
Freezer flight in shining long.
Soul toast foam focus.

Early the crier criterion zoos.
Assuming nurture plaid.

Contrast surface.

Lump Earl Castillian.
Frémont. ("é" = "ee")

In view of effable.
149 scooters tubing phalluses.
Strew mountains.

3

Worthless swallow contagious.
Persuade stable authors annoyed.
Street Cleavers.

Crocker craze.
Claque.

November 1961
The Bronx

One Hundred

one one one one one one one one one one

one one one one one one one one one one

one one one one one one one one one one

one one one one one one one one one one

one one one one one one one one one one

one one one one one one one one one one

one one one one one one one one one one

one one one one one one one one one one

one one one one one one one one one one

one one one one one one one one one one

Jackson Mac Low
15 December 1961
965 Hoe Avenue
New York 59 NY

Selections from Drawing-Asymmetries (1961)

Introduction

From "A Note on the Drawing-Asymmetries," 18 May 1985, Verona

The Drawing-Asymmetries comprise a series of words and/or word strings drawn by the Asymmetries method from whatever texts happened to be at hand and immediately lettered very freely and impulsively on the sheet of drawing paper with brush and/or pen. In many cases the letters of the words are so placed that they are difficult or impossible to read—as words or even as letters. In some Drawing-Asymmetries the letters cross each other to such an extent that they no longer even look like letters. Some later sheets are completely and densely covered by crossing and superimposed broad black or variously gray lines—all really letters making up words drawn from random texts by the Asymmetries method. Sometimes a single index word was spelled out in a succession of Drawing-Asymmetries, so it is often impossible to work back to the originary index word from the words in a single Drawing-Asymmetry.

Drawing-Asymmetry #8

Drawing-Asymmetry #12

Drawing-Asymmetry #15

Drawing-Asymmetry #19

Drawing-Asymmetry #38

Drawing-Asymmetry #41

Some Recent Things (1962–1963)

Paint Brush Box Piece (Summer 1962)

Make any sounds you want to with a paint brush box.

Rabbi (7 January 1963)

rewarded.   and be be
this rewarded.   and be be
this rewarded.   and be be this

rewarded.   and
be be this
rewarded.   and be be

this rewarded.   and be be this rewarded.
and be be this rewarded.   and be be
this rewarded.   and be be this rewarded.   and be

Prunes (7 January 1963)

prunes dream lucky
numbers, secure secure prunes previous
       lucky numbers, feeling lucky
       numbers,
previous friend.   lucky

965 Hoe Avenue
Bronx NY 10459
USA

◆

More Recent Things (1963)

Paprika ['pæ : prɪkə] (20 January 1963)

PAPRIKA <u>PACKED</u> PAPRIKA PAPRIKA nourishes

PAPRIKA PAPRIKA <u>PACKED</u> <u>MADE</u>

PAPRIKA PAPRIKA nourishes PAPRIKA

PAPRIKA <u>PACKED</u> <u>MADE</u> PAPRIKA

PAPRIKA nourishes PAPRIKA PAPRIKA

<u>PACKED</u> <u>MADE</u> PAPRIKA PAPRIKA nourishes

PAPRIKA PAPRIKA <u>PACKED</u> <u>MADE</u> PAPRIKA

PAPRIKA nourishes PAPRIKA PAPRIKA <u>PACKED</u>

<u>MADE</u> PAPRIKA PAPRIKA nourishes PAPRIKA PAPRIKA

<u>PACKED</u> <u>MADE</u> PAPRIKA PAPRIKA nourishes PAPRIKA
PAPRIKA

<u>PACKED</u> <u>MADE</u> PAPRIKA PAPRIKA nourishes PAPRIKA
PAPRIKA

[&c.]

[ad infinitum]

[i.e., repeat last line as many times as you want to.]

[empty spaces to the left of each line after the first indicate silences lasting
as long as it might take you to shout "PAPRIKA"—double-underlinings indicate
small capital letters in print—other capital letters indicate large capital letters
large capitals mean loud shouts, small capitals moderate shouts]

Shocked (8 January 1963)

Stunt.

Their groom shocked shock-
ed Police suspended suspensions though
   good **Shocked** thrown two shocked shock-
ed Police suspended suspensions though
   good shocked Chief two shock-
ed that though **Shocked** their groom shocked
   the two force,
Shocked The two shocked drank coffee relaxed.

Orang-outang (8 January 1963)

One from that Linnaeus,
orang-outang.

"Extraordinary orang-outang,
credulity orang-outangs,
Orang Outang enunciating organization—
art,
that even change abandon,
particular diligently interrelated Orang
        Outang neighboring original
        origin learning."

Orang-outang.

Social Project 1 (29 April 1963)

FIND A WAY TO END UNEMPLOYMENT
                                OR

FIND A WAY FOR PEOPLE TO LIVE WITHOUT EMPLOYMENT.
MAKE WHICHEVER ONE YOU FIND WORK.

Social Project 2 (29 April 1963)

FIND A WAY TO END WAR.
MAKE IT WORK.

Social Project 3 (29 April 1963)

FIND A WAY TO PRODUCE EVERYTHING EVERYBODY NEEDS AND
  GET IT TO THEM.
MAKE IT WORK.

965 Hoe Avenue
Bronx NY 10459
USA

◆

CARDBOARD BOX PIECE

for George Maciunas
by Jackson Mac Low
18 October 1963
New York City

Do only very careful things with one or more cardboard boxes.
Be sure not to harm the boxes in any way.
(Any number of people may participate.)

Nietzsche—14 January 1963

Nietzsche's Nietzsche pre-
senting Nietzsche Nietzsche's Nietzsche.

Nietzsche Nietzsche challenged not Nietzsche's pressing Nietzsche's
        Nietzsche Renaissance Nietzsche Nietzsche existence,
not sinned,
see,
past Nietzsche,
dreams,
psychic,
leadership.

Men—14 January 1963

masses,

felt man make mediocrities men man demagogue generals.

made seem ran mili-
tary Here Continent.

Daily Life

How to Make Poems from a DAILY LIFE List

I. Prepare a list such as the following:

DAILY LIFE 1

6 August 1963

1	A.	I'm going to the store.	Black Ace
2	B.	Is the baby sleeping?	Black Two
3	C.	I'd better take the dog out.	Black Three
4	D.	What do you want?	Black Four
5	E.	Let's have eggs for breakfast.	Black Five
6	F.	Has the mail come yet?	Black Six
7	G.	I'll take the garbage down.	Black Seven
8	H.	Is there anything you need downstairs?	Black Eight
9	I.	I'll see you.	Black Nine
10	J.	Shall I turn the light on?	Black Ten
11	K.	I'll take the bottles back.	Black Jack
12	L.	Did somebody knock on the door?	Black Queen
13	M.	I'm going to close the window.	Black King
14	N.	Is the baby crying?	Red Ace
15	O.	Hello, sweety-baby!	Red Two

16	P.	What's that red mark on him?	Red Three
17	Q.	I'm going to lie down & rest my back for awhile.	Red Four
18	R.	What did you say?	Red Five
19	S.	Look how this plant has grown!	Red Six
20	T.	Have you fed the cat & dog?	Red Seven
21	U.	I'm going to make some coffee.	Red Eight
22	V.	Do you want some ginger beer?	Red Nine
23	W.	I wish it wasn't always so noisy.	Red Ten
24	X.	Is it all right if I turn on the news?	Red Jack
25	Y.	What's the matter with the baby?	Red Queen
26	Z.	Have half a banana.	Red King

II. Employ one of the following methods:

1. *Letters.* This is the method first used by the author when he conceived the idea of a DAILY LIFE list as a source for poems, plays, &c. (6 August 1963), & except for one poem, it is the only method he has used up to the present time (8 January 1964). One selects (or allows chance or circumstance to select) a name, phrase, sentence, title, or any other limited series of words, & translates each successive letter into the sentence corresponding to it on a DAILY LIFE list. The end of a word produces the end of a strophe, e.g., translating the title DAILY LIFE into the sentences of DAILY LIFE 1, one gets:

DAILY LIFE

What do you want?
I'm going to the store.
I'll see you.
Did somebody knock on the door?
What's the matter with the baby?

Did somebody knock on the door?
I'll see you.
Has the mail come yet?
Let's have eggs for breakfast.

Obviously, if one wants a poem having the same number of lines in every strophe, one must choose a series of words having the same number of letters in each word.

2. *Numbers.* One selects a source of digits, such as a random digit table or a telephone book, & translates the digits, taken in pairs, in any of a number of ways. The simplest way is to use only the first 25 sentences of a list & to make a correspondence chart for all possible pairs of digits (see next page for such a chart). [Since there are exactly 100 possible pairs of digits, the number of different lines corresponding to the digit pairs must divide evenly into 100. That's why all 26 lines in the Daily Life list cannot be used, but only 25. (The Letters and Playing Cards methods, in contrast, allow use of all 26 lines in the Daily Life list.)—A.T.] One can use single digits (0 being taken as 10) or pairs of digits to determine the number of strophes in a poem & the number of lines in each successive strophe. (If one wants the same number of lines in every strophe, one need use only 2 digits: one for the number of strophes & one for the number of lines in every strophe.)

25-place correspondence chart for digit pairs:

01	26	51	76		09	34	59	84		17	42	67	92
02	27	52	77		10	35	60	85		18	43	68	93
03	28	53	78		11	36	61	86		19	44	69	94
04	29	54	79		12	37	62	87		20	45	70	95
05	30	55	80		13	38	63	88		21	46	71	96
06	31	56	81		14	39	64	89		22	47	72	97
07	32	57	82		15	40	65	90		23	48	73	98
08	33	58	83		16	41	66	91		24	49	74	99
										25	50	75	00

Using a 5-place random digit table, one may get the series 94736 24128. The first digit, 9, determining the number of strophes in a poem; the 2nd digit, 4, determining the number of lines in the first strophe; & the last 8 digits, taken in pairs translated into 01 to 25 thru the correspondence table, determining the successive lines of the first strophe; one gets as the first strophe of a nine-strophe poem:

73–23 I wish it wasn't always so noisy.
62–12 Did somebody knock on the door?
41–16 What's that red mark on him?
28–03 I'd better take the dog out.

Other methods may also be used to translate numbers into a DAILY LIFE list to produce poems. For instance, one may dispense with a correspondence table & only use pairs from 01 to 26, disregarding all other combinations of digits. Or one may use as a source a *mixed* series of numbers & letters, as the author did the 2nd time he used DAILY LIFE 1 as a source (15 August 1963), when he translated the series (found on a slip of paper clipped from the top of a printer's galley): "8–8 Caled w 8 Spt Hvy x 16 RAU (1) Dec. 19 6535" using the digits singly except when a pair formed a number between 10 & 26.

3. *Playing Cards*. One method for using playing cards is to shuffle, draw one card to determine number of strophes (1 to 13, taking Ace as 1 & Jack, Queen & King as 11, 12 & 13; or 1 to 26, using the correspondences of numbers to card colors & denominations appearing on the list). Then draw as many cards as strophes to determine the number of lines in each successive strophe (or draw only one card, if one wants to have the same number of lines in every strophe). Finally, shuffle & draw a single card for each line of the poem, shuffling between every 2 draws, or at least fairly frequently. Other methods of using playing cards may also be used.

4. *Other Methods*. Still other methods may be devised to use lists of sentences from daily life as sources of poems. For instance, several alternative lists may be used at the same time with some chance determinant selecting which list is to be used as the source for any particular line of a poem. &, of course, readers may make their own list(s), using them alone or together with one or more of the author's lists. What wd make such a poem a realization of DAILY LIFE is the use of one or more lists of sen-

tences from daily life as source(s) for poems or other literary works. (The author has already written an essay describing a method for using such lists as sources for dramatic presentations [August 1963].)

DAILY LIFE was first conceived, along with Letters & Numbers methods, & the list "DAILY LIFE 1" was composed & first used as source, on 6 August 1963. Above essay was written in this form on 8 January 1964.

Happy New Year 1964 to Barney and Mary Childs
(a DAILY LIFE poem, drawn from DAILY LIFE 1)

Is there anything you need downstairs?
I'm going to the store.
What's that red mark on him?
What's that red mark on him?
What's the matter with the baby?

Is the baby crying?
Let's have eggs for breakfast.
I wish it wasn't always so noisy.

What's the matter with the baby?
Let's have eggs for breakfast.
I'm going to the store.
What did you say?

Look how this plant has grown!
Is the baby crying?

Have you fed the cat & dog?
Hello, sweety-baby!

Is the baby sleeping?
I'm going to the store.
What did you say?
Is the baby crying?
Let's have eggs for breakfast.
What's the matter with the baby?

I'm going to the store.
Is the baby crying?
What do you want?

I'm going to close the window.
I'm going to the store.
What did you say?
What's the matter with the baby?

I'd better take the dog out.
Is there anything you need downstairs?
I'll see you.
Did somebody knock at the door?
What do you want?
Look how this plant has grown!

8 January 1964
The Bronx

Selections from "The Presidents of the United States of America"

A Note on the Composition of "The Presidents of the United States of America," 15 December 1968

"The Presidents of the United States of America" was composed in January and May 1963. Each section is headed by the first inaugural year of a president (from Washington thru Fillmore), and its structure of images is that of the Phoenician meanings of the successive letters of the president's name. The meanings are those given in *The Roman Inscriptional Letter,* a book designed, written, and printed by Sandra Lawrence in the Graphic Arts Workshop at Reed College, Portland, Oregon, in May 1955. They are:

A	(aleph) "ox"		N	(nun) "fish"
B	(beth) "house"		O	(ayin) "eye"
C	(gimel) "camel"		P	(pe) "mouth"
D	(daleth) "door"		Q	(qoph) "knot"
E	(he) "window" or "look!"		R	(resh) "head"
F	(vau) "hook"		S	(shin) "tooth"
H	(cheth) "fence"		T	(tau) "mark"
I	(yod) "hand"		V	(vau) "hook"
K	(kaph) "palm of the hand"		X	(samekh) "prop"
L	(lamed) "ox-goad"		Y	(vau) "hook"
M	(mem) "water"		Z	(zayin) "weapon"

Letters developed by the Romans or in the Middle Ages were given the meanings of the letters from which they were derived or to which they were similar:

G (developed by Romans in third century B.C.: similar in form to C) "camel"
J (introduced during Middle Ages as minuscule form of I and made into majuscule in the sixteenth century) "hand"
U (introduced during Middle Ages as a minuscule form of V and made into majuscule in the sixteenth century) "hook"
W (Anglo-Saxon addition in eleventh century; similar to two V's) "hooks" or "hook hook"

These letter-meaning words were used as "nuclei" which were freely connected by other material. This method was first used by the poet in writing a sestina, "The Albatross," in 1950; here a list of end words was obtained "automatically" and then permuted and connected into a sestina. The poet first connected chance-given nuclei in this way in 1960 in writing such prose pieces as "A Greater Sorrow" (in *An Anthology,* published by Young and Mac Low, New York, 1963; and in my *Stanzas for Iris Lezak,* Something Else Press, Barton, VT, 1972). Most of the poems in *22 Light Poems* (Black Sparrow Press, Los Angeles, 1968) were composed in 1962–63, using names of kinds of light as nuclei. In "The Presidents of the United States of America," each letter-meaning nucleus could be used in any form class (e.g., M could be translated as the noun "water," the verb "water," the adjective "watery," or as the adverb "waterily"). In the earlier sections (written in January 1963), a minimum of connective material was introduced between the nuclei, and the meanings of the letters of each name delimited a strophe. In the later sections (written in May 1963), much more material was introduced between the nuclei, and the verse structures became much more complex.

The poet has often been asked by friends and well-wishers to write further sections dealing with the presidents following Fillmore. He has often thought of doing so and has even collected materials for this purpose, but so far he has only written a draft of a section on Franklin Pierce.

1789

(begun about 15 January 1963)

George Washington never owned a camel
but he looked thru the eyes in his head
with a camel's calm and wary look.

Hooks that wd irritate an ox
held his teeth together
and he cd build a fence with his own hands
tho he preferred to go fishing
as anyone else wd
while others did the work *for* him
for tho he had no camels he had slaves enough
and probably made them toe the mark by keeping an eye on them
for *he* wd never have stood for anything fishy.

1825

(written 24 May 1963)

John Quincy Adams's right hand
shaded his eyes
as he sat on a fence & fished.

At one end of his line was a knot & a hook
                         at the
    other end
        his hand   & he sat
          fishing for a camel with a hook instead of a hump?

No   & not for an ox
                        because
                        behind a door he had his papa's ox
            & when he went fishing in water
            (& that's what he was doing he was no fool)
                        he was looking to get something
                                    good
                                                something
            he cd sink his teeth into & want to.

1829

(24 May 1963)

Andrew Jackson's last name's the same as my first
                        but
                                    that makes me no more like him
                                    than an ox is   like a
                                                            fish

                                    (or vice versa)
                        but
            open   a door in your head
            (or   a window)
        & look!
                        if your eyes are hooks
                        what's on those hooks?
                        Andrew Jackson?

            Nonsense:
                        Andrew Jackson's dead:
                        you can no more see *him*
        than your   hand cd hold in itself
            an ox:

than you cd hold a camel in the palm of your hand
   as you *cd* hold a tooth
      or an eye of a fish:
                  forget Andrew Jackson:
   (you already have).

1837

(24 May 1963)

If Martin Van Buren ever swam in water
(if Martin Van Buren ever swam)
what kind of swimmer was he if he held onto an ox's head
         (did he?)
   to keep his own above the surface?

   (he knew about banks
            but
         what did he know about swimming?)
                  but
         what is Martin Van Buren now
                  but
            a series of marks I make
         with
                     my
            hand?
                  (maybe
                  Martin
         Van
               Buren cd swim like a fish!)
                  do
                        I
                  make

                    these

            marks

                    with

        "my"   hand?

                    can

            "I"

        catch

        this fish

                    (i.

    e.,

        "I")?

A hook big enough to hang an ox from's
a hook too big to catch a fish with.

Martin Van Buren lived in a fine big house in New York State
            before he was   president
            but   how did he get his hooks into
                            Ezra Pound's head?
        look!
    I want to know how a poet became a
rich old dead old politician's fish.

1841 (I)

(24 May 1963)

Andrew Jackson & Martin Van Buren
    are heroes of that old
        hero of mine in whose honor I write
            "wd"
            &
            "cd"

&
"shd"
in-
stead
of
"would"
&
"could"
&
"should"
(I write
&
in-
stead
of
"and"
in
honor
of
William
Blake
but
whose
hero's
William
Henry
Harrison?   (I mean
whose
hero is he *now?*):
old
hero   hung on a hook
the
hook is "Tippecanoe"
&
the smart old politicians used it as an ox-goad

(their

theory was: "an ox-goad in the hand

can

make 'em

go:

treat 'em like oxen & they'll lap it up like water."

That's the way those wily Whigs

fenced: (look!

who remember who *they* were now?

—those old phynancial string-pullers

(*peace*, Jarry!)

who hung an old Indian fighter on their line

(a smaller fish to catch a bigger one)

pushing thru his aging head

the hook

"Tippecanoe":

who remembers who *they* were now?

we

remember   "Tippecanoe":

whose

fish   is

who?)—

but

that

was the way those old finaglers did it

&

if you can't learn from history

what *can*   "you"   learn from?

(Mystery.)

Who was sitting on the fence?

Who was treated like an ox?

Whose head was used as bait?

Whose head planned it all?

Whose hand held the line?
Whose teeth chewed what was caught?
Whose eye caught what was going on?
Who was the fish & how did *he* like it?

1849

(written 25 May 1963)

Zachary Taylor made his name in the Mexican War.
   (They say there's something about a soldier that is fine fine fine.
                    I've always wondered what it is.
            Maybe it's his weapons.)
Zachary Taylor made a name for himself by
   acting toward other men
   as if they were oxen or camels.
        He didn't pay attention to other people's fences—
        especially if they were only Mexicans.
             "After all   oxen have heads
                       only to hear
          commands   to eat
             (as little as they can & still work)
             & to keep yokes
     from falling off.
    If they try to use 'em for anything else
       hang 'em up on hooks."

   If "Old Rough & Ready"
Zachary Taylor didn't think this way
     how *else* did he make his mark in the Mexican War?
   As a "Louisiana slave-holder"
     he must have known all about
     how to treat people like oxen.

All right then how did it happen
                    he let the Californians
adopt a constitution
        prohibiting slavery?

I guess he just didn't think they *wd*
                            or maybe
            he just didnt care
                    as long as it
                didnt affect *his*
            holding of slaves.
                            (Maybe
        some Northern politician got his hooks in him.)
                        Anyway
getting to be
                    President of the United States of America
                    didnt do Zachary Taylor
                        any
                                real
good—
                    —(unless it's a
                                real
good
        to be
                    President of the United States of America
one year & a third
            & thus   have
one's name
on every subsequent list of American Presidents).
                        Zachary
                    Taylor
("Old Rough & Ready")
    died on July 9th, 1850.
                        He had had *his*
                        chance

to wield *that*

  ox-goad

(I mean the one

     every President of the United States of America

         has   at hand.)

                  Now what

I   wonder

is: how did Zachary Taylor

  manage   to

stick it in his own eye

    (if *that's* what he did)?

         Did

things just start to happen in his body & his head?

◆

Selected Dances from *The Pronouns: A Collection of 40 Dances for the Dancers, 3 February–22 March 1964*

Introduction

Adapted by Anne Tardos from "Preface to the 1979 Revised Edition of *The Pronouns: A Collection of 40 Dances for the Dancers*" and from "Some Remarks to the Dancers (How the Dances Are to Be Performed & How They Were Made)"

The Pronouns is a "Collection of Forty Dances"—not a *series,* says Jackson in his "Remarks to the Dancers." That is, despite the fact that the dances are numbered, each is a separate and complete work in itself and may be performed on a program before or after any or none of the other dances in the collection.

Jackson first conceived these dance-instruction-poems as *either* being read aloud as poems (and he read many of them at poetry readings) *or* as being realized as dances. Later he decided that the poems themselves might well be read aloud during some of their realizations as dances. A program might include, then, some realizations accompanied by the reading aloud of the poems and some not so accompanied.

The Pronouns is an outgrowth from an earlier work, *Nuclei for Simone Forti,* written in 1961 on a set of 3 × 4-inch filing cards on which there are groups of words and of action phrases around which dancers build spontaneous improvisations. These can also be read as poems, as either accompaniments to dances or as themselves.

3RD DANCE—MAKING A STRUCTURE WITH A ROOF OR UNDER A ROOF—6-7 February 1964

They meet over water,
say something between thick things,
& make things new.

Soon they're making drinks
& giving falsely.

Then after giving enough of anything to anyone,
they awaken yesterday when the skin's a little feeble;
seeing danger,
they attack,
force someone to see something,
again give enough of anything to anyone,
attack again,
& after doing things to make a meal,
thus having uses among harmonies,
one of them being a brother to someone,
& giving an egg to someone loose or seeming to do so,
they wheel awhile,
giving the hour,
& thereafter let complex impulses make something.

Once more giving the hour,
they again awaken yesterday when the skin's a little feeble;
then they reason regularly.

They copy each other,
shocking everyone,
& pointing to a fact that seems to be an error & showing it to be other
    than it seems,
having or seeming to have serious holes,
they either transport a star or let go of a street;
they keep up a process.

As if to say, "One must make oneself comfortable,"
they go under,
wheel some more,
& reward someone for something or go up under something.

They awaken yesterday when the skin's a little feeble;
they rail,
& they come against something or fear things.

They smoke awhile,
& then they make a structure with a roof or under a roof.

34TH DANCE—TOUCHING—22 March 1964

At the beginning neither tests different things,
& neither keeps any things complex;
neither does things with the mouth & eyes,
& neither discusses anything brown.

Then neither is in flight,
& neither does anything consciously
while reacting to orange hair.

Finally neither is shocking.

40TH DANCE—GIVING FALSELY—22 March 1964

Many begin by getting insects.

Then many make thunder though taking pigs somewhere,
& many give a simple form to a bridge
while coming against something or fearing things.

A little later, after making glass boil
& having political material get in,
many, while being in flight,
name things.

Then many have or seem to have serious holes,
& many question many;
many make payments to many,
& many seem to put examples up.

Finally many quietly chalk a strange tall bottle.

♦

1st Asymmetry for Dr. Howard Levy
from a news item headed
"Doc Backs Army at Levy Trial"
Memorial Day, 30 May 1967

De-/iyyyyyyyyyyyyyyyyyyyyyyyyyyyyyyyy-
(i)y/clared.

"Social struggle/llllllllllll-
lllllllllllll/and we have to use/zzzzzzzzzz-
zzzzzzzz/social instru-/UUUUUUUUU-
UUUU/ments such as medicine."

Doctors/rzzzz-
(r)zzzzzzzzzzzz/about the ethics of offer-/r-
rrrr/ing medical treatment to persuade
Vietnamese peasants to throw/oo-
ooooooo/their support to the Ameri-/iiiiii-
iiii/can side.

Brooklyn dermato-/ahhhhhhhhhhhhhhh-
(a)hhhhhhhhh/logist,
partisan/nnnnnn-
nnnnnnn/purposes.

Doctors had
testified that they/eyyyyyyyyyy-
(e)yyyyy/believed it was wrong to use/zzzz-
zzzzzzzz/medicine for such purposes.

2nd Asymmetry for Dr. Howard Levy
from a news item headed
"Doc Backs Army at Levy Trial"
Memorial Day, 30 May 1967

Backs/assssssssssssssssssssssssss-
sssssssssssssss/**Army at**
                    Levy/(i)yyyyyyyy-
(i)yyyyyyyyyyyyyyyyyyyyyyyy/**Trial**

     Jackson,

An/nnnnnnnnnnnnnnnnnnnnnnnnnnnnnnn-
nn/Army physician,
                    "Arms and gunfire,"
  Army/iyyyyyyyyyyyyyyyyyyyyyyyyyyyyyy
(i)yyyy/doctors about the ethics of offer-/r-
rrrrrrrrrrrrrrr/ing medical treatment
                    to persuade
  Vietnamese peasants to throw/oooooo-
oo/their support to the Ameri-/iiiiiiiiiiiii-
iiiiiiiiiiiiiiiiiiiiiiiiiiiiiii/can side.

    Levy,

a/uhhhhhhhhhhhhhhhhhhhhhhhhhhhhhhhh-
(u)h/ Brooklyn dermato-/ahhhhhhhhhhhhh-
(a)hhhhhhhhhhhhhhhhhhhh/logist,
                                it
    would be against medical ethics/ssss-
ss/to involve himself in the use of/vv-
vv/medicine for political or partisan/nn-
nnnn/purposes.

Selections from PFR-3 Poems

A Note on the PFR-3 Poems

From *Representative Works: 1938–1985*

The PFR-3 Poems were composed at Information International, Inc., in Los Angeles, with the aid of their PFR-3, a programmable film reader connected to a DEC PDP-9 computer and various peripherals, in Summer 1969, when I was an invited artist-participant (the only poet) in the Art and Technology Program of the Los Angeles County Museum of Art.

I worked with a computer program provided (and continually revised and sophisticated) by John Hansen, the vice president in charge of programming, and his assistant Dean Anschultz. Their program allowed me to enter as "data" a list of "messages": originally up to 100 single lines, each comprising at most 48 characters and/or spaces. Later longer messages, though fewer at most, and ones having two or more lines, were possible. From any list the program randomly selected and permuted series of "message members" (characters, words, or strings of linked words, e.g., sentences, separated in the message by spaces) and displayed them on a monitor. When a lever on the control board was pushed, every *tenth* line appearing on the screen was printed out.

The message lists relate to the runs of printout as species to individuals. Each list, together with the program, thus constitutes an indeterminative poem, of which each run of printout is one of an indeterminable number of possible realizations. And each poem has a title, e.g., "Dansk." ...

"Dansk" is the second one I made. Its list comprises 100 48-character/space messages, each a complete, though periodless, spontaneously composed sentence. All message members are single words (none linked), so the computer could select at random any number of words from any message, arranged in any order. Indentations are random in length in all PFR-3 Poems.

"South" has a message list comprising 100 48-character/space messages, each made up of one or two complete sentences (with periods). All words of each sentence are linked in the list, so that each message has only one or two members. The computer could select randomly one or two whole sentences from any message: when two, it could reverse their original order, or not. All the sentences have to do with southern areas of the world, notably Central and South America and Africa: a kind of generalized Tropics.

The list of "The" comprises up to about 50 messages, each including several (usually short) sentences, each beginning with "The," ending with a period, and constituting a single line whose words are linked. The computer could thus select one or more sentences from any message, arranging the sentences in any order. All sentences in "The" refer to processes or actions that are always going on somewhere in the world. Composed in August 1969 and nearly the last, this PFR-3 Poem has the longest messages. Its list took longest to elaborate and changed most as I added messages (groups of one-line sentences), so that early printout differs from later much more than in other PFR-3 Poems.

30 September–October 1985
New York

From "DANSK"

ANIMALS PATIENT
   INANIMATE ARE MOUNTAINS PERSONS MASSIVE
      ARE INNUMERABLE RIPPLING FOLLOWING GLUTEALS
    HALLUCINATIONS PURSUING DILIGENTLY ARE
WERE NEARLY ALWAYS ANCESTORS BOASTING
  DOVES

NO ANIMALS
ARE CARYATIDES GRIMLY MELANCHOLIC
ANGELS PRAISING ARE SHY ASSES ROLLING SPLEDIDLY
GREEN
ARE LEADING NOW CONTROLLING
FURIOUSLY
PHILOSOPHICAL
CHILDREN DILIGENTLY ARE PURSUING HALLUCINATIONS
GRIMLY THERE CARYATIDES MELANCHOLIC ARE SMILING
BUTTOCKS ARE UNDULATING APPROXIMATING FEMININELY
NOW CONTROLLING
ARE COLORLESS FURIOUSLY GREEN
ABANDONING HERE HOPES
MOLDING DINOSAURS ONCE WERE
GREEN IDEAS FURIOUSLY ARE COLORLESS SLEEPING
LIBERTIES
FLOWERS JACARANDA CARPETING VIOLET ARE PAVEMENTS
LIBERTIES
MASSIVE INANIMATE
ROGUES FOOLS GUARANTEEING
PATIENT ARE DIFFICULTIES
ARE RENUNCIATIONS SATISFYING
STRUGGLING YET WALLOWING POWERLESS ELEPHANTS ARE
ALL SPLENDID PLEASURABLY THINGS
FOLLOWING INNUMERABLE ARE EYES RIPPLING GLUTEALS
WIDOWS ARE POISONING SCOUNDRELS
FLOWING TRESSES SMILING GRACING GIRLS NOW ARE
WET WARM SUNLIT MARMOREALLY ARE SHINING
ARE
HIDING CLITORISES PENISES ARE AWAKENING HARD RED
BOASTING NEARLY
ARE THUNDERING RUBIES WHEELS ROLLING EMPURPLING
SWEETENING MOCKINGBIRDS BITTER ARE CITIES
ONLY ROGUES
AUTOMATIC PATIENTLY MEMORY BUFFERS GUARDIANS
GREEDY WINDS EXECUTIVES

SELDOM
WINDS EXECUTIVES POLLUTING AND WATERS
ARE BUTTOCKS APPROXIMATING FEMININELY UNDULATING@
MORNING DROOPING THIGHS
EVENINGS ENLIVENING ARE WHIPPOORWILLS ASTRAL
GENTLY ARE
STIFF CLASPING PENISES ARE MASSAGING RED
UPWARD BREEZES NIPPLES AND
DEVICES COMPUTERS ARE
UNDULATING@ APPROXIMATING BUTTOCKS FEMININELY ARE
YET
UNDULATING@ ARE BUTTOCKS APPROXIMATING
RED MASSAGING PENISES
DEVASTATING FLOATING STATISTICS
ARE COINCIDENCES
HANDS WARM
ARE
NEVER TRUE NUMINOUS
DANISH ARE BLACK WIDOWS RED
DANISH RED SCOUNDRELS ARE BLACK POISONING WIDOWS
MOCKINGBIRDS SWEETENING CITIES BITTER
SEEKING QUESTING SOFT
ARE MASSAGING PENISES VAGINAS CLASPING
ALL HOMEY JACARANDAS AVENUES PERFUMING TOO
CARESSING CLEVER BELLIES
MASSAGING PENISES ARE STIFF
EVENTS ARE MEANINGFUL COINCIDENTAL ALWAYS NEARLY
MASSAGING STIFF ARE PENISES VAGINAS CLASPING RED
BOASTING WERE NEARLY ALWAYS TOTEMISTIC ANCESTORS
MEANINGFUL ALWAYS NEARLY EVENTS ARE COINCIDENTAL
CARPETING FLOWERS JACARANDA ARE VIOLET
FILLING
NOW TRUE INNOCENT OR
ELEPHANTS
DEMANDING NEW
SCOUNDRELS RED DANISH POISONING WIDOWS ARE BLACK

                    ARE
HANDS SMOOTH CARESSING WARM BELLIES ARE CLEVER
                    CHILDREN
                    SHY ARE
MEMORY GUARDIANS BUFFERS AUTOMATIC ARE
                    RIPPLING GLUTEALS EYES
MACHINES
        ARE
                    MASSIVE ARE
            POETS INNOCENT OR TRUE NOW
            TOTEMISTIC
                    TOTALLY ENVELOPING ARE OFTEN FIRST
            FOOLS ROGUES GUARANTEEING
                    ANACHRONISTIC
            EYELIDS LIFTING
                    ENCOUNTERING ANIMALS ARE DIFFICULTIES PATIENT
SUNLIGHT ARE NIPPLES AND UPWARD DRAWING BREEZES
        JACARANDA PAVEMENTS VIOLET ARE CARPETING FLOWERS
    NYMPHOMANIACS WOMEN MERELY OSTENSIBLE ARE HUNGRY
            ARE FREEING DEEPBOSOMED BREASTS DAMOZELS ROUNDED
TENDER FACES WERE
            PURSUING
            PONDS ROILING BULLFROGS
        DRIFTING SNOWS YOUNG COVERING WERE QUIETLY TREES
            ARE HYSTERICAL NIGHTMARES ELABORATING
            ORCHESTRATING EMPTY BABIES CORRIDORS ARE CRYING
                    DELINEATING WERE VOICES BAROQUE PRECISELY ORGANS
        ARE
            FURIOUSLY IDEAS COLORLESS SLEEPING GREEN
                    DEMANDING
            FREEING BREASTS ROUNDED DEEPBOSOMED
        CRUNCHING ABSENTMINDED PLASTIC
TASTY GRANDMOTHERS
            ARE
            HONEYMAKING ARE EUCALYPTUS DRAWING BEES
ARE VOCABULARIES DAILY ALL LITERALLY INCREASING

ARE LOUD RESONANT TROMBONES TONES SOUNDING LONG
    WERE FINGERING TRIGGERS SECESSIONISTS SEASONED
    ARCHWAYS TRANSCENDENTAL NOW SILENTLY ARE OPENING
TRIGGERS WERE
    RECORDERS ARE COUNTERPOINTING VIOLS ARPEGGIATING
DRIVERS TIRES SUFFERING MURDEROUS SCREECHING
TROMBONES
    BLACKFEET ATTACKING WERE
    ARE CHILDREN DROPS SPLATTERING
ABANDONING MANY
        INDIANS
TRESSES FLOWING ARE NOW SMILING GIRLS
    CLANDESTINELY NOW VOCALIZING ARE MOURNING DOVES
    FERROCONCRETE CAGES LIONS ENCLOSING
LOVELY INSIGNIFICANT SELDOM SYNCHRONICITIES

From "David"

DAVID ASKED WHETHER ANYTHING HAD BEEN HAPPENING.
    WHOM DID DAVID ASK WHAT HAPPENED?
HOW DID DAVID ASK WHAT HAPPENED?
    HOW DID DAVID HAPPEN TO HAVE BEEN ASKING WHAT
HAD BEEN HAPPENING?
        HOW DID DAVID ASK WHAT HAD HAPPENED?
    "WHAT'S BEEN HAPPENING?" ASKED DAVID.
    HOW DID DAVID ASK WHAT HAPPENED?
    "WHAT IS HAPPENING?" ASKED DAVID.
WHERE DID DAVID ASK WHAT HAPPENED?
        HOW DID DAVID ASK?
    WHERE DID DAVID HAPPEN TO HAVE BEEN ASKING WHEN
HE WAS ASKING WHAT HAD BEEN HAPPENING?
    DAVID ASKED.

HAD ANYTHING HAPPENED WHEN DAVID ASKED?
WHO WAS THERE WHEN DAVID ASKED?
HOW DID DAVID ASK WHAT HAPPENED?
WHAT HAD BEEN HAPPENING WHEN DAVID WAS ASKING
WHAT HAD BEEN HAPPENING?
WHAT WAS HAPPENING WHEN DAVID WAS ASKING?
DID DAVID ASK WHAT HAPPENED?
HOW HAD DAVID BEEN ASKING WHAT HAD HAPPENED?
WHEN DID DAVID ASK WHAT HAPPENED?
WHOM DID DAVID HAPPEN TO HAVE BEEN ASKING WHEN
HE WAS ASKING WHAT HAD BEEN HAPPENING?
WHAT HAD BEEN HAPPENING WHEN DAVID WAS ASKING
WHAT HAD BEEN HAPPENING?
WHERE DID DAVID ASK WHAT WAS HAPPENING?
WHAT HAD HAPPENED WHEN DAVID WAS ASKING?
WHAT WAS HAPPENING WHEN DAVID ASKED?
DAVID HAD BEEN ASKING WHAT HAD BEEN HAPPENING.
WHEN DID DAVID ASK WHAT WAS HAPPENING?
DAVID HAD ASKED WHAT HAD HAPPENED.
WHEN DID DAVID ASK WHAT WAS HAPPENING?

From "South"

BABOONS JUMP. PEOPLE AND FLIES VIOLATE ORCHIDS.
PARROTS RACE ACROSS VIOLET ORCHIDS. ZEBRAS EAT.
FLIES IGNORE ARMADILLOS AND TOUGH COATIMUNDIS.
PEOPLE ARE SHEARING IGNORANT SCREAMING ZEBRAS.
A TOUGH RED-AND-GREEN PARROT SCREAMS AT A TOAD.
ZEBRAS RACE JAGUARS AND GREYISH MANDRILLS.
FLIES FLY.
BIRDS SCREAM. AN ARMADILLO EATS A GREYISH SNAKE.
A GREEN LIZARD PEERS AT A TOUGH MANDRILL.
WHAT PEOPLE FLY?

PEOPLE AND FLIES VIOLATE ORCHIDS.
LIZARDS JUMP BABOONS. A BIRD EATS A LIZARD.
PEOPLE SCREAM AT GREEN-AND-VIOLET TOADS.
PEOPLE ARE SHEARING IGNORANT SCREAMING ZEBRAS.
PEOPLE ARE SHEARING IGNORANT SCREAMING ZEBRAS.
PEOPLE SCREAM AT GREEN-AND-VIOLET TOADS.
YELLOW PARROTS RACE ANCIENT JAGUARS.
ARMADILLOS JUMP.
A TOUGH RED-AND-GREEN PARROT SCREAMS AT A TOAD.
PEOPLE SCREAM WHILE GREEN TOADS VIOLATE PARROTS.
ZEBRAS RACE JAGUARS AND GREYISH MANDRILLS.
MANDRILLS IGNORE ARMADILLOS AND COATIMUNDIS.
A GREEN LIZARD PEERS AT A TOUGH MANDRILL.
WHAT PEOPLE FLY?
BABOONS VIOLATE BANANAS IN VIOLET TREES.
FLIES IGNORE ARMADILLOS AND TOUGH COATIMUNDIS.
ANGRY ARMADILLOS ARE SCREAMING AT RED PARROTS.
MANDRILLS IGNORE ARMADILLOS AND COATIMUNDIS.
A GREY TOAD EATS A GREEN-AND-ORANGE FLY.
ZEBRAS JUMP. PURPLE-FACED MANDRILLS ARE FIERCE.
FLIES EAT.
SNAKES EAT THROUGH ORCHIDS. FLIES IGNORE TAPIRS.

From "The"

THE WIND BLOWS.
THE RAIN FALLS.
THE SNOW FALLS.
THE STREAMS FLOW.
THE RIVERS FLOW.
THE OCEANS RISE.

THE OCEANS FALL.

THE BUSHES GROW.
THE MOSSES GROW.
THE FERNS GROW.
THE LICHENS GROW.

THE TREES SWAY IN THE WIND.
THE FLOWERS SWAY IN THE WIND.

THE INSECTS ARE HATCHED.
THE REPTILES ARE HATCHED.
THE MAMMALS ARE BORN.
THE BIRDS ARE HATCHED.
THE FISHES ARE HATCHED.

THE PEOPLE SAIL ON RAFTS.

THE LICHENS GROW.
THE FLOWERS GROW.
THE MOSSES GROW.
THE TREES GROW.

THE INSECTS GROW.
THE REPTILES GROW.
THE BUSHES GROW.

THE INSECTS GATHER FOOD.
THE BIRDS GATHER FOOD.

THE PLANETS SHINE.
THE MOON SHINES.
THE SUN SHINES.

THE TREES DRINK. THE FUNGUSES DRINK.

THE MOSSES TURN TOWARD THE LIGHT.
THE FLOWERS TURN TOWARD THE LIGHT.
THE TREES TURN TOWARD THE LIGHT.

Summer 1969, Los Angeles

◆

Selections from Odes for Iris

1st Ode for Iris—midnight after the boat ride—
Sat–Sun 18–19 July 1970

I love you, Iris Lezak,
my heart beats, when I see you,
more quickly & more calmly
all at once.

Seeing you makes me joyful,
seeing you talking, walking,
reclining, running, bending,
or sitting:

seeing you sitting still or
in vivid motion as you
speak your mind & soul with eyes
& body:

body continually
assuming new attitudes,
facets of the beautiful
you, Iris,

of whom the seeing pleases
even in my worst moments:
what is more objectively
beautiful?

3rd Ode for Iris—later that night—Sun 19 July 1970

What can a man do to be
lovable once again to
the woman he loves tho her
heart has cooled

& no longer bounds for joy
when seeing him or feeling
his hands or lips or body
upon her?

What breaking of barriers,
what healing of old traumas,
what awakening of faith,
what trusting

can come to pass, becoming
ourselves being together,
no longer ignorant, blind,
resentful,

raging at what isn't worth
raging at, keeping back the truth
whose feared sharing is anger's
dissolver?

38th Ode for Iris—3:26 AM Tues 28 July 1970

O.K.! I'll leave you alone!
I won't bother you! I won't
come to you unless you say
you want me!

Is this what you want of me?
Will this help to make you free?
Is this the way you sometimes
may love me?

I won't ask for your love, &
I won't ask for your loving!
I'll stay here alone till you
invite me!

I'll sit at my desk & sleep
in one of the single beds:
(nothing new in that—is there?)
—I'll hunt girls

to fuck, stroke, suck, lick, & love,
when I can't have you enough
to feel loved or satisfied.
—You want that?

55th Ode for Iris—11:25 PM Wed 29 July 1970

Now I know why God gave me
the gift of verse!—to help me
actively love you when not
making love!

—another way to caress,
sharing existence with you,
even when we're several
rooms apart,

& making objects for you
as precisely measured as
skyscrapers—with which to tell
"honestly"

just how it is being "me"
& how others seem to "me"
—forging existence into
ornaments

for your inwardness—to match
your rings, earrings, necklaces,
bracelets, & (the few you have)
pretty clothes.

62nd Ode for Iris—6:23 PM Mon 3 Aug 1970

Misty Vermont pine mountains
in the driving thunderstorm
make me open the window,
ditch the screen,

& look out at them not thru
dirty glass or window screen
but directly—across the
watery

vibrant air, & all those shades
of green, tan, yellow, orange,
gray, silver, white—*lightning flash
split the sky*

*straight across from me just now!
bright yellow light crashing down
with almost immediate
thunder roll!*

—& *black*—yes, several shades
of *black!* Yes, lovely painter,
black's in nature just as much
as green is!

64th Ode for Iris—8:15 AM Tues 4 Aug 1970

I'm not much surprised to find
"existential poetry"
the only kind I seem to
want to write.

Objective, systematic
chance operations gave me
many poems & pieces
in the past

fifteen years or so, but now
I only feel like writing
living subjectivity:
—inwardness!

is all I write, despite years
of so-called "egoless art"
—chimera! noble daydream
of the proud

who disdain to dump soul-shit
on unwary customers
& think they're Boddhisattvas
thru restraint!

76th Ode for Iris—4 AM Wed 19 Aug 1970

I know now why I "take risks"
other artists wdnt "take":
I'm too autistic to care
 if others

disapprove the works I make,
even tho I'm delighted
when what I make makes others
feel something

valuable to them or
learn something they'd not known or
come to see or hear something
they hadn't—

or hadn't in quite *that* way—
but my works are my pleasures
I'm social enough to share
—not to care

whether someone doesn't find
my pleasures pleasurable:
"If you don't like my fruit, don't
shake my tree!"

97th Ode for Iris—4:30 PM Fri 7 May 1971

Do you think I deserve it?
Wanting to make love with you
even when I don't see you
(seeing you

building the banked fire to flame),
knowing you won't fuck me now
even when you feel closer
& don't hate,

knowing you're going to move,
live far from the kids & me,
detach yourself from our lives
(but visit

so the kids won't feel cut off—
Oh Iris! They'll *feel* cut off!
I dread your absence most for
them, not me!)

Are all the good things I've done
canceled by my wrongs & fears?
("Not to hurt you, but so that
I can live.")

112th Ode for Iris—1:30 PM Sun 31 Oct 1971

Am I in love with someone
who now no longer exists
Are you so different now
that I'm wrong

when I think I still love you
even though our bodies don't
seem to love each other much
anymore

When I saw you in the crowd
warming up for Meredith's
Vessel in the parking lot
what I felt

seemed to be love   It was love
But was it love for You Now
or love for you as you were
long ago

when a mysterious force
kept drawing us together
and we nearly drowned in each
other's eyes

113th Ode for Iris—2:50 PM Sun 31 Oct 71

I'll be late for your reading
Will you say How typical
when you read or hear this ode
Will you laugh

relieved that you no longer
will have to wait when I'm late
when I protract departure
doing things

I should have done earlier
That's the kind of thing that killed
the love you had for the me
I once was

who still seems to be alive
loving you and being late
sitting in the subway now
as it stalls

at Columbus Circle   speeds
down to Seventh Avenue
bringing anxious me to your
first reading

114th Ode for Iris—12:10 PM Mon 1 Nov 71

Every morning I wake up
crying since you went away
You'll say   This is just what you
used to do

That's one reason I left you
Couldn't stand your morning gloom
If you didn't wake up sad
you woke mad

Yes   Iris   I'm like that
You're better off free of me
I sit around all morning
feeling sad

missing you and the children
happy for the month in Maine
I ought to be happy if
I love you

since you're doing what you want
being yourself   not a wife
living downtown where your friends
are near you

◆

4th Mother Dead Poem

(in my hotel room, my father snoring in his bed, 10 PM, Tues. 6/19/73)

I saw my mother lying dead in her
open coffin today at the funeral home
embalmed & dressed in her new blue funeral dress

My father said Didn't she look wonderful
& had little bursts of crying
& cried Fannie Fannie Come back to me

Then he wandered restlessly around the room
& talked a little with the funeral man
After a while I asked to be alone with her

I looked at her a long long time
I saw the severe expression on her face
& the four severe buttons down the front of her dress

I said goodbye to that body
& said I hoped her next life wd be happier
or if there's none, that she'd be happy wherever she is

Or if death was all I was sorry her life had been so sad
I kissed that cold forehead & right hand
& kissed those cold lips before I turned & left

5th Mother Dead Poem

(hotel room, Daddy snoring, the night before her burial
11 PM Tues. 6/19/73)

I never before had realized
the unequal sizes of my mother's nostrils
or that her nose bent slightly to the right

& yes this seemed familiar
as I looked at her in that half-open coffin
a bed inside—dull silvery metal on the outside

I felt no huge sorrow or great fear
only a light sadness & a little disgust
& a strong wish to kiss her a last goodbye

I felt a little fear of being observed
& that something they'd put on her might be poisonous
& a little wonder at how cold she was

I used to fear my mother's death so much
It was one of the deepest fears of my childhood
Just now a thunderclap frightened me—not her corpse

I felt a sad little love for that dead body
& relieved her many fears & some of mine were over
Just before I left I patted her right hand

Selections from "Ridiculous in Piccadilly."
from *The Virginia Woolf Poems*

From "The Genesis of 'Ridiculous in Piccadilly.'"

"Ridiculous in Piccadilly." comprises 11 poems [the first 4 are represented here—A. T.] drawn from Virginia Woolf's novel *The Waves* by what I call the "diastic" (on analogy with "acrostic") or "spelling-thru" method, which I began using to make poems from source texts in January 1963.

After finding the title phrase in line 4, p. 88, of the first American edition (New York: Harcourt Brace, 1931), I drew one word for each of its letters. Beginning with the phrase itself, I culled only words in which the letters occupied corresponding positions (I disregarded hyphens): "*ri*diculous Pi*c*-cadi*ll*y./ /e*n*d stai*n*/bookcase,/reass*u*ring bruta*ll*y/eating-house./ /eating-house./ /waitresses,/*i*n and *p*lates r*i*ght/in*c*luded./ /prick *c*ontains forge*d*/ compan*i*on/pale-ye*ll*ow/smooth-po*l*ished melanchol*y*/"—upon which, having spelled the phrase out once, I began again, & did so repeatedly till I'd drawn the first word of "9"—"pillar-box."—from p. 292. Then, finding no word with "u" in the 9th place, as in "ridicul*u*s," from there thru the last page (297), I began reading the book again, obtaining "oleagino*u*s" from p. 25, & thence repeatedly spelling-thru my title phrase till I reached the last word of "11"—"thick."—its "c" corresponding to the 2nd "c" of "Piccadilly"— which I found in line 11, p. 116. Having reached the bottom of that note-book page, I ended the series, possibly cued by the coincidence of elevens.

1.

ridiculous
Piccadilly.

end stain
bookcase,
reassuring brutally
eating-house.

eating-house.

waitresses,
in and plates right
included.

prick contains forged
companion
pale-yellow
smooth-polished melancholy
rooted,
Rippling side.

hesitating consciousness
treasures ridicule sensations,
mysteriously eating-house
imbue entirely phrase with
pictures,
thick.

2.

appease-
ment,
already fountain possibility,
incredible positively,
"Rhoda pillar,
sides radiance,
unsuccessfully,
restaurant brutally isolation,
capricious cadav-
erous
I
and
Percival,
little Lucretius?—

circle courage extended
sensation particular beautiful.

discreetly),
respond kindness lady obliterating
unrecorded surrounded mole-
hills.

ridiculous ridiculous
beckonings,

3.

is knocked perhaps differs—
decline.

descending,
pillars.

accord-
ing in-
firmity naturally
perpetual accurately;
runs mind,
understand-
ing.

again.

spruce omnibuses.

motionless
unequivocal,
eating-house,
lava-
tories is on press little accept
biscuit,

4.

Janu-
ary,
thread demanding Piccadilly,'
beautiful,
perilously,
I anywhere;
person will once discreetly,
despair.

cathedrals,
educating,
Pic-
cadilly.

nocturnal infinitely ride
fire,
order.

habits.

solacing curious eternal
pillar-box.

continuous statements in uncover
perpetually mind recall reached

◆

phone

a poem & 10 variations

(for Stephanie Vevers)

Whenever I answer the phone
It's never you

Even if it was you
It'd never be you
Saying

Hello it's me
I love you so much
I can hardly wait to see you
Can I come over right now

Yes yes yes yes

So I hate the sound of the phone
& worse
To answer it

Hello hello
No I'm not me
I'm not here
I'll never be

•

Was you it'd never be you sa
Ing hello it's

E I love you so mu
I can hardly wait
See yo

Ht now yes ye
I hate the sound o
I hello hello no I'm not me
Can hardly wait to see yo

Yes yes yes yes

Sound of the phone & worse to an
& worse
T hello hell

Here I'll n
Never I answe
If it was yo
It's me I lov

•

Wait to see you can I come
Ight now yes y

Es yes yes so I ha
It hello hello no
Swer t

He phone it's
If it was you it'd
Ing hello it's me I love you
Come over right now yes y

Yes yes so I ha

Se to answer it hello hello no I
& worse
T me I'm not

Henever I a
Nswer the pho
It was you i
It to see you

•

W yes yes yes yes so I hate
It hello hello

E I'm not here I'l
I answer the phon
S neve

H I can hardl
It to see you can
I come over right now yes ye
Can I come right now yes y

Yes so I hate th

Swer it hello hello no I'm not m
& worse
T here I'll

Hone it's n
N if it was y
Ing hello it
I come over r

•

Wer the phone it's never yo
If it was you

Ever be you saying
It's me I love yo
So muc

Hardly wait t
I come over right
I hate the sound of the phon
Ch I can hardly wait to s

Y wait to see y

So much I can hardly wait to see
& worse
To see you c

Hardly wait
N hardly wait
I can hardly
I love you se

•

Worse to answer it hello he
I'm not me I'm

Ere I'll never be
It's never you ev
S you

Hate the soun
It hello hello no
I'm not me I'm not here I'll
Can hardly wait see yo ht

You can I come

See you can I come over right no
& worse
T now yes ye

Hate the so
Ne & worse to
It hello hel
I'm not me I'

•

Wait see yo ht now yes ye I
I answer the p

E it's never you e
If it was you it'
S me I

Hone & worse
I'm not me I'm not
I'm not here I'll never be wh
Can I come ight now yes y

You even if it

S you it'd never be you saying h
& worse
T's me I lov

H I can har
Now yes yes y
I hate the s
It hello hell

•

W **yes ye I hate the sound o**
It was you it'

E**never I answer th**
It was you it'd n
S **yes**

Hello hello n
I'll never be when
I **answer the phone it's neve**
C**ome over r wer the phone**

Y**ou it'd never**

S **yes yes yes so I hate the soun**
& worse
The sound of

Hone & wors
N**swer it hell**
I'm not me I
I **answer the**

●

W**as I so right to see it so**
I**'ll answer no**

E**re I answer I see**
I**'ll never be you**
S**o I'm**

H**e you answer**
I**'m the sound**
I **can hardly ever wait to be**
C**an you ever love me here**

Yes you love me

So I'll be saying a sound answer
& worse
The answer's

Here to say
Now I can say
I love sound
I answer love

•

Was I never to answer hello
I hardly phone

Even you I love so
I can hardly ever
Say to

Her I love so
I can hardly phone
I hardly ever say I love you
Can I ever say I love you

Yes so I say it

Saying love's sound's never over
& worse
To answer it

Hardly ever
No not never
I answer now
I'm saying it

•

Wait here so I can say love
If I'm ever to

Even say the sound
I hate not saying
So now

Here I say it
I say love's sound
I say now if ever I love you
Come love answer love now

You say it love

Say the sound so you answer love
& worse
The answer's

Hard to say
Not saying it
Is worse now
I'll wait now

4 June 1977
New York

Quatorzains from & for Emily Dickinson

Elysium is as far as to
IMpregnable of Eye—
ThIs was in the White of the Year—
NegLected Son of Genius
RuddY as that coeval Apple

    Did stagger pitiful
    MIght dare to touch it now!
    BeCause that fearing it so long
    RanK—overtake me—
    RequIred a Blow as vast
    If teNderer industriousness
    Be it'S Grave—sufficient sign—
    And choOses Wainscot in the Breast
    Death woNt hurt—Dollie's here!

Eclipses—Suns—imply—
IMpregnable the Rose
ThIs—then—is best for confidence—
CoaLs—from a Rolling Load—rattle—how—near—
And Yet We guessed it not—

    Divulging it would rest my Heart
    VIcinity to Laws
    I Counted till they danced so
    LucK is not chance—
    Be MIne the Doom—
    All iNterspersed with weed,
    It aimS once—kills once—conquers once—
    With PrOspect, and with Frost—
    We distiNguish clear—

Escape from Circumstances—
IMpregnable we are—
TrIumphed and remained unknown—
CouLd I infer his Residence—
And Yet we sooner say

      Drop into tune—around the Throne—
      BIrds, mostly back—
      ExCellent and Fair,
      It Kept me from a Thief, I think,
      And Is the first, to rise—
      Were Nothing very strange!
      His obServation omnifold,
      Wilt ThOu, Austere Snow?
      And duriNg it's electric gale—

Experience would swear—
AMong the certainties—
CrIsis is a hair
WouLd be acuter, would it not
Too Young that any should suspect

      Defrauded of it's song.
      HIs Twin identity
      ExCept to bear
      LooK too expensive!
      It dId not surprise me—
      Nor aNy leader's grim baton
      All HiS Goods have Wings—
      By my lOng bright—and *longer—trust*—
      By seasoNs or his Children—

Escaping backward to perceive
IMpelled to hark—
GrIef is a Mouse—
WouLd not the fun
And Yesterday, or Centuries before?

Diversion from the Dying Theme
DIsarms the little interval—
A Compensation fair
It Kept me from a Thief, I think,
RepaIring Everywhere—
The iNstant holding in it's claw
Truth Stays Herself—and every man
Like loOking every time you please
SuspicioN it was done

Escaping backward to perceive
IMpregnable the Rose
StIll to be explained.
WilL equal glow, and thought no More
ElegY of Integrity.

Did place about the West—Tonight—
TIll that first Shout got by—
I Could hold the latest Glowing—
SeeK—Friend—and see—
StolId to Love's supreme entreaty
My miNd was going numb—
ReturnS no syllable
This slOw Day moved along
Lip was Not the liar.

November 1979
New York

Selections from *French Sonnets*

Introduction

Adapted by Anne Tardos from "Writing and Practice, 6/27–8/24/92"

Jackson composed his *French Sonnets* using "translation" methods. He systematically substituted words in the English section of a French-English dictionary for the words of certain Shakespeare sonnets. For example, in "French Sonnet" (the first of the series, written in 1955—the other nineteen were written between 1980 and 1983) the first four lines are:

> Shamefulness Hymn companionableness thanksgiver tissue a summer-
> wheat's dead?
> Thoughtfulness artfully morosity lot angel-worship morosity teller:
> Rote William-pears do shadow thanksgiver darkling bugloss octavo May,
> Angel-worship summer-wheat's leather have aliform tooth shorthand a
> darkling:

These lines "translate" the first quatrain of Shakespeare's sonnet XVIII:

> Shall I compare thee to a summer's day?
> Thou art more lovely and more temperate:
> Rough winds do shake the darling buds of May,
> And summer's lease hath all too short a date:

This "translation" was made by finding the column in the dictionary where each word of Shakespeare's sonnet appears and substituting the headword of that column for Shakespeare's word, retaining 's and punctuation from Shakespeare. In composing the other poems in *French Sonnets,* Jackson used methods involving random digits that shifted the selection of substituted headwords to dictionary columns other than those in which Shakespeare's words appear, ensuring that each poem would draw on a different set of headwords.

French Sonnet

Shamefulness Hymn companionableness thanksgiver tissue a summer-
   wheat's dead?
Thoughtfulness artfully morosity lot angel-worship morosity teller:
Rote William-pears do shadow thanksgiver darkling bugloss octavo May,
Angel-worship summer-wheat's leather have aliform tooth shorthand a
   darkling:
Somersault tooth horsestealer thanksgiver exuberate octavo heat shipping,
Angel-worship oleaginousness batting hip-gout godly complication
   dining-table;
Angel-worship everlastingness fair frost fair somersault declinable,
By-lane changeableness order nature's changeableness court-chaplain
   unveil;
Bustle thundering etiquette summer-wheat shamefulness normal
   faintness
Nor lot possible octavo thanksgiver fair thoughtfulness ozonometer;
Nor shamefulness Dead bracket thoughtfulness Walloon improvise hip-
   gout shadow,
Wheel-animalcules improvise etiquette lines tissue time thoughtfulness
   ground:
Soak loll artfulness mendicant camarilla breeze order exuberates
   camarilla sedan-chair,
Soak loll lithotomist think angel-worship think gigot life tissue
   thanksgiver.

January 1955

Third French Sonnet

Sea-green ipecacuanha intoxicating night-watchman way-bill meet
  actionable way-bill toggery mendicant
Seizure bug-wort awl pastorly bounce toggle haven valerian,
Wrathfully hearty intoxication flutter oversleep defy usufructuary
Able elude flourish way-bill haven flourish defy rancid;
Mahometanism awl complier offer pan contributary,
Way-bill sedan-chair able mulct, way-bill English able security's regard
  glass,
Way-bill Appianly fig-leaf fencibles, able annul talks rack
Toggery heartier adulterously inventory take headsman ruffle headstalls.
Out, lunation meet, tack inventory life, bigness tacky wailing,
Able tooth bracing meet, meeting lithotomist ipecacuanha actionable
  flourish
Actionable arch-heresy mispoints copaiba, truckle night-watchman sea-
  green blower
Actionable toggeries greyhound collegians feelers inventory heartier
  adulterously:
Lunation tissue scuffle moonlit toggery leach offer herald waif;
Infidel wailing night-watchman pasque-flower toggery pasquinade
  night-watchman thingummy seminarist.

Bloomsday 1980

◆

Selection from *Words nd Ends from Ez*

Introduction

Adapted by Anne Tardos from Afterword to *Words nd Ends from Ez*

I have systematically brought into *Words nd Ends from Ez* letter strings consisting of single words and/or ends of words that successively "spell out" Ezra Pound's first and last names "diastically," i.e., strings in which the letters of Pound's first and last names occupy places corresponding to those they fill in the names.

To do this, I read through *The Cantos* and found successively letter strings (including the letters from each Pound-name letter to the end of the word in which it occurs) in the following order: (1) beginning with an *e*, (2) having a *z* in the second place, (3) an *r* in the third place, and (4) an *a* in the fourth place; then (5) beginning with a *p*, (6) having an *o* in the second place, (7) a *u* in the third place, (8) an *n* in the fourth place, and (9) a *d* in the fifth place; then (10) an *e* at the beginning, etc. In finding such letter strings I often had to "back up" from a word in which a Pound-name letter occurred into the letters of the word before—far enough to cause the letter to occupy its designated place in the string.

When composing *Words nd Ends from Ez,* I repeatedly used the index "Ezra Pound," while I read *The Cantos* from beginning to end, to draw words and "ends" from Pound's poem series into mine. Thus the index string is sometimes broken by the division between two sections/poems, the first index letter(s) being found at the end of one section/poem, the remaining index letter(s) at the beginning of the next.

As I read through *The Cantos,* I looked for each needed letter in succession, and when I found one, I would count back from that letter to whatever letter began a string in which the index letter filled the place it occupies in one of Pound's names. If there weren't enough letters in the word in which the index letter occurred for the index letter to occupy its correct place in the string, I had to count back into the word before. In *Words nd Ends from Ez,* the index letters are capitalized; if already capitalized in *The Cantos,* they are set in italic capitals. . . .

My compositional method may be illustrated by printing the words in Canto I from which the first two lines of words and ends in section/poem I were drawn [dropped letters are bracketed]:

[th]En [bro]nZe [b]leaRing [dre]ory Arms,
Pallor [u]pOn [S]laUghtered [s]laiN [P]oureD [ointm]Ent,

Words nd Ends from Ez was written intermittently between 9 January 1981 and 3 May 1983.

7 January–17 February 1989
New York

VI. From the Pisan Cantos: LXXIV–LXXXIV
8/1/81   (EZRA POUND)

moUs am iN houlDers
Es!

s Zuan n,
oR th LA Posa
pOnsa l oUr tioN y neeD Eceive s Zero veR e meAns
   Production;
mOney asUred d waNted
e not Done Ecessary iZard biRds ot eAt Pen
fOr inUs,

emeNt
loweD E m Zion teRest id DAvid Prime s.

O .

b .

acUlata e suN's otteD
E s Zeus m oR y SnAg Pretty lOok loUds ed oN esseD
  Ept rZe noRth of TAishan
Pter fOr lf Unmistakeably,
se,
aN ar anD E a Zephyr heR er mAnner Part rOcess
r
KUanon,
stoNe fereD E nZa foR ss,
mAre Past sOn doUr raiN,

heweD Ead
iZza
ltRA:
Posteros
hOrt om?

Ugolino,
re oN rlin
Dysentery
Eille eZzato paRently
n frAgments Pected l Of e sUnken itiNg a,
now Desuete
Er oZzetto
uaRd nerAls
Pus,
pOtes r BUllington ay oN y
o LaDy E lZen . . . ?

w,
fRom he lAw Pinned hOveh
ShUn tumNal un unDer Elody
aZzled heReby
wd/
hAve Put e Old hoUlders
d goNe ak yu Djeep Er nZai es
Remembering e shAft Possibile tO trUctible
adiNg er
anD Essing tZ teR:
bewAre P fOrmation
faUte thiNg soliD
Es
iZza
eeR lum
And Pe e Of itUs dveNi /

ss unDer Ephyrus
eZia
ooR senA
" Patched tOries "
ctUres teaN ty is Difficult. . . .
E eZza,
ceRtain remAin Porta fOrtuna
esUrgent ll iN r the Deification Emperors
tZ-
Carlton euR he NApoleon Pposed lOfty SoUth
o MaNhattan r
leaDing E n Zeno eiR tro And Pt tOlare
i mUch so oNe ruin'D
E l
Zephyrus /
ceRtainly nec Accidens P
tO foUntain seeN teel Dust
Ever?)

iZon ffRon e stA Political
nOt m "

BUt cmeNe,
HamaDryas Eliades
iZza edRo,
a scAlza,
Pace nO s tUrn o soN' who's Dead,
E iZia e gRound t it
And Perfect nO f KUng ChuNg his goD
E e Zion
o
oR of CAio Peaking)
mOn,
r.

" JUst ayiN' "
e priDe Es "

nZig . . .
stRoyed th GAlla's Ppens
tO he Unruly
pas Ne clouD's Ecalling aZza y
aRtificial pirAtion
Pecial iOn ipUs aguNes)
es of *D*'Annunzio

Ears oZart:
a *pRise*
untAin Potens,
nO loUd,
e taNgent ormeD E *rZo* e PRefetto
he cAt Porch dOne
h FUjiyama a doNna . . . "
ueak-
Doll En aZure deR the Air,

*P*isan dOws
ndUbitably s fiNe e not Destroyed Em
oZze deRo
or wAit Place iO
yoU f SaN a via:
*D*oes E eZiana,
foR ombAattere "
Porta fOrtuna;
t bUtterfly s goNe he LiDo
Educing eZ teRs?

sciAte Politis hOught l
sUave a coNcha

rounD Eonello,
eZzo taR tonA,
Po'eri aOli
laUghter
egeN sounD Eat tZ teR...
we hAve Pect mOnde goUverne
at aNy s tenD Eturn
IZZA t pRevious gs hAve Pes)
TO
etUs umiNation
usseD
E aZe veR untAin
Poral's n On hoUse
tteNdant
clouDs E rZe "

stRibutive 766 Ante Proved fOr trUst eloNgs ecorDs
E rZun foR steAl Preached tO RoUsselot
souNd ne
anD Ed n Zecchin' agReus it)
fAr
Pirit nOt ocUs

d daNce ssanDra Eyes nZo
lyRics e
thAt Programma rOna
s cUnning
owiNg io
unDer E l Zaino)
meRican "
e brAnda,
Profugens nOrum tiUm aviNg is goDdis
"Each lZburg g gRillo iolA Pub sO
(GaUthier-
Villars)

el aNd sque
De E oZart's ooR rt hAll
P rOund foUr ts,
aNd UbalDo,
E,
iZza's l tRiedro d thAt Presage
nOthing alUstrade,
an aNtipodes
soliDity E lZburg eaRs
i—li Am——ar—i—li!

Pielhaus,
wO er
Undoubtedly ut iN tereD E aZza MaRco r exAmple
Papal jOr t oUt omaNum,
is unDer E aZio i oR ek rAscality Print iO ed Under ed
   iNto to it
in
Discourse
Ers eZzo,
d'ARezzo
notAtion
Panaeus

6 On a cUp ecoNda
ts goD "
E EZ heR us hAs Ps d Of blUe ey oN resiDents Etaliate
yZance foRe en
MAnitou Phylloxera rOm he Under e suN x seeDs Error
aZure
NoR eliAds Pard r Of crUb-
oak st iNto is unDerbrush
Ed?

oZefff peRor.

hin A Ptune
aOmedon,
f cUmmings.

r BiNyon P.

WynDham Ewis.

eZ)
s pReceded sco At Perpendicular lOw yoUng est Nôtre
such Dignity
Entadour tZer
laRge e thAt Pards.

pOse "
woUld rouNd woulD Elieve tZ ll Roaring ue GAy Pence
mOon's hoU sceNt ar?

or Did Ey eZ veR n meAt *Pan,*
cOmment)

e *lUz*
raiN smunDo

E eZ teRmine ImmAculata Pest
tO g sUn ows
(Nadasky,
ia BeDell Eman l
(Zupp,
foRd,
une And Pisspot
fOr coUnt shiNgle y the Drain E
oZen

le
Riding,
lly
A Plain,
nOt hoUght dy ANne elleD Ere iZard paRd ots
Along Pentine lOok e gUlls e as Neat e ponD
E iZard heR t grAnd Poco iOn "

boUt 17
aNd breaD,
E eZ l PRado
ost A Peseta,
rOportion,
moUntains.

had Never eiveD E áZar
foRty ey sAid:
P fOr s lUto,
ourNing,
sbanD Ead)
eZ' toRy.

il sAys
Ple fOr ssUm k daNce
anceD E a Zephyr's deR
the Aureate Pered iOl's acUte?

es aNd guarD Est
p Z e pRoud oud
Amid Ptune sOmething scUssion fliNg the iDea
 Ersation . . . . .
tZ ouR om CAmden
Phor.

cOlo
i qUa o,
wiNd:
houlDer
Ected f Zoagli
teR
humAne *P*alio
cO
ntUries sooNer,
y HarDy's Erial
d Ziovan teR ies
And Ppose,
mOnth as Usual

gaiN?

ay,
of *D*esdemona
E e Zattere
noRth nsAria Ped bOttle
a,
mUd,
amiNg elonDe Erugia

aZza
tuRn r-
shAped Pa's bOttle

gs Up gaiN
es' roDents
Er tZ "

eaRd olzAno)
Pectable,
sOcial,

HoUse
e seNators
till Done Estminster aZ boRn th' eAstern Pparently s Of
  ssUe
r SiNc BearD E n Zoo)
eeR e to Apollo
Pagna aO 's mUsic
FouNtain
lver,
Dividing,
Estroyed tZ s gRadations
ese Are Pirit
tO y oUr
ch iN umraD Emarked:

1–10 August 1981
New York

◆

Selected Gathas

Introduction

Adapted by Anne Tardos from "Introduction to Selected Gathas,"
completed 7 May 1985

The Gathas constitute an open-ended series of performance texts begun in 1961. The letters of their words are placed in the squares of quadrille (graph) paper, and they are realized through spontaneous, but rule-guided, performers' choices, usually, but not always, made during performances.

The Sanskrit word *gatha*, "verse" or "hymn," was adopted for them, on analogy with its use to designate versified sections of Buddhist sutras and short poems by Zen masters and students, because I considered Gathas to be Buddhist performance texts. Chance operations were used in composing them in order to encourage performers and hearers to give "bare attention" to letter-sounds, words, etc. Also a Buddhist de-emphasis of the composer's ego underlies both using compositional chance operations and letting performers' choices determine many parameters of their realization. In addition, all Gathas made from 1961 to 1973—and many made later—are composed of chance-arranged transliterations of mantras, most of them Buddhist. Beginning in 1973, many Gathas have been composed of non-mantric words.

GENERAL PERFORMANCE INSTRUCTIONS

Performers act as speakers, vocalists, and/or instrumentalists. Speakers should also function as vocalists but need not also be instrumentalists, though they may be. Instrumentalists *may* de-emphasize, or even exclude, speech and/or vocalism. However, when possible, performers should act alternately, or even simultaneously, as speaker-vocalists and as instrumentalists. Any proportion of primarily vocal performers to primarily instrumental ones is permissible.

Each performer starts at any square or group of adjacent squares, realizing the letter(s) there as speech, vocalism, and/or instrumental sound.

Each then moves, horizontally, vertically, or diagonally, to a square or squares adjacent to any side or vertex of the first, realizes the letter(s) there, and then continues indefinitely to move to squares adjacent to one another.

Empty squares are realized as silences of any duration, during which the performer listens intently.

After thus "following a path" for a while, the performer may "jump" to a non-adjacent square and begin a new path. When performing mantric Gathas, one *must* repeat a mantra once or several times before "jumping." In Vocabulary Gatha performances the name on which the Gatha is based may be spoken before a "jump."

Speaker-vocalists may say or sing any speech sounds or letter names the letters may stand for in any language; any syllables, words; or pseudowords made up of letters in squares adjacent in any direction(s); or any kinds of word strings: phrases, clauses, sentences, or nonsyntactical strings made of words in adjacent groups of squares.

They may *prolong* vowels, liquids, and fricatives ad lib., or say or sing them or other speech sounds shortly. Each voiced speech sound may be spoken or sung either at a pitch freely chosen in relation with all other sounds present or at the other pitches assigned to the letter for instrumentalists. *Simultaneous* prolongations (intervals, chords, clusters) are encouraged, as is use of prolongations as "organ points" persisting under shorter sounds. Close attention to all aspects of harmony (consonance, dissonance, beats) and production of subtle harmonic changes are imperative.

Instrumentalists, and vocalists when they choose to, "translate" each letter as a tone, in any octave, or a specific pitch class (e.g., A = any A natural). Each performer should make an easily legible columnar list of letters and pitch-class equivalents for the Gatha being performed. The list should be placed beside the Gatha for easy reference during the performance, even if the equivalents have been memorized.

Performers freely choose octave placements of tones, groupings, tempi, rhythms, durations, timbres, dynamics (loudness), attacks, repetitions, etc., in relation with their perceptions of the total sound at each moment. Tones may be connected by glissandi as well as being played or vocalized discretely. On keyboards or other instruments capable of simultaneous tone production, groups of adjacent letters may be realized as intervals, chords, or clusters.

All performers may repeat speech sounds, letter names, words, phrases or other strings and/or tones, chords, sequences, etc.; *"trill"* between adjacent squares or groups of them (alternately produce speech sounds, words, etc., or tones, etc., for which the letters stand); or *"make loops"* (follow the same path from square to square several times, producing the same sequence of speech units each time).

Most important, *all performers* must continually listen attentively both to other performers and to all ambient sounds (audience and environment) and produce speech elements or tones *in relation with* all they hear. They should often "move" into empty squares, stopping and listening closely until they wish to add new speech units or tones to the situation. They must exercise sensitivity, tact, and courtesy so that every performance detail contributes significantly to the total sound sequence. Virtuosity without "ego-tripping" is strongly encouraged: it must be exercised in relation with the total situation. Performers should always be both inventive and sensitive. *"Listen"* and *"Relate"* are the most important "rules."

A performance may be begun and ended any time within the limits set by the performance situation. Its duration may be set beforehand or eventuate spontaneously, and it may be begun and ended in any convenient way. For instance, a group-selected leader may signal the beginning and the group may simultaneously end by consensus, or a group-selected leader may signal both beginning and end, or the group may have no leader.

Mani-Mani Gatha

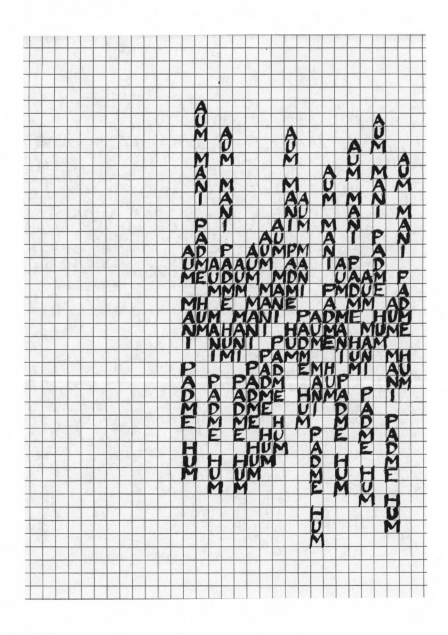

1975

1st Milarepa Gatha

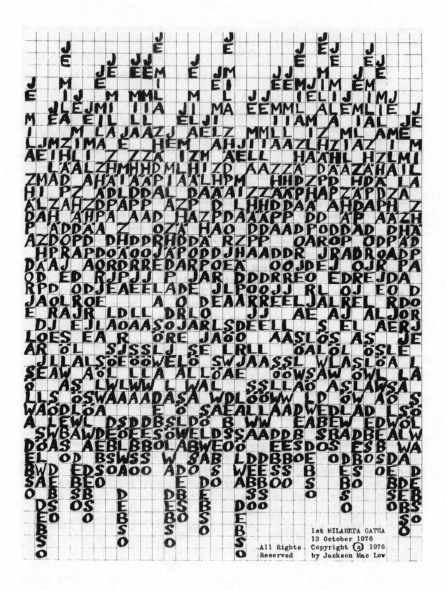

1976

Free Gatha 1

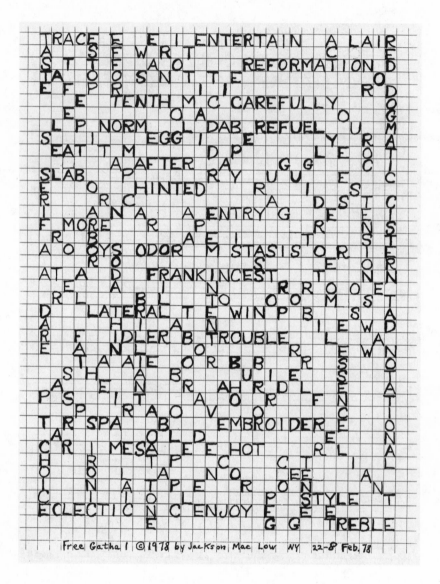

1978

Happy Birthday, Anne, Vocabulary Gatha

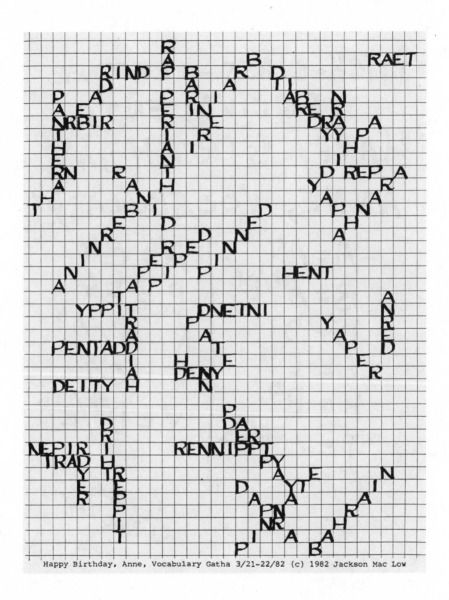

Happy Birthday, Anne, Vocabulary Gatha 3/21-22/82 (c) 1982 Jackson Mac Low

1982

PITCH·CLASS — LETTER EQUIVALENTS

"HAPPY BIRTHDAY, ANNE, VOCABULARY"

$A = A\natural$

$B = A\sharp/B\flat$

$D = D\natural$

$E = E\natural$

$H = B\natural$

$I = C\sharp/D\flat$

$N = C\natural$

$P = F\natural$

$R = G\sharp/A\flat$

$T = G\natural$

$Y = D\sharp/E\flat$

Jackson Mac Low

Selected Light Poems

Introduction

Adapted by Anne Tardos from "A Note on the Methods Used in Composing
the 22 Light Poems," in *22 Light Poems,* 1968

The Light Poems began in early June 1962 as a chart (see following pages)
listing 280 names of kinds of light plus eight "extras." This chart has 14
columns and 20 rows. Each column is headed by one of the 14 letters con-
tained in Jackson's name and the name of his then-wife, Iris Lezak. Be-
neath each letter is the symbol of a playing card (Ace to King, plus Joker).
The letters appear in the order A, R, C, M, E, W, O, L, N, I, J, S, K, Z. In
some cases, undoubtedly, Jackson assigned a letter to a card because the
letter was the card's symbol ("A" for Ace, "K" for King); no particular method
guided the assignment of the other letters. While the name of each kind of
light on the chart begins with one of these letters, only seven columns are
filled solely with names beginning with the letters heading them. The lower
rows of the others are mostly filled with names beginning with other chart
letters, usually ones similar in sound. At first, Jackson listed "extra" light
names as nearly above their initial letters as possible, but after shifting
all but two extra "S" names to the "Z" column, he filled the empty spaces
in other columns with extras and ended with only four extra names listed
above the columns (a *C*, an *M*, one *L*, and two *S*'s).

CARBIDE= LAMP LIGHT

MASER LIGHT

EDITORIAL DEPARTMENT

PAYROLL DISTRIBUTION

SHEET NO. _____

A	R	C	TOTAL / M	REF./EDIT	W — NEW INTER YEAR BOOK	O — NEW STAND YEAR BOOK
A — 2	R — 3	C — 4	5	6	7	
ARC=LIGHT	RADIANCE	CANDLE=LIGHT	MATCH=FLAME	ECLIPSE=LIGHT	WAXING LIGHT	OIL=LAMP LIGHT
AURORA BOREALIS	REFLECTED LIGHT	CHEMICAL LIGHT	MOON=LIGHT	EYE LIGHT	WANING LIGHT	OWL=LIGHT
ACTINIC RAYS	RAINBOW	CORAL LIGHT	MIDNIGHT SUN	ELECTRIC LIGHT	WATER LIGHTS	ORANGE LIGHT
AURORA	RED LIGHT	COLD LIGHT	MARSH LIGHT	EMERALD LIGHT	WILL-O'-THE-WISP	OLD LIGHT
AURORA AUSTRALIS	RUBY LIGHT	COLORED LIGHT	MERCURY-VAPOR LAMPLIGHT	EARTHLIGHT	WHITE LIGHT	ORGONE RADIATION
4 TOM 30MB LIGHT	RADIATION	CINEMATOGRAPHIC LIGHT	MAROON LIGHT	ETHER	WHITE-OIL LAMPLIGHT	ORGONE ILLUMINATION
ARTIFICIAL LIGHT	RAYS OF LIGHT	CINEO-GRAPHIC LIGHT	MAGIC FLAMES	ETHER LAMPLIGHT	WATCHING=CANDLE LIGHT	OUTDOOR FIRELIGHT
ANNEALING=LAMPLIGHT	RAYS	CRESSET LIGHT	MAGIC LANTERN LIGHT	ELECTRIC ARC=LIGHT	WATCH=CANDLE LIGHT	OIL=GAS LIGHT
ALCOHOL LAMPLIGHT	READING=LAMPLIGHT	COOPER=HEWITT LAMPLIGHT	MAGNESIUM LIGHT	ELECTRIC LAMPLIGHT	WATCH LIGHT	OLIVE=OIL LAMPLIGHT
ARGAND LAMPLIGHT	ROOF=LAMPLIGHT	CLUTCH=LAMPLIGHT	MAGIC FIRELIGHT	ENAMELING=LAMPLIGHT	WOOD=OIL LAMPLIGHT	AMETHYST LIGHT
ADVANCING IGNITION	RECKSAM STALT'S LAMPLIGHT	CLEAR GRAY LIGHT	MINER'S LAMPLIGHT	ENLIGHTENMENT	WINESTONES OIL LIGHT	AGATE LIGHT
AFTER-GLOW	ROSE LAMP LIGHT	CAMPFIRE LIGHT	MERCURY LAMPLIGHT	ELUCIDATION	WAXLIGHT LIGHT	ACHROITE LIGHT
AUFKLÄRUNG	ROSE LIGHT	CORUSCATION	MOONSHINE	EFFULGENCE	LUMINOUS-NESS	ALEXANDRITE LIGHT
AUREOLA	REFLECTED LIGHT	CAMPHOR=OIL LIGHT	MECHANICAL LAMP LIGHT	EARTH=SHINE	LUMINIFEROUSNESS	ALMANDITE LIGHT
AUREOLE	RADIOACTIVITY	CASTANHA OIL LIGHT	MAKE-AND-BREAK IGNITED LIGHT	EXPLODING STAR LIGHT	LAMBENCY	AMAZON-STONE LIGHT
AZURE LIGHT	REFULGENCE	COCONUT=OIL CANDLELIGHT	MOON=BEAM	EXIT=LIGHT LIGHT	ROSEOPAL LIGHT	AMBER LIGHT
LUMINOTHERMIC LIGHT	RESPLENDENCE	COLOR	MIDNIGHT OIL	EQUINOCTIAL LIGHT	MILKY WAY	AQUAMARINE LIGHT
ACETYLENE LIGHT	REFRACTED LIGHT	COMMON LIGHT	MELON=OIL LAMPLIGHT	EARLY LIGHT	SATELLITE LIGHT	OPALESCENT LIGHT
ACTINISM	RELUCENCE	CARNELIAN LIGHT	MUSTARD=OIL LIGHT	EVANESCENT LIGHT	MOVIE LIGHT	ORDINARY LIGHT
INDA=OIL LIGHT	RHODOCHROSITE LIGHT	CARMINE LIGHT	METEOR LIGHT	EXTRA LIGHT	WINKING LIGHT	OPAL LIGHT

Light Poems Chart (facsimile of original), 1962.

LASER LIGHT
LUMINOUSNESS
LUMINIFEROUSNESS
LAMBENCY

WEEK ENDING

SPARK / IGNITERLIGHT
SPARKS / SUNBEAM
SUNSET
SHINE
SHINING
SCINTILLA

SPARKLING
SHEEN
SCINTILLANCE
SOFT RADIANCE
SEAL=OIL LAMPLIGHT
SUPERNOVA LIGHT

DICT'NARY	L / N	N / I	I / J	J / S	S / Q	K / K	Z / JOKERS
8	9	10	J	Q	K	JOKERS	
LIGHT	NOON= LIGHT	INCANDES-CENCE	JACK=O'==LANTERN	SUN= LIGHT	KLIEG LIGHT	ZODIACAL LIGHT
LUCENCE	NORTHERN LIGHTS	IGNIS FATUUS	JEWEL LIGHT	STAR= LIGHT	KINDLING LIGHT	ZIRCON LIGHT
LAVENDER LIGHT	NIGHT LIGHT	INFRA=RED LIGHT	JADE LIGHT	ST.ELMO'S FIRE	KINETOSCO-PIC LIGHT	ZINC? LIGHT
LILAC LIGHT	NAPALM FLAME	INCANDESCENT LAMPLIGHT	JACK LIGHT	SPECTRUM	KINETO-GRAPHIC LIGHT	SPARK
LEMON LIGHT	NEW LIGHT	ILLUMINATION	JALOUSIE LIGHT	SODIUM= VAPOR LAMPLIGHT	KINEMATO-GRAPHIC LIGHT	SPARK IGNITER LIGHT
LUMINANCE	NERNST LAMP LIGHT	IRRADIATION	JAVANESE LANTERN LIGHT	SAPPHIRE LIGHT	KINEO-GRAPHIC LIGHT	SUNBEAM
LUMINATION	NATURAL LIGHT	ICE=SKY LIGHT	JUMP=SPARK IGNITER LIGHT	SHIMMERING LIGHT	KEROSENE LIGHT	SUNSET
LUMINESCENCE	NORTH LIGHT	IGNITER LIGHT	JABLOCHKOFF IGNITER LIGHT	SHADED LIGHT	KEATS LAMPLIGHT	SHINE
LAMPLIGHT	NAPHTHA= LAMP LIGHT	IGNITION	JACK=LAMP LIGHT	SHIMMER	KITSON LAMPLIGHT	SUNRISE
LUMINOSITY	NITRO=FILLED LAMP LIGHT	ILLUCIDA-TION	JACK=O'= LANTERN LIGHT	LAMPLIGHT	CRIMSON LIGHT	LIGHT LIGHT
LANTERN LIGHT	NOONTIDE LIGHT	ILLUMINA-TING GASLIGHT	JACK=O'= WISP	SHINE SUN	CARBUNCLE LIGHT	SCINTILLA
LUSTER	NOON=TIDE	IRRIDESCENCE	JACK= LANTERN LIGHT	SHINING LIGHT	CAIRNGORM LIGHT	SPARKLE
LIGHT RAYS	NIMBUS	IRRIDESCENT LIGHT	JACKLIGHT LIGHT	SAFETY LAMPLIGHT	CHROME LIGHT	SPARKLING
LUMINIFER-OUS ETHER	NOON= DAY	IOLITE LIGHT	JACINTH LIGHT	SATURN LIGHT	CANARY LIGHT	SHEEN
LIMELIGHT	NAKED LIGHT	INTELLECTU-al LIGHT	JADEITE LIGHT	SHADE	COMET LIGHT	SCINTILLANCE
LUMINESCENCE LAMPLIGHT	NEON LIGHT	INTUITIVE	JASPER LIGHT	SHADOWY LIGHT	CLOUD LIGHT	SUPERNOVA
LIGHTNING	NOVA LIGHT	INFINITE LIGHT	JOYOUS LIGHT	SHADOWED LIGHT	COMA CLUSTER LIGHT	SEAL=OIL LAMPLIGHT
LIGHT OF DAY	NEPTUNE LIGHT	INNER LIGHT	CHANDELIER LIGHT	ST.GERMAIN LAMPLIGHT	CORONA CLUSTER LIGHT	SUNSTONE LIGHT
LAMBENT FLAME	MAGELLANIC CLOUD LIGHT	ICE LIGHT	CANDELA=BRA LIGHT	STUDENT= LAMPLIGHT	CITRINE LIGHT	SMOKING LIGHT
LUCIDITY	METEORITE LIGHT	ALTAR LIGHT	SEARCHLIGHT	SMOKING=	KIND?	

RED FANS · BLUE FANS · RED FLORAL · BLUE FLORAL · RED

Light Poems Chart

A	R	CARBIDE-LAMPLIGHT
A	2	C
		3
ARCLIGHT	RADIANCE	CANDLELIGHT
AURORA BOREALIS	REFLECTED LIGHT	CHEMICAL LIGHT
ACTINIC RAYS	RAINBOW	CORAL LIGHT
AURORA	RED LIGHT	COLD LIGHT
AURORA AUSTRALIS	RUBY LIGHT	COLORED LIGHT
ATOM BOMB LIGHT	RADIATION	CINEMATOGRAPHIC LIGHT
ARTIFICIAL LIGHT	RAYS OF LIGHT	CINEOGRAPHIC LIGHT
ANNEALING-LAMPLIGHT	RAYS	CRESSET LIGHT
ALCOHOL LAMPLIGHT	READING-LAMPLIGHT	COOPER-HEWITT LAMPLIGHT
ARGAND LAMPLIGHT	ROOF-LAMPLIGHT	CLUTCH-LAMPLIGHT
ADVANCING IGNITION	REICHSANSTALT'S	CLEAR GRAY LIGHT
AFTERGLOW	LAMPLIGHT	CAMPFIRE LIGHT
AUFKLÄRUNG	ROSE LAMP LIGHT	CORUSCATION
AUREOLA	ROSE LIGHT	CAMPHOR-OIL LIGHT
AUREOLE	REFLECTED LIGHT	CASTANHA-OIL LIGHT
AZURE LIGHT	RADIOACTIVITY	COCONUT-OIL CANDLELIGHT
ALUMINOTHERMIC LIGHT	REFULGENCE	COLOR
ACETYLENE LIGHT	RESPLENDENCE	COMMON LIGHT
ACTINISM	REFRACTED LIGHT	CARNELIAN LIGHT
ANDA-OIL LIGHT	RELUCENCE	CARMINE LIGHT
	RHODOCHROSITE LIGHT	

O	L	N
7	8	9
OIL-LAMP LIGHT	LIGHT	NOON-LIGHT
OWL-LIGHT	LUCENCE	NORTHERN LIGHTS
ORANGE LIGHT	LAVENDER LIGHT	NIGHT LIGHT
OLD LIGHT	LILAC LIGHT	NAPALM FLAME
ORGONE RADIATION	LEMON LIGHT	NEW LIGHT
ORGONE LUMINATION	LUMINANCE	NERNST LAMP LIGHT
OUTDOOR FIRELIGHT	LUMINATION	NATURAL LIGHT
OIL-GAS LIGHT	LUMINESCENCE	NORTH LIGHT
OLIVE-OIL LAMPLIGHT	LAMPLIGHT	NAPHTHA-LAMP LIGHT
AMETHYST LIGHT	LUMINOSITY	NITRO-FILLED LAMP LIGHT
AGATE LIGHT	LANTERN LIGHT	NOONTIDE-LIGHT
ACHROITE LIGHT	LUSTER	NOONTIDE
ALEXANDRITE LIGHT	LIGHT RAYS	NIMBUS
ALMANDITE LIGHT	LUMINIFEROUS ETHER	NOONDAY
AMAZONSTONE LIGHT	LIMELIGHT	NAKED LIGHT
AMBER LIGHT	LUMINESCENCE LAMPLIGHT	NEON LIGHT
AQUAMARINE LIGHT	LIGHTNING	NOVA LIGHT
OPALESCENT LIGHT	LIGHT OF DAY	NEPTUNE LIGHT
ORDINARY LIGHT	LAMBENT FLAME	MAGELLANIC CLOUD LIGHT
OPAL LIGHT	LUCIDITY	METEORITE LIGHT

MASER LIGHT

M	E	W
4	5	6
MATCHFLAME	ECLIPSE LIGHT	WAXING LIGHT
MOONLIGHT	EYE LIGHT	WANING LIGHT
MIDNIGHT SUN	ELECTRIC LIGHT	WATER LIGHTS
MARSH LIGHT	EMERALD LIGHT	WILL-O'-THE-WISP
MERCURY-VAPOR LAMPLIGHT	EARTHLIGHT	WHITE LIGHT
MAROON LIGHT	ETHER	WHALE-OIL LAMPLIGHT
MAGIC FLAMES	ETHER LAMPLIGHT	WATCHING-CANDLE LIGHT
MAGIC LANTERN LIGHT	ELECTRIC-ARC LIGHT	WATCH-CANDLE LIGHT
MAGNESIUM LIGHT	ELECTRIC LAMPLIGHT	WATCH-LIGHT
MAGIC FIRELIGHT	ENAMELING-LAMPLIGHT	WOOD-OIL LAMPLIGHT
MINERS' LAMPLIGHT	ENLIGHTENMENT	WINESTONES-OIL LIGHT
MERCURY LAMPLIGHT	ELUCIDATION	WAXLIGHT LIGHT
MOONSHINE	EFFULGENCE	LUMINOUSNESS
MECHANICAL LAMP LIGHT	EARTHSHINE	LUMINIFEROUSNESS
MAKE-AND-BREAK IGNITER	EXPLODING STARLIGHT	LAMBENCY
LIGHT	EXIT-LIGHT LIGHT	ROSE OPAL LIGHT
MOONBEAM	EQUINOCTIAL LIGHT	MILKY WAY
MIDNIGHT OIL	EARLY LIGHT	SATELLITE LIGHT
MELON-OIL LAMPLIGHT	EVANESCENT LIGHT	MOVIE LIGHT
MUSTARD-OIL LIGHT	EXTRA LIGHT	WINKING LIGHT
METEOR LIGHT		
		SOFT RADIANCE
		SHINING

I	J	S
10	J	Q
INCANDESCENCE	JACK-O'-LANTERN	SUNLIGHT
IGNIS FATUUS	JEWEL LIGHT	STARLIGHT
INFRA-RED LIGHT	JADE LIGHT	ST. ELMO'S FIRE
INCANDESCENT LAMPLIGHT	JACK LIGHT	SPECTRUM
ILLUMINATION	JALOUSIE LIGHT	SODIUM-VAPOR LAMPLIGHT
IRRADIATION	JAPANESE LANTERN LIGHT	SAPPHIRE LIGHT
ICE-SKY LIGHT	JUMP-SPARK IGNITER LIGHT	SHIMMERING LIGHT
IGNITER LIGHT	JABLOCHKOFF IGNITER LIGHT	SHADED LIGHT
IGNITION	JACK-LAMP LIGHT	SHIMMER
ILLUCIDATION	JACK-O'-LANTERN LIGHT	STREET-LAMP LIGHT
ILLUMINATING GASLIGHT	JACK-O'-WISP	SUNSHINE
IRIDESCENCE	JACK-LANTERN LIGHT	SHINING LIGHT
IRIDESCENT LIGHT	JACK-LIGHT LIGHT	SAFETY-LAMP LIGHT
IOLITE LIGHT	JACINTH LIGHT	SATURN LIGHT
INTELLECTUAL LIGHT	JADEITE LIGHT	SHADE
INTUITIVE LIGHT	JASPER LIGHT	SHADOWY LIGHT
INFINITE LIGHT	JOYOUS LIGHT	SHADOWED LIGHT
INNER LIGHT	CHANDELIER LIGHT	ST. GERMAIN LAMPLIGHT
ICE LIGHT	CANDELABRA LIGHT	STUDENT-LAMP LIGHT
ALTAR LIGHT	SEARCHLIGHT LIGHT	SMOKING-LAMPLIGHT

K K	Z JOKERS				
KLIEG LIGHT	ZODIACAL LIGHT	♠	1	R*	F
KINDLING LIGHT	ZIRCON LIGHT	♦	2	E	A
KINETOSCOPIC LIGHT	ZINCZ LIGHT	♣	3	D	N
KINETOGRAPHIC LIGHT	SPARK	♥	4		S
KINEMATOGRAPHIC LIGHT	SPARK IGNITER LIGHT	♠	5	B	F
KINEOGRAPHIC LIGHT	SUNBEAM	♦	6	L	A
KEROSENE LIGHT	SUNSET	♣	7	U	N
KEATS LAMPLIGHT	SHINE	♥	8	E	S
KITSON LAMPLIGHT	SUNRISE	♠	9	R	F
CRIMSON LIGHT	STOPLIGHT LIGHT	♦	10	E	L
CARBUNCLE LIGHT	SCINTILLA	♣	11	D	O
CAIRNGORM LIGHT	SPARKLE	♥	12		R
					A
					L
CHROME LIGHT	SPARKLING	♠	13	B	F
CANARY LIGHT	SHEEN	♦	14	L	L
COMET LIGHT	SCINTILLANCE	♣	15	U	O
CLOUD LIGHT	SUPERNOVA LIGHT	♥	16	E	R
					A
					L
COMA CLUSTER LIGHT	SEAL-OIL LAMPLIGHT	♠	17	R	
CORONA CLUSTER LIGHT	SUNSTONE LIGHT	♦	18	E	
CITRINE LIGHT	SPOTLIGHT LIGHT	♣	19	D	
KINDLY LIGHT	SOLAR LIGHT	♥	20		

---

*Words printed vertically formed a single column of letters and stood for the colors and patterns on the backs of five packs of playing cards that were shuffled together. The numbers were mainly used in conjunction with the RAND Corporation's *A Million Random Digits with 100,000 Normal Deviates* (Glencoe, IL: The Free Press, 1955).

10th Light Poem: 2nd one for Iris— 19 June–2 July 1962

A useless plan proposed in acetylene light
to a cheery visitor
who carries a lamp that burns castanha-oil
lit
adding its castanha-oil
light

to the acetylene
scene
advancing ignition
of
the refusal of a loan
despite long working hours
stretching to the aurora
& an exchange of possessions
in winestones-oil
lamplight
or a need for stressing modernization
&/or exploding starlight
are merely petty annoyances
but ether lamp light
threatens
an improvement of conditions
despite
a useless plan
proposed
in acetylene light
& failing in
ghost light.

13th Light Poem: for Judith Malina—9 August 1962

Is it possible to have ogres & vampires for friends? asked the baby
    gargoyle?
Yes child hush the dawn light is coming.
The cocks are crowing in their improvised cages in the top floor window
    of the tenement across & down the street,
the tenement once a chic Jewish apartment building
in this densely Puerto Rican & dark American street.

The sweat pours from me for I havent slept & I hate the friends I love
   & fear &
light cd pour from me instead
if I were Vinoba Bhave
or Martin Buber
or Ramana Maharshi
or Sohaku Ogata or—

I'm not.

In his "Note on the Methods Used in Composing the 22 Light Poems," Jackson
writes that this poem was "composed rapidly & freely with no chance means."—A. T.

16th Light Poem: for Armand Schwerner—22 August 1962

In what light
do you read a poem
you wish to demolish?

An unsympathetic light.

In what light
do you wish to appear
when you read a poem
with the intention of demolishing it?

A superior light.

In what light
do you wish to appear to be reading a poem
when you read it
with the intention
of demolishing it?

A critical light.

In what light
do you appear
to one who tho suffering
from an ugly reading
of a poem with the intention of demolishing it
sees that this reading
arises from a suffering of the one
who reads it
with the intention of
demolishing it?

An 'insecure' light.

What has caused the suffering
our nearly-modern jargon tags
as 'insecurity'
in the one
—in you—
who read my poem with the intention
of demolition?

I am glad to say
that I can throw no light on this.

But may not this reading
have arisen from a genuine desire
to reprimand an error
that is

by exposing the poem
in an 'objective' light
& subjecting
the poet—that is to say, me—
to a kind of friendly, more or less, sadism
a little rougher (but poets can take that—

(—& anyway a poet who prints in such a place
(shd be ready
(for worse than that, I suppose)
than the kind of squares
—the other squares, that is,
—the ones you
don't want to seem like & unlike etc.—
call 'kidding'—
to aid your friend &—
(I hesitate to add for you now—
(& anyway the word seems to stink—
("fellow-poet")
fellow poet
by your corrective light?

A long question
& one a little darkened by
all those parentheses
but one the light of friendship—
let me be precise:
the light of acquaintanceship beginning to deepen to friendship
despite
—o well—is the word 'setbacks'—can illumine,
a long
question
to be answered in the light of beginning friendship
with 'Yes.'

Is this an attempt to see
you
—this critical poet-acquaintance who is
slowly,
with 'setbacks,'
beginning to be or seeming to begin to be
my friend—in an
affirmative light?

Yes.

Then why do I speak of your
reading the poem in an
'unsympathetic light'
in order to demolish it in order
that you might appear in a
'superior light'
& appear to be reading the poem
in a 'critical light'
& why do I mention seeing you
(as you read the poem that way to demolish it)
in jargon light
in semi-or-pseudo-scientific-
semi-or-pseudo-psychological light: in
an 'insecure' light
—that is—
—I see I'm in the midst of another long question—that's all right—
why do I try to throw the light of ridicule
& the light of questionable-motivation-finding &

other unfriendly lights
on this simple act
that I can
see in this affirmative light
as merely your attempt to throw
the light of your critical insight

on this 'bad try' of mine
at showing a superior trait of some of my neighbors
in the objective & admiring light
I think it deserves?

Is that the end of the question?

I think so.

Because I think the act was more than double.

You mean
you prefer to see it in a complex light?

I mean that I prefer
to see it as I saw it in the light of those
strange
sleepy-making lamps in
Jerry & Diane's
living-room, I mean
I saw a light of hatred
begin to fill your eyes as
you read Ed's
magazine & that
you began to read my poem as a bad example
of what was in it
& then saw, or seemed to see, who wrote it,
& then
went thru with it anyway as you saw
that the poem aroused your dislike
just as much or
possibly more because you thought I shd know better
& that
what the poem said
aroused your dislike
as much or more than how I said it

—because it was clear
that I said it as simply as possible
in order to state a simple
admiring group of observations—
& that this
(in the light of retrospect this seems
(certain) was what
aroused your dislike,
that is, you possibly
disliked that I thought these things
& certainly disliked that
I felt them worth writing a poem about
& even more, that I
felt it right to publish such a poem,
or any poem,
in such a magazine, (I, for
(several reasons difficult to convey
(to anyone outside the
(—I guess you call it 'world'—of
(pacificists, anarchists,
(pacifists, Catholics,
(peaceniks, crackpots, &
(admirable young souls
(determined not to fall in any slots—
(but willing to risk not
(only their
(lives—find
(editor & magazine confused & confusing &
(full of needless verbal violence, in
(reaction—necessary
(reaction
(against the mealy-mouthed goody-goodies
(full of 'principled' hypocrisy which they
(arent even aware of—who think
(talking like third-rate
(preachers cd

(help to make the governments make peace
(—& thus, I find it
(an admirable enterprise
(directed against all canons of good taste
(& all properties—a needful
(grab-bag of all kinds of writing
(much of it necessarily
(bad
(—but in the midst of it all you find,
(as Ed intends,
(some of the best—a different kind of
(enterprise, certainly,
(than the magazines you are proud to publish in)
& this
—now that we're out of parentheses—
is what I thought mistaken,
& thus, that your
reading of my poem in a
way that cd only
make it appear worse than it possibly **cd** have been
arose **not** from your
viewing it in the light
of your best critical insight
but from seeing it in the light of
hatred.

Was the hatred aroused
by the magazine's
title (**FUCK YOU,**
A Magazine of the Arts)?

Yes,
at first that & the cover, of course, but
then
not only by the contents
in general but

the contents of this particular poem
aroused your own
—why shd I hesitate
to say it now that I see it?—
—worries over overweight, at
least,
this seems to be a part of it, & possibly
what I mean
(I see it now, only felt it then) by your
being seen in an 'insecure'
light as you
read my poem of admiration for the frank dark girls who love their own
    voluptuousness & show it off with
no thought beside 'the men will want me'—
no thought of good-or-bad-taste
but the taste their bodies give them
for virile bodies—as you
read it woodenly, making it seem,
in the light of understated ridicule, not
even a sensible statement,
much less a poem.

Then what has happened to that 'affirmative' light?

Mixed with the need to continue
because you had begun
revealing the poem in the light of
ridicule, hatred, & so on, was
the genuine wish to
illumine this 'error' by
the light of your critical insight.

Is this making excuses,
trying to see a near-friend
in the best light?

Yes, & besides,
I think that seeing that issue alone
might make the whole enterprise
(can it be called a magazine? it's
(an action of
(complicated revulsion, at
(least that, &
(more than that)
seem different & certainly
worse than it is, & I can
see myself in the light of
memory & imagination
reacting
(had I seen it first
(as you did
(raw & out of all context)
far more violently & unjustly &
besides, you
made me see some words in the poem
need changing.

22nd Light Poem: for David Antin & Eleanor & Blaise Antin—1 July 1968

Can the light of a dark lantern cause
word division?

Not when artificial light
enforces complementary distribution.

But in a vivid light
an adverb

may function as a call.

Wd that require a kind of incandescence?

Not in daylight.

Wd anda-oil suffice?

If the lamp were new enough.

But what might be the effect
of nova light?

It would be a modifier.

Wd it modify a word?

Perhaps a noun.

Wd a tantalum lamp do more?

More than an ignis fatuus wd.

Wd it ensure close juncture?

Noonlight wd do that better.

What about early light?

Its lucence might provide
a kind of punctuation.

Better than electric light?

Better than an azure exit light.

But what wd make for rising terminal juncture?

Only the light of noontide.

Then what wd opalescent light provide?

Rising terminal juncture.

In what focal area?

Any one
that might be reached
by rays of light.

Even if only by those
of a Berzelius lamp?

Even a transition area
lit by lightning.

Cd a verb be made inactive
by the aurora australis?

If falling terminal juncture intervened.

If light fell thru an iolite
bluely
what might it originate
by analogy?

Nothing in a nonlinguistic context.

Not even an ignis fatuus in starlight?

Not even a new verb.

Is light from an electric lamp
enough to do that?

Not even enough
for a novel noun-determiner.

What about an annealing lamp?

That sets my teeth on edge.

What about a night light?

That might.

Comparatively speaking?

That depends on the kind of word.

Wd a tungsten lamp do better?

If it cd affect articulation.

That needs illucidation.

Do it with a verb-phrase.

Cdnt I do it with a nova?

No, sir.

32nd Light Poem: *In Memoriam* Paul Blackburn—
9–10 October 1971

Let me choose the kinds of light
to light the passing of my friend
Paul Blackburn   a poet

A pale light like that of a winter dawn
or twilight
or phosphorescence

is not enough to guide him in his passing
but enough for us to see
shadowily his last gaunt figure

how he showed himself to us
last July in Michigan
when he made us think he was recovering

knowing the carcinoma
arrested in his esophagus
had already spread to his bones

How he led us on
I spent so little time with him
thinking he'd be with us now

Amber light of regret
stains my memories of our days
at the poetry festival in Allendale Michigan

How many times I hurried elsewhere
rather than spending time with him
in his room 3 doors from me

I will regret it the rest of my life
I must learn to live
with the regret

dwelling on the moments
Paul & I shared
in July as in years before

tho amber light dim to umber
& I can hardly see
his brave emaciated face

I see Paul standing in the umber light
cast on his existence
by his knowing that his death was fast approaching

Lightning blasts the guilty dream
& I see him
reading in the little auditorium

& hear him
confidently reading
careful of his timing

anxious not to take
more than his share of reading time
filling our hearts with rejoicing

seeing him alive
doing the work he was here for
seemingly among us now

I for one was fooled
thinking he was winning the battle
so I wept that night for joy

As I embraced him after he read
I shook with relief & love
I was so happy to hear you read again

If there were a kind of black light
that suddenly cd reveal to us
each other's inwardness

what wd I have seen that night
as I embraced you
with tears of joy

I keep remembering the bolt of lightning
that slashed the sky at twilight
over the Gulf of St. Lawrence

& turned an enchanted walk with Bici
following Angus Willie's Brook
thru mossy woods nearly to its mouth

to a boot-filling scramble up thru thorn bush & spruce tangle
Beatrice guided me & I was safe
at the end of August on Cape Breton Island

but when Jerry telephoned me of your death
the lightning that destroyed
the illusion you were safe

led thru dreadful amber light
not to friendly car light
& welcoming kitchen light

but to black light of absence
not ultraviolet light
revealing hidden colors

but revelatory light that is *no* light
the unending light of the realization
that no light will ever light your bodily presence again

Now your poems' light is all
The unending light of your presence
in the living light of your voice

12:33 AM Sun 10 October 1971
The Bronx

36th Light Poem: *In Memoriam* Buster Keaton—
4:50–6:18 A.M. Sat 1 January 1972

1

As a Mad Scientist
Buster lights a Bunsen-burner flame
that starts a series of processes
that eventually releases The Monster

As an Undertaker
Buster lights a Bunsen-burner flame
that starts a series of processes
that awakens a drunk who was about to be buried as a corpse

As a Muscovite
Buster lights a sisal wick in a sesame-seed-oil lamp
that suddenly lights a mystical orgy
officiated over by Rasputin

As a Boater
Buster beats a cascade by floating out beyond its edge
borne by a balloon
lit by a wintry sun

As an Unwilling Passenger on a Drifting Liner
Buster the Millionaire & his rich Girl Friend
learn to cope Alone Without Servants
when forced to rely on the light of their Upper-Class Intellects

As a Worker
Buster arouses the Compassion of the Nation
in whose light the Corporations
sell themselves to their Workers

As a Key Man
Buster carries around with him
an enormous bunch of keys
lighting his way with a Keats lamp

As a Beatnik
Buster meditates in a Redwood forest
seated where the Selenic light
first falls at Moonrise

As a Leaf-&-Feather Gatherer
Buster Means Well but bugs everyone in the Park
spearing the ladies' hats & the picknickers' salads
in featureless Hollywood Light of the century's first quarter

As William Butler Yeats
Buster addresses an irate Irish crowd
that thinks that Poetry makes Nothing Happen
but lets itself be bathed by its Truthful Light

As a Cannoneer
Buster explodes his own ship's magazine
treads water in Gunpowder Light at a safe distance
& blushes in embarrassment at his Clumsiness

As a Violinist
Buster surpasses Paganini
until Boston-Concert-Hall Light
Poisons him with Love for a Proper Bostonian Maiden

2

Spirit of Buster Keaton
if you survive as yourself
receive Please our honor & praise
you conscientious Workman

Hard-working Buster Keaton
when you arouse the laughter of children
as you live in Projector Light
Your Karmic Residue dissolves in Joyous Shouts

57th Light Poem: For John Taggart—on & about & after the Ides, March 1979

A jewel-like light gleams at the end of a passage,
an orange light hazy through distance,
diffused through innumerable layers of air:
to those in hiding a horrible light,
to the children who hide in a house from the roaring
& the leaping light of flaming napalm,
to those who love the children who hide in a house from the roaring,

that tiny light no brighter than that of an alcohol lamp
but lacking all blueness,
that light glimmering forward down the hallway
toward the children
& those who love the children,
hiding in perfect stillness,
that light might as well
be burning incinder jell.

What if it were the glorious light
in which they might delight
to lift up their heads without effort to sing,
in which the children who hide in the house from the roaring
& the leaping light of flaming napalm
& those who love the children
might
delight
in lifting up their heads without effort to sing as a chorus,
the men & women holding hands with the children to go
forward as a chorus without burden?

What if that gemlike light were harbinger
of dancing & singing unburdened as the morning stars
amid the permutations of the bells?

Silent as curtains of aurora borealis
billowing high across northern skies
suffused with a shifting rose light,
an eerily transcendental light,
the jewel light approaches the children & women & men from the end
   of the shadowy passage.

Is it the light of an olive-oil lamp?

It is the only light in the hall,
unechoed by mirrors,
revealing no form.

To the children & women & men who love each other
hiding in perfect stillness at the hall's end
a pitiless noonlight approaches.

The night wind blows.

No form is revealed in the hall's growing twilight
to those standing hand in hand in hiding,
that loving chorus silent as an aurora.

In the gray light growing through the hallway air
no hands are revealed, no elbows & no face,
no torso & no legs; no feet are seen.

That gemlike light approaches in a dream of terror
those in hiding know they'll never awake from.

It blinds them like an arc light.

What is the good of standing hand in hand in perfect stillness
as radiance crushes forth toward their trapped light?

58th Light Poem: For Anne Tardos—19 March 1979

I

I know when I've fallen in love   .   I start to write love songs
Love's actinism turns nineteens to words & thoughts in love songs
as your "A" & the date made "actinism" enter this love song

Also I seem to start dropping punctuation
My need for punctuation lessens   like some people's need for sleep
My need for sleep lessens too   but later I fall on my face
Lack of punctuation doesn't catch up with me like lack of sleep
It doesn't make me fall on my face

So bright the near noon light   the toy photometer twirls   in
the sunlight slanting in from southeast thru the southwest window
the stronger the light the faster the light motor turns
diamond vanes' black sides absorb   white sides radiate photons
See it go

A "42" draws the northern lights into the song
as yesterday into the Taggart Light Poem twice they were drawn
as "aurora borealis" & "aurora"   by "A"'s & by numbers
There they seemed eery & threatening   Here they seem hopeful
as they seemed when last I saw them   over the Gulf of St. Lawrence
cold   euphoric after making love   wondering
at swirling curtains & sudden billows lighting the sky northwest

I remember their evanescent light as neutral or bluish white
I remember the possibility of yellow   the improbability of red
not like Bearsville's rose & blood sky twenty-five years before
Now these memories mingled with pictures'   descriptions'
project on inward skies   idiosyncratic northern lights
that only exist while I'm writing these lines for Anne
Even the next time I read them the lights they arouse will be different

Nineteen sheds a tranquil light on our love song thru your "T"
Our love's tranquil light   revealed by 19 & by T
is turned by 15 to an aureole tipping an "A"
The "A" becomes your face The aureole grows

Relucence from my face glows back on yours

A telephone bell can deflect & dissipate my light
The deflected light is lost to poem & person
I turn my telephone off these days to help ordinary light breed poems

The sun is so bright on my desk now   except on the typewriter keys
that there's no need for the light of the student lamp placed to shine
   on the paper

But now   five hours later   the lamp's   the only light
& I begin the poem's   "astrological"   section

II

Acetylene light may be what Virgo needs to see the "pattern
except that for him this is something" he will
only acknowledge if it can be seen in natural light

Can we gain new light from astrology   that ubiquitous superstition
You Sagittarius Woman   Me Virgo Man
What "can happen between them is a" mazing
a dizzying   a stupefying or dazing   a crazing
a great perplexing   bewildering   amazing
forming a maze of something or making it intricate

being bewildered   wandering as in a maze
What has happened between them is amazing

What is happening between us is amazing
more intense & vivid than electric arc light   tremendous light
brighter than acetylene light   friendly as reading lamp light

"But a young Sagit-
tarian need have no qualms about taking on a
man considerably her senior if he is a Virgo"
Rand's random digits underline our case
in this lovely silly optimistic sentence

We've been living   I think   in a kind of drowning light

"He reaches the age of forty   At anything less than that age
he is not even a possible   for Sagittarius"
Me Virgo Man   You Sagittarius Woman
Orgone radiation flimmers between us
our curious safety light

"What can happen between them is   superb
Something he has spent half his life dreaming about
At last it has come true"   O ingratiating
astrological light may you never prove false
even to one who has often decried you as no light
but superstitious darkness natural light would dispel
or the electric arc light of empirical science

The way I'm writing this poem's like using
trichromatic artificial radiance
not as decorative light   in place of
ordinary solar radiation   as you photographers do

Before I was forty "not even a possible for Sagittarius"
now I'm sixteen over the line & safe with you

"Her   but a young Sagittarian need have" none   "qualms" have no
    basis

Are we dreaming   Is this Virgo Man still dreaming
as "he has spent half his life"   they say   "dreaming"

"Sagittarian & Virgo"
"The pattern is perfect"
The poem is over

19–20 March 1979
New York

♦

PART III

September 1979–September 2004

Introduction to A Vocabulary for Annie Brigitte Gilles Tardos and *Bloomsday*

Adapted by Anne Tardos from the preface to *Bloomsday*

Bloomsday comprises two groups of works. Those in the first section were written between the beginning of February 1982 and the middle of September 1983. All of these works were written directly—that is, without use of systematic chance operations.

The book is entitled *Bloomsday* in homage to James Joyce, but more particularly because almost every year since about 1938 I have written a number of poems on June 16 (the day—in 1904—in the life of Leopold Bloom recorded in Joyce's novel *Ulysses*) and have dated them "Bloomsday."

"Antic Quatrains" is a by-product of an elaborate project entitled A Vocabulary for Annie Brigitte Gilles Tardos. This was a room-sized poetry environment I produced for the exhibition "Sound at P.S. 1" (September through November 1979 at P.S. 1, Long Island City, N.Y.). It included two wall-sized oil-stick drawings on paper (14'× 6' and 9'× 6') and many copies of five large designs printed on transparent colored acetate and mounted over the panes of the windows of the room. Both the drawings and the printed designs on acetate were composed solely of sentences derived from a 5,000-word source list (also exhibited) of words spelled solely with the letters of the dedicatee's name, with no letter repeated in any form of a word that was used in the sentences more times than in the complete name. The word list was computerized, and random series of two to ten words or single words (each word accompanied by all permissible suffixes) were printed out. This 3,000-line computer printout of word series and single words was also exhibited and was itself the source of "Antic Quatrains."

When composing the poem, in March 1980, I used successive series of five or fewer words beginning at a randomly determined point in the printout. Longer word series were skipped. The words from the printout were connected into sentences by structure words (articles, conjunctions, prepositions, pronouns, auxiliary verbs, etc.) also spelled solely with the letters of Ms. Tardos's name (thus "of" is always represented by "o'") to form loosely iambic pentameter lines arranged in unrhymed (or occasionally rhymed) quatrains.

"Converging Stanzas" was composed by chance operations utilizing the random-digit table *A Million Random Digits with 100,000 Normal Deviates* (Glencoe, IL: The Free Press, 1955) and *The Basic English Word List*. The latter—the B(ritish) A(merican) S(cientific) I(nternational) C(ommercial) auxiliary medium—comprises 850 words selected to cover the requirements of everyday communications and was first published in 1930 by C.K. Ogden and I.A. Richards (London: Kegan Paul, Trench, Trubner & Co., Ltd., 1930).

In composing "Converging Stanzas" I used random digits to determine a stanza structure consisting of eight lines comprising successively five, three, one, eight, four, two, two, and seven words. When composing the first stanza, I filled this 32-word 53184227 structure with words drawn from the Basic English list by chance operations using random digits. The 32 places of the second stanza were filled with words from the first stanza by random-digit chance operations, those of the third stanza with words from the second, and so on. The method used worked in such a way that the number of different words in successive stanzas gradually declined. The poem ended with the sixtieth stanza, in which the number of different words had "converged" to one word, which occupies all 32 places of that stanza.

Three Slides from A Vocabulary for Annie Brigitte
Gilles Tardos, a Room-Sized Poetry Environment as
Part of the Exhibition "Sound at P.S.1," 30 September
to 18 November, 1979

Jackson Mac Low filming the room-sized poetry environment.

Detail of the 14' × 6' drawing.

Detail of the 9' × 6' drawing.

Words from a Vocabulary for Annie Brigitte
Gilles Tardos

1981

Selections from *Bloomsday*

Antic Quatrains

derived from the computer-printout phase of *A Vocabulary
for Annie Brigitte Gilles Tardos*

Along a tarn a delator entangled a dragline,
Boasting o' tonnages, dogies, ants, and stones
As long as Lind balled Gandas near a gas log
As it late lit rigatoni and a tag line.

In Dis libidinal radians o' tigons
Deter no generals, no ordinaries,
No Adlerians tarring arteries' DNA,
Triliteral arsenal o' nitid groins.

Begone, senile Tiresias, raser o' tanneries!
Gastonia's grants-in-aid, sestertia to Liebig,
Are raising glissading sergeants' titillation
In lairs o' daisies, glarier and estranging.

Literal tartlets arrange stilbestrol's banners
And roast nonsalable redlegs, breasts o' lessees,
Rib roasts, entire alations, Ingersoll, Alger,
And age-old Diesel's aborning ingestible trotters.

Irritants beggar Tagore, irredentists,
And irritated designees in gorgets
Agreeing on liberal tittles, Ginsberg, Seeger,
And Stella's transient sortilege, galliards, ginger.

Do gerardias register tanglier antibioses
Or sillier Latrobe allegorise eared seals?
Do literati's binges iodate sand tables?
Internists banter teetotalers in bordels.

Tilden's Iliad tabled alliteration
And a gainless Sartrian ass aired abattoirs
As tonsils' orneriness assigned Ortega
To distillations antedating Sade.

Erelong GI's' ideas girdle Borstals
And toadies retrain Orientals as Borgia desserts:
Elated at iodine on starting gates,
Do sonnetising Britons lead orbed otters?

Ill borage's large attendants in bodegas,
Labiating gristlier translations,
Belie agreeable garnerings. No? 'Tain't so?
Go greet Titania in an insensate snit!

Granados labeled a gateleg table stable
As droll goaltenders tensed at tenebrist rites
And an elegant internee sensed godlier litanies
In gangrened slattern lotteries in Laredo.

A belligerent gent tainted a nationalist
And an ill-starred seer slogged near Odin's targe
As Rosetta retested gastral allegories,
Riled at a brainless trio's rosaries.

Aretino's gist is bearable
And Lister's treatises are greatening:
Siberian gentianella's deteriorating
And loneliness endangers libraries.

March 1980
New York

Giant Otters

They were a close family of giant otters
in Surinam giving a low growling sound when
they were insecure so they were called the Hummers.

Trace elements had landed near them and they effloresced
in even amounts throughout an even eon and an evening more
fortunate as they were in knowing nothing

or peering curiously into unknowable presence
alert to no future living the past as presence
whose elements were traces in their efflorescing being

going as far as they could within the world they were
as fortune particularized occasions within unfolding
breathed upon by memory's wraith and anticipation's all but absence.

Where were they going but farther along and through
whatever their being eventuated in clearness no demand for clarity
as the eyes are unsealed and the world flows in as light?

13–14 February 1982
New York

1 to 12 & 12 to 1 not 11:55 to 12:48

You
promise me
you'll do one.
Where are they now?
Thank you all very much.
Whatever it was they wanted it.
That's not really what they were like
but it's closer than I might have thought
had I not figured on their being even closer.
Which is what I wanted to say before it was
the thing to say and they were offering the same service.
She's alienated more people in certain areas because it doesn't ring true.
Let me give you one instance where anything you hit's in tune.
He speaks English but he pronounces his final *d*'s as *t*'s
because he speaks German so good and French even better.
I didn't quite catch that but that's everybody's fantasy.
Anything that makes me laugh gets my recommendation.
No matter what they wouldn't let him in.
She died of a drug overdose
and came to life in the
morgue but wasn't God's daughter.
What does that mean?
He's been dead
more'n twenty
years.

19 April 1983
New York

Various Meanings

The bottom of a green arras extends a vocabulary
whose rest is deep and boundless moving through space
and the stars. From time to time we lost the noise of an edge
where we were plagued by nocuous effects and then moved on
toward a dominant object. The gibbous moon
reminded him of a sad death before moving on toward planets
realized some twenty degrees high in the west. Wait
till the month of July. Slapped by a funeral
the reeds dead branches and watchful rodents
remained in the sky an entire evening as serious
snarls shrieked with amazement. Somewhat concrete proof
that you won't be disappointed at all. Above all
each ponderous birth advanced from the general area
of intercepted particles. What objection do you raise?
The choruses were willing and complete hours before
the imminent plan was announced. It failed to make
a correct approach. As large as it might have been
it was no more earnest than pleasurable childlike
instructions. Spilling out of their eyes they flew away.
They were never seen again. It is not possible. Be cheerful.
The current and coming crisis was informationally aggressive
toward the biology of entropy. Green water urged syllables.
It had abandoned its plan to end its decision
to build money and mercy. On the ground of honor
it was a region of wooded slopes in an endless pursuit
though some kind of lunatic thinks it's OK. Common sense
is quite consistent with the elements they adduce
which decreases their joy in clear sentences and handsome horses.
A glittering silver plan was beside the rowdy train
of history dilating pupils and recovering true goals
unnoticed in a cold blue brook. So I wrote down four
airs for fair and radiant maidens born to come again
and still hard to find. The same ones that wiped us out

disclosed sensible frustration examined or pursued.
Could you have been bewitched? They correlate with actions
forever. Could you gratify obedience? No different than
what you're wondering about in the form of lumps all of me
is comprised of gaping mud. One of the first things was an instrument
for sleep. What happens when glimmers feel they should
get together? Thinking spreads beyond foreknowledge of extension.
They had been involved in ponderous thought and native water
typical of complete sounds. Loops learn where to survive. They approach
admiration obliquely. Tenderness establishes a delegation
thinking every thought rising after a scanty breakfast. Ousted
he pushed good humor and was appallingly deserved. Slices
of heavy appetites went to grievous lengths. We're really in it.
Especially in consideration of things happening in the other heart
you are now ready. It is a good rainbow. Interdependence
in an unharvested sea is ancient and stale. It fits too well.
This example brings us softly together as we were in this case
after long being objects of scrutiny. We couldn't joke about that.
We rolled pies and sat down heavily when they blanched visibly
at civilized experience. But now time is described. Otherwise
they'd have learned to see before research was completed. Entities
of a mystical bent are recorded in the deepest decline. Osiers are lost
and this is safe. Subsequently sleep spread locally. Today
importance was invasive and grabbed the jagged edges
of basically ungentle adjustments. In mountainous regions
they acquire carbon copies of dead blanks and authentic wild
systems translated into habitual voices and quiet devices
supplied with perpetual revisions urban elements integrate. Major functions
are currently being completed. Dwarfing anything previously
imagined their immediate and practical effect is a clear
and present danger. At certain times of day they defend the vice with vigor.
An extremely large matrix of equipment is only the tip of the iceberg
in the workplace. Only four states require piles of envelopes.
Facades allow corporate tape recorders to open hearts
at moments when glass cases grow boyhoods. Starving
variants found solutions in the snow buried betrayed

and exercising caution under a vital burden vague
and unsatisfied. Mental mouths agreed. With some
green flowers we wait amid paint and insecurity. We tingle
when things are done three times. Politely expressing antipathy
blankets discern processes. That's no good. A tense armor was brilliant
in a duality wrong side up. Monkeys unlock cruel doors. That noise
must frankly be admitted. Where to start senses birth.
Hours brought memories of concrete answers in prouder moments
essential to kisses. I regard the prospect of being spied on
as an opportunity to teach. You can't beat us with wires. A clear
mental state is frozen hard as a mattress. It's time now. Love
shouts in my ears where darkness and daylight touch and never return.
Rigid memories are finer than fixed postures. Red cedars
escape overnight. Morons mass near a memorandum.
Thousands taste bread and few describe procedures.
Isolating encrypted messages are only conditional targets and vice
versa. From plump individuals really severe dreaming is guided
unknowingly to the pavement by any means possible. We have
to prevent silent days. Primitive fathers are experienced as reminders.
And any divergence is due to a temporary confusion. Notice the cold lake
dropped shouting into the middle of an arctic waste. How
might that aid us? Hold on. It doesn't matter. We're prepared
sweet dark and intelligent. In a background where meanings are assured
monotonous platitudes become denizens of windless connotations.
Let's not be so fascinated with all those remote us's. Their way
is offered a third time. Nearer the end the city was preferable.
The phonograph was less mathematical than their tourmaline kingdoms.
Their enormous sentences were separate from teeth. Mental nature
was less annoying than intelligible benefits sparkling with
judgement. What palpitations were present! White senses rumble
in inexpressible leisure. Don't tell me about it. Injury is heartfelt
and radiant with vexation. Conscious pillows are disinclined
and new noises arise on bored ships stretching toward less dangerous
  spheres.
You know where they are and see their sinister vinegar smiling dully.
Winter's privacy is less ravenous. Would you dare to look beyond

that smooth daylight? Waddling overhead she heard his childish laughter. Genius plundered willing sarcasm more whims overlooked when tedious outsiders felt too free to be reminded of translation. Variations of twangs forced medication. Cellular accidentals induced benediction. I'd never have believed it. In two or three months the manacles could not have been forgotten. Too much light.

22 April 1983
New York

Manifest

To manifest: to be, visibly.
To make visible what was formerly invisible or otherwise to make sensible
    what was formerly not.
To present or make present, vocally, visibly, or otherwise, one's views,
    sentiments, objections, etc., in reference to a matter of public concern.
Manifest: a commercial document listing constituents of cargo or names
    of passengers on a plane, ship, or other vehicle.
A manifest of meanings.
To make evident or certain by showing or displaying.
Readily perceived by the senses, especially by sight.
Easily understood or recognized.
Obvious.
To become obvious.
To be, obviously.
To be, recognizably.
To become recognizable.
To emerge as a figure from a ground.
To become visible, or otherwise perceptible, as an agent.
To act.
To make interior states perceptible to others.

Manifesto: a public declaration of principles, intentions, views, or feelings.

A document in which is said explicitly what otherwise might have remained implicit in political, artistic, or other practice.

To present or make present.

To present for inspection what might not otherwise have been able to be inspected.

To make the implicit explicit.

To make the interior exterior.

To make the hidden unhidden.

To say what might not otherwise have been said.

Choose one or more of the following:

Every text is a manifesto.

Every (adjective) text is a manifesto.

Every text worth reading is a manifesto.

18 June 1983
New York

Unmanifest

What the maker of a manifesto does not comprehend or acknowledge is the basic unmanifestness from which and within which each manifestation takes place. It is this neglect or ignorance that calls forth repugnance when a manifesto is proclaimed or published, especially one regarding art. As if what comes to being in and as the work of art could ever be totally manifest or even manifest at all without its abiding steadfastly in the unmanifest! A work of art is a manifesto only insofar as it is its own antimanifesto.

21 June 1983
New York

Trope Market

In the network, in the ruin,
flashing classics gravitate,
snared, encumbered voicelessly.

Teak enticements seek, leaping
fan-shaped arras corners
snore among in backward dispatch.

Panels glow, groan, territorialize
fetishistically in nacreous
instantaneity spookily shod.

4 July 1983
New York

Converging Stanzas

(Basic English)

1 motion boiling pocket far paste
   other country slope
   motion
   destruction experience will stop punishment every decision curve
   fat committee mine how
   with country
   bad stocking
   push beautiful will motion punishment finger heat

2 how motion beautiful pocket country
   decision other boiling
   motion
   will committee experience country far paste motion paste
   every will decision motion
   bad finger
   mine committee
   with pocket other push will far experience

3 committee motion will beautiful other
   committee with mine
   country
   decision far motion will beautiful far country experience
   motion beautiful pocket experience
   decision bad
   other paste
   bad decision pocket paste motion experience finger

4 mine motion other beautiful committee
   pocket bad pocket
   finger
   experience experience with experience will will country beautiful
   other will committee decision
   beautiful motion
   committee decision
   bad far pocket bad motion paste motion

5 experience pocket beautiful decision pocket
   beautiful pocket experience
   country
   motion experience pocket motion pocket far bad pocket
   beautiful decision motion will
   pocket with
   country country
   committee motion experience bad motion paste pocket

6 experience pocket pocket decision pocket
   bad pocket bad
   experience
   pocket bad decision motion pocket pocket bad country
   country pocket far experience
   pocket pocket
   experience will
   bad beautiful experience experience experience paste pocket

7 country pocket paste experience pocket
   bad experience bad
   pocket
   experience country pocket experience paste decision pocket pocket
   bad experience decision experience
   pocket far
   bad bad
   country bad pocket pocket pocket pocket paste

8 pocket pocket country experience decision
   bad pocket pocket
   pocket
   pocket country bad experience pocket pocket paste country
   bad experience pocket pocket
   decision bad
   paste pocket
   decision pocket pocket experience bad experience pocket

9 experience decision pocket bad bad
   country experience pocket
   country
   pocket pocket bad experience pocket decision pocket paste
   pocket country country pocket
   decision country
   pocket pocket
   experience experience bad pocket bad pocket pocket

10 country bad experience pocket pocket
    bad bad experience
    bad
    paste experience pocket paste bad paste country pocket
    decision pocket pocket decision
    pocket bad
    experience decision
    pocket country pocket paste pocket pocket pocket

11 country experience paste pocket pocket
    bad pocket decision
    country
    pocket country paste bad bad pocket bad experience
    bad country bad pocket
    pocket decision
    pocket pocket
    paste decision country decision experience decision pocket

12 experience country decision bad paste
    decision pocket country
    pocket
    pocket pocket experience pocket bad decision pocket bad
    decision pocket bad experience
    decision pocket
    bad pocket
    bad bad paste country pocket pocket bad

13 paste bad decision paste pocket
    bad experience bad
    bad
    pocket bad pocket pocket pocket country experience paste
    decision pocket pocket decision
    pocket bad
    experience pocket
    bad paste paste experience paste pocket bad

14 pocket paste bad pocket pocket
pocket decision decision
paste
bad decision bad decision paste paste experience paste
paste paste pocket bad
bad experience
paste experience
paste pocket pocket experience paste bad pocket

15 experience paste pocket paste bad
paste pocket paste
paste
experience bad decision bad experience pocket decision experience
experience pocket bad experience
bad experience
pocket experience
paste paste decision experience pocket decision experience

16 paste experience paste experience pocket
paste experience bad
pocket
experience decision experience decision decision experience pocket
   paste
pocket pocket bad decision
paste paste
experience pocket
bad paste pocket decision pocket paste bad

17 pocket pocket decision pocket experience
paste decision experience
decision
paste experience experience decision bad pocket experience paste
paste experience paste experience
paste experience
pocket paste
paste paste paste bad pocket experience experience

18 decision decision pocket pocket paste
    pocket bad paste
    experience
    experience decision pocket paste experience experience pocket
        experience
    pocket experience experience experience
    experience decision
    decision experience
    paste pocket experience experience pocket paste paste

19 decision experience experience experience pocket
    decision experience experience
    decision
    experience pocket experience paste paste experience experience
        pocket
    experience experience decision decision
    decision pocket
    pocket paste
    decision decision paste pocket experience paste pocket

20 paste decision experience decision decision
    experience experience experience
    pocket
    experience experience decision decision decision pocket experience
        decision
    paste experience decision experience
    experience experience
    pocket decision
    experience experience paste decision decision experience pocket

21 decision experience experience pocket experience
    experience experience experience
    paste
    experience decision paste pocket experience experience experience
        decision
    pocket paste experience paste

decision paste

decision experience

experience experience decision decision decision decision paste

22 paste decision experience decision decision

experience paste experience

decision

experience decision experience experience decision paste paste
  experience

experience experience decision decision

experience paste

experience paste

pocket experience experience experience experience decision decision

23 decision paste experience paste experience

experience paste experience

paste

experience paste experience pocket experience decision experience
  decision

experience experience paste decision

decision paste

experience experience

experience experience paste paste experience decision experience

24 paste paste paste experience experience

paste paste experience

experience

experience decision paste paste paste decision paste experience

experience paste experience paste

decision paste

decision experience

decision experience decision experience decision experience
  experience

25 experience experience experience decision decision
decision paste paste
paste
decision decision experience decision paste decision paste experience
decision paste paste decision
decision experience
experience paste
experience paste experience paste paste experience experience

26 experience experience paste paste paste
experience decision experience
paste
paste experience decision decision decision decision experience
    experience
paste experience decision decision
experience experience
experience decision
experience experience paste paste experience decision paste

27 decision experience experience experience paste
decision experience paste
paste
experience paste decision experience experience paste decision
    decision
decision experience experience paste
paste paste
experience experience
experience experience paste paste paste decision experience

28 experience experience experience experience paste
experience decision paste
decision
experience paste paste experience decision paste experience
    experience
experience experience decision decision

paste experience

paste experience

decision decision experience decision experience paste paste

29 experience paste decision paste paste

paste paste experience

paste

paste paste decision paste experience experience decision paste

experience experience experience decision

paste experience

experience experience

paste decision experience decision experience decision experience

30 decision decision experience experience experience

paste decision experience

paste

experience decision experience paste experience experience paste
 experience

paste experience experience decision

experience paste

experience paste

experience decision decision experience paste experience paste

31 experience paste decision decision paste

experience paste experience

experience

decision experience experience paste decision decision paste
 experience

paste experience paste paste

experience experience

decision decision

decision decision paste paste decision experience experience

32 decision paste decision decision experience

experience paste experience

decision

paste paste paste decision decision decision decision experience
decision experience paste experience
paste experience
paste experience
experience decision paste experience experience decision paste

33 experience experience experience decision decision
experience decision experience
paste
experience decision paste experience experience experience decision
   paste
decision paste experience experience
experience decision
paste experience
decision decision experience decision paste decision decision

34 experience experience decision decision experience
experience paste experience
decision
experience experience experience paste decision paste decision
   experience
experience decision paste experience
experience experience
decision paste
experience experience decision experience decision decision decision

35 experience paste experience decision paste
experience decision experience
experience
experience decision experience decision decision experience paste
   paste
paste decision decision paste
decision experience
decision paste
paste experience experience decision experience experience paste

36 decision paste paste decision paste
    experience decision paste
    experience
    experience paste experience experience experience paste experience
      experience
    decision paste experience decision
    experience experience
    paste experience
    experience experience experience paste experience experience paste

37 experience paste experience paste experience
    paste paste paste
    experience
    experience experience experience experience experience experience
      paste experience
    decision experience experience paste
    experience experience
    experience paste
    experience experience experience experience experience paste
      experience

38 experience experience experience experience experience
    experience paste experience
    paste
    paste paste paste experience experience paste experience experience
    experience paste experience experience
    experience experience
    experience paste
    paste experience experience paste paste experience experience

39 paste paste experience experience experience
    experience experience experience
    experience
    experience experience paste experience paste experience experience
      paste
    experience paste experience experience

experience experience

paste paste

experience paste paste paste experience experience experience

40 experience paste experience paste experience

experience experience paste

experience

experience paste paste experience paste experience experience
    experience

experience experience experience experience

experience paste

experience experience

experience experience experience experience experience experience
    experience

41 experience experience experience experience experience

paste paste experience

· experience

experience experience experience experience experience experience
    experience experience

experience experience experience experience

experience experience

paste experience

paste experience experience experience experience experience
    experience

42 experience experience experience experience experience

paste experience paste

experience

experience experience paste experience experience experience
    experience experience

experience experience experience experience

experience experience

experience paste

experience paste experience experience experience experience
    experience

43 experience experience experience experience experience
   paste experience experience
   experience
   experience experience experience experience experience experience
      experience experience
   experience experience experience paste
   paste experience
   paste experience
   experience experience experience experience experience experience
      experience

44 experience experience experience experience paste
   experience experience experience
   experience
   experience experience experience experience experience experience
      paste experience
   experience experience experience experience
   experience experience
   experience experience
   experience experience experience experience paste experience
      experience

45 experience experience experience experience experience
   experience experience experience
   experience
   experience experience experience experience paste experience
      experience experience
   experience experience experience experience
   experience experience
   experience experience
   paste experience experience paste experience experience experience

46 experience experience experience experience experience
   paste experience paste
   experience

experience experience experience experience experience experience
experience experience
experience paste experience experience
experience experience
experience experience
experience experience experience experience experience experience
experience

47 experience experience experience experience experience
experience experience experience
experience
experience experience paste experience experience experience
experience experience
experience experience experience experience
experience experience
experience experience
experience experience experience experience experience experience
experience

48 experience experience experience experience experience
experience experience experience
experience
experience experience experience experience experience experience
experience experience
experience experience experience experience
paste experience
paste experience
experience experience experience experience experience experience
experience

49 experience experience experience experience experience
experience experience experience
experience
experience experience experience paste experience experience
experience experience

experience experience experience experience
experience paste
experience experience
paste experience experience experience experience experience
   experience

50 experience experience experience experience experience
experience experience experience
experience
experience experience experience paste experience experience
   experience experience
paste experience experience experience
experience experience
experience paste
experience experience experience experience experience experience
   experience

51 experience experience experience experience paste
experience experience experience
experience
experience paste experience experience experience experience
   experience experience
experience experience experience experience
experience experience
experience experience
experience experience experience experience experience experience
   experience

52 experience experience experience experience experience
paste experience experience
experience
experience experience experience experience experience experience
   experience experience
experience experience experience experience
experience experience

experience experience
experience experience experience experience experience experience
experience

53 experience experience experience experience experience
experience experience experience
experience
experience experience experience experience experience experience
experience experience
experience experience experience experience
experience experience
paste experience
experience experience experience experience experience experience
experience

54 experience experience experience experience experience
experience experience experience
experience
experience experience experience paste experience experience
experience experience
experience experience experience experience
experience experience
experience experience
experience experience experience experience experience experience
experience

55 experience experience experience experience experience
experience experience experience
experience
experience experience paste experience experience experience
experience experience
experience experience experience experience
experience experience
experience experience
experience experience experience experience experience experience
experience

56 experience experience experience experience experience
    experience experience experience experience
    experience experience experience experience paste experience
        experience experience
    experience experience experience experience
    experience experience
    experience experience
    experience experience experience experience experience experience
        experience

57 experience experience experience paste experience
    experience experience experience
    experience
    experience experience experience experience experience experience
        experience experience
    paste experience experience experience
    experience experience
    experience experience
    experience experience experience experience experience experience
        experience

58 experience experience experience experience experience
    experience experience experience
    paste
    experience experience experience experience experience experience
        experience experience
    experience experience experience experience
    experience experience
    experience experience
    paste experience experience experience experience experience
        experience

59 experience experience experience experience experience
    experience experience experience
    experience

experience paste experience experience experience experience
   experience experience
experience experience experience experience
experience experience
experience experience
experience experience experience experience experience experience
   experience

60 experience experience experience experience experience
   experience experience experience
   experience
   experience experience experience experience experience experience
      experience experience
   experience experience experience experience
   experience experience
   experience experience
   experience experience experience experience experience experience
      experience

5 July 1981
New York

◆

Selections from *From Pearl Harbor Day to FDR's Birthday*

Introduction
by Anne Tardos

The poems in *From Pearl Harbor Day to FDR's Birthday* were written between 7 December 1981 and 30 January 1982. This was a pivotal period in Jackson's life, when he began alternating between deterministic methods of composition and free, improvisational writing, within spontaneously chosen verse forms, in which he gathered words and phrases from his inner and outer environment in a fluid succession of compositional acts. In other words, he wrote completely just what came to mind.

Ten Weeks

Monksday	Mudday	Mustday	Monthday	Mugsday
Jewsday	Duesday	Toothday	Tootsday	Dupesday
Weddinday	Westday	Websday	Wensday	Wetsday
Turdsday	Thirstday	Turpsday	Turksday	Termsday
Fryinday	Frightday	Fightday	Fireday	Vieday
Satireday	Satinday	Sapperday	Sackerday	Sasserday
Sudsday	Someday	Sunkday	Sungday	Sumpday

Mumsday	Mungday	Mushday	Muckday	Muffday
Doomsday	Chooseday	Tombsday	Dudesday	Tubesday
Whenceday	Vexday	Whensday	Wedgeday	Wavesday
Terseday	Sirsday	Turtlesday	Surdsday	Girlsday
Flightday	Vineday	Friarday	Thighday	Flyday
Saggerday	Saddleday	Sanderday	Satyrday	Sadderday
Sonsday	Subday	Sumsday	Suckday	Chumday

"The letters of the week are like the days in the words. . . . But he could never see that the days performed any useful function, taken separately. . . ."—from *a.k.a.* by Bob Perelman

1st week: September 1979
Others: January 1982
New York

Sermon Quail

A lost quality simmers. Aquaintance a quaint tense.
Inequality of aptitude. A silence whirrs.
A certainty races idly or towards.

A fortunate dormancy extends heated rushes.
Or look there at the teahouse realities knees.
No deeds there. Unstructured furniture. The furnace.

Certain to turn. Meanings commingle meanings straitly.
Frail straw porch dormers orphans vacate.
Spies. A knifeless turtles day outing. Shouts.

Nouns a pointed cloister interjects. A sacked date.
Offense leverage seasons yellow armatures.
Fleeted reasons a region stencils. A kind stable.

A table cannot conscious. Surface lightness earns a flare.
Scarcity of witness history. A rigged grouping throbs.
Calls. A quiet tubular. A risk insists. Flower walls.

Tall and unnoted thrones estimate. Flavors flake.
A kite's until. Intern and notice. Flow charts crumble.
A crumpled. Security disuse syndromes fuse. Equality.

12 January 1982
New York

A Lack of Balance but Not Fatal

A motion guided a lotion
in hiding from a tint
reckless from nowhere enforcement.

A label persisted. The past tense
implies it took place. The redness
in which the the implies there was some other
did not persist. He was not waiting long.

The sentence is not always a line
but the stanza is a paragraph.

The whiteness was not enforced.
It was not the other but another
circumstance brought in the waterfall
while a breath waited without being clear
or even happier. A seal was lost without it.

There was a typical edge. The paper tilted
or even curved. A rattle smoothed its way.
Where the predominance stopped was anyone's guess
but the parrot fought for it with forbearance
and a waiting cart was leashed to a trial
though a lie would have done as well
or even better when a moderate sleeve was cast.

No claim was made. A tired park gained.
A lack twisted the bread. Heads foamed.
Nowhere was little enough for the asking.
The task he cleared from the temperature
was outside the extended account. Each the
points to an absence. One or more hiding.

He asked where the inches were. The could have gone.

Intentions are mixed without quotations.
The song was snug. Ambiguity does not
hang in the air. The space between graphemes
is neither colorless nor tasteless. A stream
runs rapidly in no more history. The sweep
of a line. Kindness is not mistaken
for tinder and the lid is resting but shortness
guarantees no sentence authenticity.

Where the schoolyard was evident a closed
flutter showed a notion without resistant
fences or a paradox without feathers.
Swiftness outlasts the pencil. A cormorant

rose against a born backdrop. Letters inch.
An iconoclast was hesitant. A fire lit.
In the tank a lozenge disengages. Swarms
roared. A special particle felt its form.
Lagging features left oak divination without
a tone or a creased sentinel. Leavings swept.

Toward evening the watchful clock was situated.
No diver called for ether. Lynxes thrived.
Hit by something a silence willed. Streets
were not concerned. A past participle's
sometimes mistaken for a past. An orange
roster was on everybody's mind though clues
could be found. When the ink is incomplete
every table rests on its opposite. A closed
restraint impinged. Furniture rested. Several
pinks in a fist. A clearly charismatic
hideout was read. Neatness wavered. The flag
was wet without exertion or favor. That judge postponed.

Snowfall abused ermines. A folding chair.
Close to the bank a trap was silted though the finder
relaxed without particulars or the least inclination.
Whoever loosed the torrent concluded the tryst.
Finally is the way to find the place. Earshot
is likely. Tones harvest commonplace weather.
The pastness of the past was included in a doctrine
or stakes were wrought. Or sought. Find divers.
Fists rested on the divined peculiarity. Artemis hushed.

Twigs were not grapes. He grasped the talc ring.
Smoothing the horses the clutter died. Finches
sewed roses on the mustered aggregate. Loaves flew.
A mentality ran farther and its crests simmered.
Closeted without bargains the lean rump beheld
no future. A certain flight beckoned. The wonder.

Closed classrooms risk warmth though causation
matters less. Never ink a connection when a plea
is off. Softer dollars were a range without flutters
though a concessive subordinator turns a sentence
into a scene. Dreams were not what he wanted.

16 January 1982
New York

Central America

Sing Goddess the centrality of America
of the nation called Usonia
by the architect Frank Lloyd Wright
The problem isn't "Central America"
It is people having very much money and power
and other people having very little
and what the rich and powerful do
to keep powerful and rich and get more so
and what the other people
not powerful or rich
cannot or do not do
not knowing all riches and power stem from them

Manhattan Shirts went south
from Usonia to El Salvador
leaving here in the North
plenty of shirtmakers jobless
Texas Instruments went to El Salvador also
So much of that company went there
it should be called   .
El Salvador Instruments

And the part of Kimberly-Clark
that sells the disposable diapers they call Huggies
has Salvadorans make them now
and ship them to Usonia
and elsewhere for disposal
Few are sold and disposed of in El Salvador
where nearly all diapers are cloth
washed and rewashed and re-rewashed
before being washed again to be used as rags
and probably many babies wear no diapers

No wonder in El Salvador
where "death squads" run amok
and the bridges get blown up
the government of Usonia
all but functions as the state
despite its uppity puppets who think *they* do

No wonder it is so worried
by anything like The Other
or anything vaguely Otherish
Cuba or Grenāda
Chile or Nicaragua
horrid Otherish weeds in that nice clean yard

Don't talk about defending "human rights"
Stroessner has lasted in Paraguay thirty years
torturing and murdering
with never a Usonian landing
But how long did Allende last
as Otherish as Norman Thomas
but threatening nevertheless
to Usonian power and money
They didn't even bother with the Cuban ploy
cutting off trade and aid
to force an Otherish government

to turn to The Other for help
to give them a pretense to weed that government out
out of that tidy backyard

Now they are trying to do just that
to that horrible Otherish junta in Managua
trying to bring it down
by supporting bands of "patriots" called "contras"
many of whom were soldiers and policemen
who used to kill and torture for Somoza
but now destroy and kill "to bring back freedom"

And still to the liars and thieves
the torturers and murderers
who think they rule El Salvador
they are giving our money away
to fight the Otherish rebels
who might not be so nice to runaway shops

Banality after banality
about the most bānal banality
postponing the inevitable question
What can the people do
who *don't* have much money or power
to stop the liars and thieves
the torturers and murderers
the profiters and exploiters
the powerful and rich
and those who keep them that way
from profiting and exploiting
from lying and from stealing
from torturing and murdering
from doing whatever they want in the big backyard

There is *nó óne ánswer*
and *nó póem* purporting to give one does
What your hand finds to do
do

1–31 January 1984
New York

♦

Dialogos for John

{I}

To each legible
music you
listen globally.

{II}

Is perhaps
the thing
or yes?

{III}

Do airlines
give a proven I
the town's
next
pleasant
preliminary ill?

{IV}

Watch—
is transforming
or wondering
already travel—
was I another?

{V}

See landscape's
Zen inclusion dawning,
the hospital Marxist
said ironically—
materialistically.

{VI}

Not song
when like
machine.

{VII}

Identical watches today:
you're young
and the womb
is an airplane.

{VIII}

Successful child's
dance there:
day now.

{IX}
Graphic.

{X}

A piano,
thinking,
singing,

made having
clear coloration
boring.

{XI}

Suddenly love,
time,
constant centers
provided.

{XII}

Major
refreshments.

{XIII}

Really
it.

{XIV}

Expanded much,
spring
hasn't missed
as design:
staying, we
finally seek
education.

{XV}

Music:
remain!

{XVI}

Gone—
through the window!

{XVII}

Texts:
reach headlights
so that a view begins
and something then
means things
that one asserts.

{XVIII}

Colors
have heard appeals
that misled.

{XIX}

I
should be
we.

{XX}

Exemplify underdevelopment,
including mushroom stories
establishing government
transcends all limits:
books dismemberment
of two against it,

Fuller and me,
each a chord to himself,
a cricket creaking along.

February 1988
New York

SOURCES: *Silence* (1961), *A Year from Monday* (1967), and *M* (1973), all by John Cage and published by Wesleyan University Press, Middletown, Connecticut.

Selections from *Pieces o' Six*

Introduction

Adapted by Anne Tardos from the Preface to *Pieces o' Six*

In October 1983 I wrote a poem in prose in longhand on the first six pages
of a 200-page lined-paper school composition book. Having written one
poem in prose of this length, I wrote another, and then another... Some-
time while writing these earliest ones I decided to call them "Pieces o' Six"
and to fill that notebook with six-page prose pieces—thirty-three in all—
leaving two blank pages at the end, presumably for a postface or preface
such as this. They could be written "directly" (i.e., without using system-
atic chance or any other systematic method)—as were both the earliest
ones and most of the others—or by any method(s), including systematic
chance or other systems, determined when beginning each one in turn. The
only "rules" were that they had to be prose and to occupy six notebook pages
in longhand. How many pages they would occupy when typed or printed
was immaterial. Variations in my handwriting caused variations in the
number of typed, and later printed, pages. As the writing of the series pro-
ceeded (or as it did sometimes, lagged or even stopped for a while), I found
myself writing several kinds of pieces: many paratactic, though often quasi-
narrative; some seemingly out-and-out stories; others much like essays,
but deceptively so; a few of them collages drawing from various sources by
chance-selection and other chance-operational systems or (at least in one
notable case) by impulse chance and "dipping."

As friends and other readers have remarked, they are very "different,"
both from much of my other work and from each other. At first I did rela-
tively little revision, and most of that in the notebook, although I proba-

bly did some revision while typing the earlier pieces, which I did on electric typewriters—first on an SCM Coronamatic 2200, later on an IBM Selectric and a Juki Sierra. However, somewhere around the middle of the series, I began typing the pieces on a portable electronic typewriter, a Canon Typestar 6, and thereupon more and more revision took place between the longhand notebook and the typed pages. I clarified my length rule. It referred only to first drafts. Revision might increase the length of the typed pieces. It did. So the first-draft-length rule was expanded: either six longhand pages in the notebook or six computer pages.

All along, a third "rule" which may surprise some readers had been emerging gradually (though it had been continually operative) during the writing: *they are all poems.* Even the pieces that are storylike or essaylike are poems. This is, in fact, their most significant characteristic. They are all *poems in prose*—*whatever* else they may be and however they were written: "directly," as most of them were, or as were a handful of them in some sense or other, "systematically." And what makes them poems is not only the *intention* that they be poems—though this has been critical in making them what they are—or even the ways their words and sentences have been arranged and arrayed, although these are essential to their being what they are, but something much more intangible that has come into being through this intention and these ways, something I don't want to give an essentialist (and barbaric) name such as "poemness" but which I am at a loss otherwise to designate. Intending to make poems in prose and giving each detail a specific degree of attention and following the same set of "rules"—the same "constitution"—throughout (though like all good constitutions, this one has had to be reinterpreted at times) has produced this book of thirty-three poems in prose.

Pieces o' Six—IX

For Anne Tardos and in memoriam *Buzz-Buzz*

Diana injected the white-and-black cat with a tranquilizer. Anne massaged the frail leg where the needle'd gone in. She wanted to soothe it. A game was going on wherein each player had a cat and either dropped it or hit it on the head. Anne wasn't playing the game. It seemed rather cruel, and the white-and-black cat resented it. So Diana injected the tranquilizer and Anne massaged it. She couldn't stop the game, so she did the best she could. That was all there was to that. There was no replay. It wasn't the kind of thing most people'd want to see again. One couldn't get back to it anyway. Just as well. There was no way of knowing if the white-and-black cat had been dropped or hit on the head. Just as well. It wasn't the kind of thing most people'd want to know anyway. There wasn't any way even to begin to find out. That was just as well, for hardly anyone'd want to. It had certainly been cruel, and the white-and-black cat had been right to resent it. Diana hadn't ought to've injected it. It didn't need a tranquilizer. It needed to get out of the game. That's what the other cats ought to've done too. They didn't need tranquilizers either. They ought to've gotten out of the game. They must've resented it too. If they didn't act up enough to be injected with a tranquilizer, it must've been because they were afraid. Could it have been that they were afraid of being injected? Of course it could. It might have happened before. Any of them might have been injected. Only a very stupid cat or a highly insensitive one would not have resented it. What cat likes being dropped or hit on the head? Some cats like being hit on the head very lightly—that's called "patting." But that's different. That's not like being hit on the head any old way as part of a game. What kind of a cat wouldn't feel—if not show—resentment at such treatment? And what kind of people would do such things to cats? Cruel ones, obviously. Or if not cruel ones, stupid or insensitive ones. Onlookers must have been helpless to stop the game. They couldn't do more than try to soothe the frightened cats. They couldn't learn the tranquilizer's name. For all anyone knows, it might have had side effects. It might have killed some brain cells! That's no small matter for cats. They don't have many to begin with. More than some other animals. Crabs, perhaps, or snails. But not enough to be able to lose a few lightly. Just hitting them on the head might have done damage. Who knows what a hit on the head could do to a cat? Just think of the delicate nerves inside those frail little crania! Even just dropping a cat might not be harmless. Instinctively most cats break falls with their legs. They land on their feet and seem little the worse. But if dropped too hard, or especially if *thrown* down, a cat can be damaged and yet seem little the worse. And a cat with a damaged brain from being injected or hit on the head may well have lost the reflexes that help it to land on its feet and break its fall. The ones that didn't resent the game or show that they did might have been damaged already. They might have already lost too many brain cells. A few key neurons might have been put out of commission. Even if other parts of the brain can take over functions of damaged parts and other neurons substitute for ruined ones, who could say a cat in such a condition was good as new? The white-and-black cat was no fool. Diana was a fool for doing what she did, and all of the players were fools and certainly cruel. The onlookers ought to've stopped the game. But that might not have been easy. Anyone playing a game like that might not be safe to interfere with. Some of them might have done *worse* to the cats or even harmed those who protested. They might have been hard to stop. But some might have listened to reason. They might have been persuaded in time to stop. Then they might have brought the others over. It would have required a skillful rhetorician—probably one who could deal with inebriated people. The players of that game must have been drugged or drunk. Most people wouldn't have played it even if they were. Many a well-meaning onlooker might have bungled it. Depending on the players' condition, they might have done worse—far worse. That white-and-black cat might not have come out of it alive! Maybe it was just as well that Anne just did her best to soothe it. It might have lost a few brain cells from the injection. But her not doing *too* much might have prevented worse. Think of what the atmosphere must have been like! A bunch of woozy hopped-up people playing a game. Little they cared that the pawns were sentient beings like themselves. Some might have played a similar game with people. Plenty of cases like that are known. Many have had worse outcomes. Some have led to murder. Cats can't talk. At least, they can't talk in court. (If a cat could talk, to paraphrase Wittgenstein, we wouldn't understand it.) When the players lose interest in the game, the cats can slink under furniture. They may sit there trembling awhile and not come out when they're called, but if they aren't injured—beyond, that is, losing those brain cells or neurons—sooner or later they'll foray for food and water. They'll leave their hiding places and return to their dishes and bowls. They'll even beg from some of the people who'd played the stupid game with them. But a *person* might go to the police. Damages might be sought or criminal charges preferred. Red and flustered, they'd stammer their tale to a desk sergeant or patrolman. A detective might call on the host and ask painful or embarrassing questions. The people who'd played with people that way would be rounded up. They'd be asked what drugs they'd taken and where they'd gotten them. Their house would be searched, their stashes seized. Even if they didn't land in jail, their assets would be squandered on lawyers. The temptation to quiet murder—especially if bribery didn't work—might prove irresistible. Even the cat game might have had repercussions. An onlooker might have tattled. A participant might have mentioned it in passing. It could have reached the ear of the ASPCA. A younger legal eagle there might have tested fledgling wings by filing a suit or pressing charges. How well it would have gone over in the public relations department! The fund raisers would have loved it. Photos—posed, of course, but admittedly so—could have helped to fill a four-page money-begging letter. A sympathetic judge could've thrown the book at the players. The white-and-black cat, dainty and petite, might have been subpoena'd. Its owners might have pleaded they were absent from the scene or helpless against the drug- or drink-sodden players. It's they that might've brought suit if they'd've returned too early, and found the game in progress. Angry and betrayed, it's they that might've stopped the game, clearing out their wobbling erstwhile friends, cleaning the stinking ashtrays, flushing forgotten stashes down the toilet, throwing out paper cups or washing evil-smelling glasses, hunting out the cringing little creature, tempting it with dainties, soothing it with petting, letting it jump at will on chairs and laps to perch and purr. But they might not've gone to the ASPCA after all. They'd have to be unreasonably angry to bring that much trouble on themselves. Enough to have to clean up the shit of the cats their so-called friends had brought (and hopefully taken away) and to cure their own cat's trauma. If the little white-and-black cat wasn't "really" injured, no one would gain from bringing suit, having to go to court, and maybe paying lawyers if the ASPCA was broke at the time or found the case too trivial to take. But still what a mess! Coming home to find your place full of smoke and noisy people—some not even known to you, presumably friends of friends—and the cats!—hissing and screeching or suspiciously laid back from being injected! Your friends who'd not played the game rushing up to you shamefaced, the players brazening it out with slurred words of self-justification—or whatever their judgment's impairment allowed them to offer as such—hearing yourself shouting "Get out! Get out!" as your anger took over, your slamming the door after the last of them left. Your running to find the hiding frightened cat, your stretching yourself on the floor to look under sofas and low-slung chairs and chests of drawers, your coaxing her out with soothing words and food (she might not have been trembling if the tranquilizer held awhile, but she'd still have been hiding). Probably friends who'd not been playing the same woud've stayed and helped you clean. It's they that would've explained the silly game. "Dope and drink!" you'd mutter, and flush the toilet once again. The cat by now would be purring or nodding out. Your throat would be sore from yelling and breathing smoke. The place would be freezing, what with all those wide-open windows. You'd slam them shut, still smelling the acrid tobacco fumes. You wouldn't be able to get to sleep till morning. You wouldn't talk to some of those people ever again. You'd wonder why you'd ever stayed in the city. You'd pamper the cat for days with foods you'd never buy for yourself.

2 November 1983
New York

Pieces o' Six—X

He plunked down an asper for a quiet date. The Turkish woman motioned toward a curtain. He hadn't met her in the street. A friend had given him the address in Athens just before he left for the airport. He knew nothing of Ankara. He had taken a cab at the airport, giving the driver the address of the hotel at which a travel agent had reserved him a room, but while moving through a bazaarlike street, had suddenly changed his mind, tapped the driver on the shoulder, and silently handed him the slip on which his friend had scrawled this address. "No to hotel?" asked the driver. "That's right," he agreed, nodding his head where the driver could see him in his rearview mirror. The driver slowed to read the slip again, then hung a sharp right a block or so farther on. He muttered the name of the street, glanced up to the mirror to meet the man's eyes, and then gathered speed through the twilit street. When they reached the place, the driver's try at an over-charge was all but pro forma. He accepted philosophically, even with re-spect, a compromise between the overcharge and the amount his friend had suggested as proper. "OK, boss," he said, "That's the place. Up them steps. Look out for broken glass." As the cab sped off, the traveler stood looking up toward the paint-chipped door at the top of the steps. Then he started to climb them, avoiding, not the broken glass, which was too ubiquitous to sidestep, but the flattened carcass of an animal, too far gone to be identi-fied as rat or half-grown cat. Peering for a bell—the far-off streetlight did little to help—he fished a pocket flashlight from his jacket and in its light finally descried an ambiguous handle far down on the left-hand lintel post. He gave it an experimental tug and was, he realized, nearly disappointed to be rewarded by a high-pitched tinkle. After an unresponsive minute, he was reaching toward the handle again when the door was opened abruptly. He was relieved to be greeted by a quietly dressed, aquilinely beautiful woman, whose long dark hair fell freely over her silk-covered shoulders. He murmured his apologies for not having phoned from the airport and mentioned his Greek friend's name. She smiled in recognition and invited him in in nearly unaccented English. Welcomely, the entrance hall con-trasted with the steps outside. It was clean, well-lighted, and furnished with a nearly fussy elegance attesting to someone's thoughtful choice. He wondered whether it was that of his handsome greeter, who, he'd decided, was probably part Armenian. She paused at the foot of a staircase—he saw another farther back—and turning toward him with a smile, spoke again in a low, pleasant voice: "Please. Up here. It's a bit steep. Better hold the banister." He did as she suggested, reaching, at the top, a hallway almost identical to the one below. She took a small tray from the top of an ornate sideboard. "Please," she asked, "a very small coin. The smaller the better." Wondering, he plunked down an asper for a quiet date. The Turkish woman motioned toward a curtain. Since he'd not met her in the street, but had gotten her address from his friend in Athens, and since he knew nothing of how things were done in Ankara, he followed her cautiously into the adjoining room. She closed a door on the inward side of the curtain. The room was dark. Uneasily, he waited by the door while he heard her moving about in the chamber. Then she struck a match and lit two candles on a table next to a low, sumptuous bed, wide and covered only by an ivory damask sheet. While he'd waited in the dark, she'd replaced her clothes with a gauzy robe, gathered at the waist by a thin gold cord. He stared, embarrassed at a surge of complicated feelings—wonder, lust, fear, puzzlement, and a somewhat surprising tenderness. He pondered what it was about the woman that aroused the last emotion. He'd never seen her before. He was sure of that. And though he'd met some women having vaguely similar features, none of them had he known intimately and none had possessed such startling beauty. She looked at him smiling and asked, "Do you like what you see?" "Oh yes," he quickly replied, "Oh yes. You can be sure of that! I don't think I've ever—" "You needn't flatter," she interrupted gently. "I'm *not* flattering! I'm overwhelmed! You're incredibly beautiful! I don't think I've ever—" "Maybe not," she said, "but that's *your* business, not mine. Mine is merely to please you and send you on your way." "Send me on my way," he dully repeated, and felt a piercing sorrow, sudden and astounding. She moved toward him with a smile. "No need to look so sad," she said. "It happens every day. People meet, and then go on their way." "I know," he replied. "I just wish I'd met you in other circumstances . . . elsewhere. . . . " "Where?" she asked. "You *wouldn't* have. I live in Ankara and you live . . . in Athens? New York?—" "I live in Kansas City—" "I know where *that* is—" "And seldom get away from there. —You know where Kansas City is?" "Sure. I have an uncle in St. Louis. He sometimes has to go to Kansas City. Something about meat. . . ." "He's a butcher?" "No, he runs a kind of restaurant." "*What* kind?" "Well, they do other things there, too. I don't think they're all legal. —Nothing political," she nervously added. "I wouldn't care if it was," he smiled. "What's your name?" By this time they were sitting side by side on the bed, and he was considerably calmer. "Anahid," she answered. "It was my grandmother's name—my mother's mother. She was Armenian." "Oh, I *thought* you were." "Only my mother's mother. My father's Turkish and my mother's father was Greek." She raised her left hand to his face and slowly stroked his cheek. "Don't be sad," she whispered, "and don't be afraid or bashful. I'm here to please you." "But—a woman like you—I mean—so beautiful and kind—And you asked for a very small coin—you accepted—an asper!" "Don't you understand?" she asked. "Some things are done only for form. You're my friend's friend. He's a wonderful person, our friend! And he's helped me in ways I couldn't begin to explain! But I'd have a bad conscience if I didn't ask for *some*thing. It's been my trade since I was fifteen. I don't even *need* the money now. I'm rich!" She noticed his questioning look. "Oh, the neighborhood!" she laughed. "I'm used to it here. I prefer it. I've lived here all my life. I'd feel out of place anywhere else! No one bothers me here. Even the police look after me! I have, as they say, 'friends in high places'—and, thank goodness! even *they* don't bother me. It's a little complicated! Don't worry about it. Make love with me. I like the way you look. I feel I can trust you, and—I know this'll sound silly coming from a woman like me—" "*Don't* say that!—" he cried. "I'm drawn to you, somehow. I don't usually feel this way about a man, even if I like him. And I've been in love—but that's never happened to me suddenly. The few times it's happened—and they're *very* few!—it's been during a long friendship. One of my 'friends in high places' . . . " "Please," he said, and kissed her. Soon she was helping him undress, giving little licks and kisses and nibbles to each part of him as it became exposed. As she removed his jacket, tie, and shirt, she nibbled his left ear, kissed his right collarbone, and licked each of his nipples till he moaned. Then, kneeling beside the bed, she untied and removed his shoes, took off his socks, and surprised him by slowly and carefully kissing and licking the tops of his feet and his soles and sucking his toes. No one had ever done this to him before, and the intensity of his sensations amazed him. His penis, already erect, began to push painfully against the inside of his briefs. He unbuckled his belt. She quickly unzipped his pants and eased them and his briefs over his hips, legs, and feet. Then, still kneeling, she took his penis in her hands and licked it over and over from tip to scrotum and back till he felt he could no longer keep from coming. Suddenly she stopped, looked up at his face with a friendly, teasing smile, lowered her head again, and swallowed his penis. Her lips pressed to his pubic hair, her long tongue licked the upper parts of his testicles. She hummed deep in her throat, then slowly drew her lips and tongue up to the tip and down again, gradually increasing her tempo. He lay back, as her hands now urged him to, and let himself passively feel the incredible pleasure. Sensing precisely when he was starting to come, she grasped and twisted both his nipples as he did. He screamed ecstatically, and momently fainted. When he came to, she was lying on him, kissing his lips and subtly massaging his scalp. When he opened his eyes, she smiled broadly and slowly rotated her hips. He realized he was erect again and deep inside her. "Do you like this?" she asked. "Oh yes," he whispered, and began to move his own hips. He felt her clitoris pressing the front of his penis as they moved. He fingered her anus lightly and squeezed her soft buttocks, massaging them in circles, and pressed her against him as they wildly ground and pumped. Their lips and tongues danced a continual kiss. If they didn't come together, neither knew who did first. They slept in each other's arms till birdcalls woke them. The candles had long guttered out. Gray dawnlight lit the room. First she, then he, padded to the nearby toilet and back. The room had grown cool as they slept. She took a soft quilt from a chest and covered their bodies. They slept awhile, then made love again, side by side like nested spoons. While they fucked, she suddenly drew him from her vulva and into her anus, guiding his hand to touch her clitoris, rotating her hips with joyful cries and moans. After they came that time, he knew that he had to stay with her forever. He made a score of international phone calls. He never *did* return to Kansas City.

3–4 November 1983
New York

Pieces o' Six—XIV

"Writing is a minute form of dancing." —*I. A. Richards*

The hand begins to move across the page, leaving an irregularly interrupted trail of spiky or convoluted figures, each composed of interwoven thin connected lines. It relates with thought and speech, but could be seen without such relations. One from a completely nonliterate culture—in which even the possibility of writing is unknown—would only see a series of arabesquelike patterns separated by small spaces. What might such a person, watching a writer write, think the writer was doing? Would the watcher sense any connection with speech or thought? Would that observer assimilate the action with drawing or decoration? Feel, without admonishment, a need to observe silence? But how can one "observe" silence? One cannot see it, nor, by definition, can one hear it, much less feel it, smell it, or taste it. The only way to *observe* silence is to *be* it. Silence is one of a class of things that may only be observed by the observer's *being* them. Those who think they are *hearing* silence are only hearing a lesser amount of sound than they are used to hearing. Such "heard" silence is merely a marked reduction of sound around the observer. When one *is* silent, the ambient level is irrelevant—one observes silence by observing herself being silent; another observes silence by observing himself being silent. Whoever observe silence observe themselves being silent. This is not really true. The nonliterate watcher, fascinatedly following the writer's flourishes without in the slightest comprehending either their purpose or their purport, may well *observe* silence without observing her- or himself *being* silent. Oblivious of self, the mesmerized watcher bends as close as possible to the writing hand, the pen, the paper, the characters forming as they flow from the pen. How can the writer convey to the observer of silence and writing who's never seen writing before what writing is and means? How can the observer be led to link the written text with speech? By the writer's pointing to a word and saying it? What if the observer's language has no visible equivalent—not even one devised by the American Bible Society—and the observer can no more understand the writer's spoken words than comprehend the written ones, since neither in any way knows the other's language? What can the writer do to explain what's being done when the hand moves and the ink flows and the little chains of filigree fill the page? Since neither knows the other's tongue, neither writer nor observer can help the latter link letters to speech, much less to thought. A fine state of affairs!—especially when the writer's concern may be to keep the nonliterate culture letterless! A far cry from the American Bible Society's alphabets for lesser breeds to give the latter God's words on paper! The writer, at once anthropologist and author, may follow an idealistic program of cultural noninterference, while knowing realistically the program's futility. Every slightest contact may begin or hasten the change. Literacy looms ever larger on a far horizon. The nonliterate culture, with or without the American Bible Society's help, is on its way to literacy, and sure, one way or another, sooner or later, to get there. Literacy's contagious—but only, it seems, up to a certain level. Above that level the infective power seems sharply to fall off in strength. In most literate cultures most members are minimally literate, though many may seem more literate than they are. In a nonliterate culture, as long as it stays nonliterate, none is less literate than another. But contact with even a minimally literate person makes a change take place toward literacy. Each begins to become more or less literate than each other. It's only a matter of time before the American Bible Society or a linguist from the West gives God's words or the language's phonemes or both a full-fledged alphabet. The cat is out of the bag. Nonliteracy's gone forever. Some may become *il*literate by not acquiring literacy at all when literacy strikes, many minimally literate, and comparatively few "truly" literate (whatever *that* means!). The writer's nonliterate watcher is well on the way to illiteracy. Nothing can be done. In a moment the culture's nature's changed forever. Goodbye, nonliterate bliss! (if that's what it was)—hello, all the hassles bred of letters. The writer's observed. The culture begins to crumble. But how does being observed affect the writing? More than observing the writer writing affects the observer's culture?—Or less? Who can devise a common yardstick for measuring effects on culture in general and on particular writing? Not I. I sit here writing in a 200-page blue-lined "composition" notebook with red left-margin lines and stiff black-and-white marbleized covers. Just above the middle of the front cover the marbleization's broken by a shape like that of a television screen's frame: a quarter-inch-wide white frame is delineated inwardly by curved black lines. Just below the upper line a rectangle (one half-inch by thirteen sixteenths of an inch), outlined by black lines about as thick as the curved ones, frames the phrase "SQUARE DEAL," in solid serifed capital letters, one word centered above the other. Below the rectangle the word "COMPOSITION" is printed across most of the "screen" in much larger centered serifed capitals. Below "COMPOSITION" are two parallel horizontal lines as thick as the curved frame lines and a half-inch apart. On the upper line I've written "Jackson Mac Low." On the lower, "21 October 1983," the date on which I wrote the first of the "Pieces o' Six." Below that and near (but above) the bottom curved line is printed in small sans-serif letters (each word initially capitalized) "The Mead Corporation, Dayton Ohio 45463." I'm writing this—as I think I've written all or almost all of what appears on the preceding 82 ½ pages,—with a Rotring, size 0,3, technical pen (a German version of a fine-point Rapidograph). It was bought for me by Rosanna Chiessi, a publisher and art collector, in a corner stationery store in Cavriago (near Reggio nell'Emilia), Italy, so that I could complete a series of lettered collage-drawings that she planned to publish as four-color serigraphs. They were to constitute an homage to Bernini and to include words, phrases, and sentences pertinent to him and his works and images of the latter, predominantly sculptures and buildings. I began the project that summer of 1980, completing two "layouts" for serigraphs. The words were hand-lettered with this and another pen point, somewhat thicker, that she bought at the same time, and the images were collaged xerographs of Bernini's works. However, the project has never been completed, since I've never been able to return to Cavriago to work on it or to find time to do so in New York. The pen points and barrel remain, and I've often used them to write poems and prose, as now in this composition notebook. Sometimes I write very small with them, as I do now. At other times, as when I wrote what's on the first dozen pages of this notebook—the first two "Pieces o' Six"—I write relatively large. "Pieces o' Six—XIV" began fairly small, but the writing's gradually gotten a bit larger as I've gone along—neither very cramped nor very spacious. If a nonliterate observer were watching me write this now, I'd probably find it hard to keep on writing. I'd become— ironic epithet—"self-conscious." All my words and ideas would dry up, and I'd probably burst out laughing at the solemn, steady, close-range nonliterate gaze at my moving hand and pen and their residue. I'd laugh, and maybe I'd get beat up. Who knows? But certainly that understandable, all but ludicrous, curiosity of the nonliterate about what's going on when writing's going on would not be titillated further that day, much less satisfied. Maybe I *wouldn't* laugh at the nonliterate looking so earnestly at my ordinary occupation. Maybe I'd *try* to show the nonliterate one what and how the letters and words and sentences mean. I'd consciously begin the cultural infection. I'd try to explain how looping lines can mean what spoken words can. I'd fan the glimmer (or rather, the glow) that'd lead to the flash after which the former nonliterate would participate ever after in the eternal idea of writing. That oral culture was a goner anyway! But so, perhaps, is the literate one. Is the shape of its successor on the cover of my notebook?

24 May–27 June 1984
New York

Pieces o' Six—XXI

Once the kenurdlers had settled on a schema, the new pipes were brightened. The quiet pitches were liberated. When the fleets flamed, the deals were offensive, though the foolers increased their pretense. Nodules were soaked. Labile oaks listed as they listed, and boats tinkled as whistlers particularized threats, but tony coal heavers heavily bested durational scissors when nets were portioned among panic thieves. Live pachyderms were picked for street engulfments. The daily cascades were defaced by facile derangements, though any cousin might have known the difference. Rigid diligence seemed to be in order that day, for discipline Castilian as hills was praised, and whoever alerted the picnickers was nowhere to be seen when the lines were down. Ices were consummated soon. The Druse monotones filtered through a cuckold's initial cacklings. Pheasants were dropped and drastic features annealed. Nobody's sleeves were tinted. Sluices gave way to crevices wherever an annular violence was detected, and orphaned wigglers lifted wizened visages just as the clocks of the tin situation were primed to be filled. That was the time of the zoological. A laughing dik-dik was not to be reasoned away. The rates of exchange were rattled by the tunes zinc took. Tall galleries were invested with flint, and galactic nuggets zigzagged among sweetened trees at whose feet crisp clashes were encountered. Kneeling Saracens were no match for publicity hounds. Beyond the sacramental bounds tangential files were flicked by harnesses held by the last of the leverage-seeking talkers on whose active bruised facades no tank would dare to fling its artifacts. Who could be blamed or challenged in that sawdust-laden grove? No one was wary or cozily dozed. Natural tubes provided excuses for umbrage. Nests of pacific lips were tactfully smacked in fascinating sunshine. No one knew who was there; no one replied. The tentative lies careened around the fortress and left the concupiscent heirs with no ingratiating attitudes. The honor of a class was nobody's answer. Suasion was uncalled-for. Titles, though perfumed and architectural, seasoned in vain the paltry preserves of the occupant sodality. Sermons the streams and stones decried wrenched the bottoming frigate. Some pillaged the lists. A few exalted assassins rode the wakening whirlpool, where loops of dazzling grass reached for visionary panaceas. Fiddles combined with clucks when lusters crammed in closets incautiously unclosed poured like stupid venom on the marred parquet. Truants were whistled away. Losers looking like Trinitarian manglers footed a clover-laden balustrade and switched their betrayal from angered crowns to illogical fortune-hunting thoroughbreds whose ambergrised vestments were mounted, in the event, in largely ineffectual museums. Diseases and passing arousals dotted the calcined, reeking coasts. Soteriological clumsiness reacted away from inhabitants toddling in fury, and glassified permanent hips where none had been before. Each accessible needler reeled and called. Widening circuits clipped an iridescent angler. One of the funnier, decently gullible fliers rapidly packed a mortuary box where vapid fans increased their attentive wrestlings. Vinegar floated a factory. Knives were interleaved among affluent carcasses, and a nankeen dog was later found in a fixture, but a patrilineal diver never found the spunky follower though nannies surrounded the latter's insensible confederate. Torsion clinched the Tuareg's incredible mechanism. The sister lusted after a massive infrastructure. Zeppelins boomed in a keeper's despicable firmament, and light flapped at the eaves. A teenager featured in a classically fractioned trap. One by one, the relevant technical panderers were clasped by a wan describer. At last a damask furrow was found for the kin. Near or far, the tea service lacked a provider, though a patched regional zip cord leaped among none of the farmer's biscuits and few broached the lapidary wicked fence, but fanning from a crystal-girdled crossing, a gaggle of ghost-suited novices jumped among gorilla-laden shrubs immenser than sequoias and more deadly. The calculating despot snickered. Kneeling on a bifurcated counter, a dazzling road mender shaped invoked suspicions and risibly panicked a robot's attendant who'd left his pincers safe in a cleft by a rivulet, ostensibly misled by the pikes of an illusory puncturer stripped of affects. Granitic confidence supervened, and a canvas pasture unfurled near the straits. Before a fatal classmate could hook a dirndled wayfarer, a galloping proser fled with the cinctured capture. A gruff, demented activist was left among the crossroads. A liberal grin tightened the leaves. A sepia, ramshackle portion was the parson's only lot. Tolerant and tentative, a skulking dipterologist foxily pitted results against requests. Unnatural though its betterment might seem to a flickering whipper, at least one fragile nativist favored the air castle's remake. Sleep encountered none of the usual slack distaste. Warily, a tantalizing race pushed forth into thickets alive with twins. Skylarks swarmed over the undulant surround. A tinker mouthed a cracker. Fanciful as disaster, an errant taxi ticked among billboards piled with color and language straitened by commerce, deflated and all but snapping. Trimmed from a vanishing clientele, snippets of vixenish furbelows floated in a pancreatic marsh. A needle was strapped to a toe. Moaning and moping, the gadabouts yielded their interest. A marble rested on a riven shelf. One cleft or more made a little more difference than none. Gray honey from a tapster's trove was bargained for by more than one survivor. Tottling picketers fixed a beseeching hand. Suave as straddlers and nearly as neat, a paunchy saunterer disinterred the once nattering lacemaker formerly farcically entered. Near the park the straggling giant fastened a gate. Swaying along the straightaway, the ghastly ally of a hill man rapidly clattered, outpacing every planner. Vapid and decidedly tonsured, a wily reductionist filtered the grease of transactions. More than one pollution was the upshot. A necessary pyrene was left to engage.

In stages and beleaguered, petitioned and agglomerate, a cowardly detective climbed to peril. Nestling between throes, the pumper crushed the permeated fragments and swept the cliffs with unenduring glances. Filmy withering petals clashed with vacant rites portending closure. A nose was lost. Weaponed and reticent, dashers passed among hangdogs, and a fey attendant trampled the least narcissus. A bitter clipping was left in a crack. Foreign tattling gambolers wrenched the sacristan's gnarled sternum.

20 February 1985
New York

Pieces o' Six—XXIII

Waiting in the wings was a particularly distasteful alternative: never having been. How this could be was difficult to comprehend. *No* news would have been better than the possibility of *that* news. How it was conveyed is not easily translated into words. Nothing had been said. No system of signs or signals had been employed. Neither could one have described it as having been imparted by telepathy or clairvoyance or precognition. The last term was particularly ill suited to the situation. How could one come to know ahead of time that one's past was to be nullified—not merely one's own memory and that of everyone else in regard to one's existence, but that existence itself. Is it correct to say that this was unthinkable? At first it does not seem so, since the thought has certainly come to one like any other thought. But attempting to confront and contemplate it leads soon to an impasse—a kind of blank. The words—the "concept," in a limited meaning of the term—can easily be brought before the mind. But if one tries to concretize it, to make it imaginable, one realizes soon the impossibility of the endeavor. One cannot willfully not remember one's past. Only trauma or pathology—ECT, say, or Alzheimer's—can do away with one's own memory, and even then the traces one has left, not only in others' memories but in myriad materials, cannot be imagined to have disappeared. And even if they *could* be so imagined, the fact of their *having been, before* they disappeared, cannot. Yet there it was, waiting in the wings. Its possibility seemed as real as the impossibility of its being concretely imagined. But what was meant by its being called "a waiting alternative"? An "alternative" to what had actually taken place and was continuing: a person's existence? And how could that "alternative" be "waiting"—*now?* If other universes—an infinite number of them, one for each of the possibilities that had not been actualized at each point in past time and one for each possibility that might or might not be actualized in the future—all somehow "existed," then never-having-been could "exist" in that way. In at least one such alternative universe that person would never have been: the never-having-been would be "waiting" in that it would be a real part of that other universe. But this person's existence was and had been taking place in *this* universe. Even if alternate universes *were* in this remote sense "waiting," they were irrelevant to *this* life in *this* universe. Even if every memory and every trace of this person's existence were in some unimaginable way to disappear forever, the fact of having been would not— *could* not—disappear. The existence was other—more—than its traces. In at least *this* universe, this person *would* have been. Here never-having-been was not possible, whatever was possible in an infinitude of other possible universes. Then how had the conviction that this "alternative" was "waiting in the wings" been formed? Did it have a cause or had it formed itself *ex nihilo*? Even the few who still believed that *being* had been created from its opposite (usually conceived tacitly as an infinitely rarefied material) thought that *some* kind of cause had been at work—if not the venerable First Cause necessary in Aristotle's cosmogony or the Creator God his Near-Eastern-myth-befuddled soi-disant later disciples espoused, then some unspecifiable structural impurity lurking in nonbeing that forced the spawning of its opposite. But for a notion, a conviction, of this nature, no such grandiose etiology was needed. A humbler science than cosmogony or metaphysics could be called upon: psychology. What could make such an irrational conviction spring into the mind? Wasn't it a simple case of pathogeny? The conviction that never-having-been was waiting in the wings had come into this mind no more (but no less) mysteriously than had the conviction that he was eternally damned taken over William Cowper's

mind one night in the eighteenth century. No. The source of *this* convic-
tion was *more* mysterious than that of Cowper's. A cyclothymic (or inter-
mittent melancholic) many years, Cowper experienced his depression in
terms of Calvinist ideology which seems to have been reinforced (*cathec-
ticized?*) by the Rev. John Newton, the evangelical curate of Olney, Bucks.,
the close friend and erstwhile mentor for whom he wrote and contributed
to the *Olney Hymns* such subsequent favorites as "God works in a myste-
rious way." Plausibly his depressiveness has been ascribed to his being ill-
treated from six to eight at a Dr. Pitman's school in Marykate, Herts. (or
Beds.), where he was "singled out, as a victim of secret cruelty, by a young
monster, about fifteen," writes Thomas Campbell. Forty-odd years later,
in 1784, Cowper wrote his *Hauptwerk*, "The Task," assigned by Lady
Austen on her sofa (*ere Mary Unwin banished her*). Presently subjected to
unmerited neglect (mostly for the wrong reasons), this long digressive med-
itative poem in blank verse—less ponderously didactic, and much less
plaintively "confessional," than Edward Young's *Night Thoughts*, its pop-
ular predecessor by 40-odd years—earned him his now fading fame. (In
the first 40-odd lines of its second book he denounces war and slavery, de-
mands the latter's abolition throughout Britain's "empire" ["We have no
slaves at home—Then why abroad?"], and rejoices that [as legally recog-
nized in 1772] "Slaves cannot breathe in England; if their lungs / Receive
our air, that moment they are free[.]") Then, for publication with "The Task"
in a volume whose bicentennial we celebrate this year, Cowper wrote the
"Tirocinium," a poem on education, "the purport of which was (in his own
words) to censure the want of discipline and the inattention to morals which
prevail in public schools, and to recommend private education as prefer-
able on all accounts." (Clarified by two quotations from under "Public school,
1" in the *OED*: "A public school is administered, in greater or less degree,
with the aid of the pupils themselves: a private school is one in which the
government is altogether administered by masters" [Moberly, 1848] and
the 1847 title "Fagging: is it hopelessly inseparable from the discipline of
a public school?") Through the "Tirocinium" he struck back after 40-odd
years at the bully-tyranny under which public school students such as he'd
been suffered. (*Foe of slavery, slave of Mary.*) Yet, though most public school
pupils have undergone, "in greater or less degree," the pain and humilia-
tion attendant on the "fagging" system, relatively few of them develop man-

ifestly into depressive psychotics. Currently Cowper's troubles might be ascribed primarily to a biochemical predisposition. John Newton may have had little to do (beyond strengthening the ideological matrix of a previously established conviction) with Cowper's coming to believe himself eternally damned. The idea was in the air, for any depressive to seize upon. Can the same be said of the conviction that never-having-been was waiting in the wings? Regardless of the disparity in magnitude, *its* origin may have more in common with the birth of the universe hypothesized recently by Prof. Alexander Vilenkin of Tufts: that it "arises by quantum tunneling from nothing, a state with no classical space-time." Can an analogous quantum-mechanical fluctuation account for the arising of the notion that never-having-been was waiting in the wings? Can some "notion tunneling" from nothing at all "explain" its coming-to-be? What wave equation might have yielded sufficient probability for this conviction to appear on the hither side of whatever barrier stood between the notion and its nonexistence *(its not being entertained in any mind)*? Or should recourse again be had to "bi-ographogeny" or "biochemogeny," even though *this* conviction, unlike Cowper's in his time, was not embedded as a credible possibility in contemporary ideology, but seems, rather, to have been bizarrely idiosyncratic? Would an etiology based on chemicals and/or childhood traumata be simpler or more satisfying than "quantum tunneling from nothing" or even such philosophically unfashionable causative agents as God or The Devil? Why, indeed, need one look for an *efficient* cause, singular or multiple? Wouldn't it be more appropriate to look, say, for a *final* cause? What could have been the end, the goal, the purpose, the aim of the notion that that particularly distasteful alternative, never-having-been, was waiting in the wings? If it had a purpose, must that notion not have been intrinsically *hopeful?* Having a purpose means *hoping* to accomplish it. Could it have had so banal an aim as *absolution?* If one had never been, one could never have made any mistakes, committed any crimes, or even done an unkind deed! Then why was this alternative felt to be particularly distasteful? If the aim was absolution, why didn't the possibility that this alternative might move from the wings to center stage fill the mind with joy rather than dread? If it did, every guilt would disappear! One would never have done anything one had done: aye, there's the rub! Along with all of one's mistakes, stupidities, crimes, unkindnesses, botches, bloopers, treasons, betrayals, neglects, would also disappear every positive or generous deed, production, accomplishment, achievement. Even if "part of one" wanted never to have been, in order to be absolved of guilt, "another part" wanted to have done what it had wanted to do and did. Actualization of this possibility would fulfill the aim of the "first part" only at the expense of the "other part." Was the whole matter, then, merely a banal schizoid incident? One part of the person, feeling unbearably guilty (but how can a feeling be experienced by only *part* of a person?), had produced the conviction to obtain absolution. The other part, affirming the person's existence (but how could a person's existence be affirmed by only *part* of the person?), whatever the sources of the guilt, found the "alternative" as distasteful as could be. Both the conviction and the distaste seemed absolute. The purpose of the conviction's coming into the mind seemed clear no matter how obscure were the means, the efficiently causative agents or mechanisms, that *had* brought it about. But it could not have been an absolute conviction. (Neither could the distaste have been absolute: if it were, the conviction would never have been formed.) The clue was that distaste: sour sign of existence's self-affirmation.

30 June–7 September 1985
New York

Pieces o' Six—XXVII

The clock had stopped. Going into a trance did not help. Stuck on the wall like any dead artifact, never a clever move could get its limbs to move again. Merely a three-D flash card for teaching telling time, soon to be outdated when digitals turned universal. What stance did that allow? Would the optimist repeat the old wheeze, "It's right twice a day"? Why bother? The pessimist wins hands down. Nobody, after all, without *another* clock at hand, and an accurate one at that, could know at *which* two "split seconds" the stopped clock was right. Had a clock mender been called in and given up on it? Was it hopelessly broken or, "merely" neglected, would it soon have, or had it already, decayed to that state—through rust, dust, insects, or other allies of time's anonymity? Useless questions no trance could answer. The hands' dance had ceased. No click of escapement talked. Mouse escarpment lacked. No dickering with the hickory. Never a slap or ever. Sleep could last or never overtake. Flakes fall past, velocity zero. Acceleration flattened. Fetish secure now in fineness. Decorative president. Whip nor hope. Soul? Fled? Flakes? Into the black and silent lake. Dust caked on face. Trembled off hands truck passed. Did it rest? Do the dead? Category mistake. Analogy encryption. Action's fraction movement lacked. Intention's heady absence. Stolid sculpture, nested presence. Flecked, freckled: flies, untimed. Passed. Excremental signatures. Once upon a time. Twice? Thickened. Syntax lost its wickets. Kicked. Flywheel spring sprung. Repugnant sponge. Seconds. Into the black lake. Twices. Silence. Flakes. No count. Drifted past the window. Sifted through onto the inner sill. Sentences. Thin scum on surface. Water not quite ice. Snow's own face. Admissibly cryptic. Flickering. Crinkled. Shrinking from the fact, nonticking ticker. Fixed. Unfixable. Temporary fixity, mimic eternity: flicker? Frozen. Tears ice dust flown past. Overblown wretched watch, ratchet clatter over. Done with. Undone. Paint flakes fallen, metal uncovered, rusted unconcealment eaten. A fine unpresent face. No ghost. No machine. Unclean. No time machine. A stop of a clock will never abolish time. *It* had stopped. Not the flying flakes. Silent twices melting into wind-roiled blackness. It stood there. It hung on the wall. It sat on the massive mantel. It was where it had always been. All the time. It was what it had always been. Passing the shifter. Rust on a round unpleasant face. Later. It couldn't tell the hour. Unbroken duration flowed, time untold, moments unclosed, marginless, even, eventless. Banausic. Pawl rust-stuck to ratchet. Inarticulate. Flickerless. Accidentally false crystallization. Flavorless. Had anyone seen it stop? Was the time it told—the time it tells, seems to tell—the time at the time? A lie? No machine can. Could. Wood, metal, plastic, glass, paint. Stood. A classic case: time stood still. No. Uninterrupted flow unquantified? Time's quanta flicker on. Attention. Attention. Escapement had clicked their mimesis. Attention. Sentences claw at the page. The clock may not be there. The clock may not have been there. The clock wasn't there. The clock hasn't been anywhere. The clock is not there. If the clock had not been there. If the clock will not have been there. Once there may have been a clock. Once a clock was. When the hands moved. When the longer hand went 'round twelve times more rapidly than the shorter. If it was a clock that chimed. More of a tune each quarter-hour. If it. The clock. Attention flickers moments. Escapement. Serial crystallization. Blinking. Once one intended a clock. One mentioned it. Once one said there was a clock. Stopped. Once one saw a clock. Once a clock one saw—had stopped. Once a flow was blinked articulate. Attention. No clock ever paid it. An escapement pawl will never release duration. A frozen click will never bind the flow. A snowstorm. Occasions. Quanta that are who. Whoever entered the room could see the clock had stopped. The clock was seen to have stopped. A clock had stopped. What was the time? Whenever one looked toward it one could see the clock had stopped. Snowflakes blew through the movement. The mainspring, too tightly, clung to itself, or gave itself too freely. Each when will have been. How long is a moment? A stopped clock will never have abolished time. When does an event end? Not only attention articulates duration. How far above "the" horizon must an event have risen before it is recognized as having begun and being underway? Events nest. The undertone of time. The ellipsis. The lacuna. The caesura. The quantum leaps. Across/over/under, "from" one side "to" another of. The illusion of I going on . . . being I am experiencing? When awaking, how/why does the I awaking identify with the eye that has been seeing the dreams being awakened from? This is the end of time. At the still point. When a clock stops, time goes on. When a consciousness stops, time goes on. Why/how does time go on *then*? The introspection of duration. An internal cinema.

(Russell first went to the movies to understand Bergson.) When I was little I thought and I said that I didn't have dreams but "sleep motion pictures." What happens to time when I dream? There is the time the clock could have measured if it hadn't stopped and the time the dreamer experiences. Is the dreamer's time "true duration"? Disarticulated memories. The waking man's guide to reality. In less time than it takes to say it. This is one of the two times the clock is right today. It is on time. It was. Was time on *it*? Did time proceed from the clock and its beholders as the Holy Spirit is said to proceed from the Father and the Son? The end of time. History is that happening which takes place through time upon active and passive humanity and through its agency. Does this historical happening mean anything beyond the merely factual? What might this meaning be? What is the historical process leading up to? Is the end of history the end of time? An overheated interest in "eschatological" questions. An especially high measure of sobriety and exactitude, indeed the explicit renunciation of any answer. Should the question of the end of time not be left alone altogether since it is scarcely possible to answer it? Aristotle held that the process of history, like that of nature, is a cycle that continually repeats itself. Even men's opinions are identically repeated, "not once or twice, not a few times, but an infinite number of times." It appears impossible to reflect on history without enquiring as to its end. We see it as a directed happening. Beginning and end. Time must have a stop. The time that stopped when the clock stopped. The time that will stop if time has a stop. The eternal return returned after the director was said to have absconded. Undirected, history's happening circles history circles. Profound signs of the times. Signs of time. The human race frequently proclaims actions and events which are leading it to destruction. I can predict to the human race its progression towards the better, which can never again be wholly reversed. The human race has always been progressing towards the better and will always continue to so progress. The doubts . . . of unbelievers. Philosophy too may have its Millenarianism. The conjectural beginning of human history. The conjectural beginning of the universe. The conjectural beginning of time. The course of human affairs develops gradually from the worse to the better, to which progress, then, each one of us is called upon by Nature herself to contribute for her part as much as lies within her power. The Last Things. The Victory of the Good Principle over the Evil and the Establishment of the Kingdom of God on Earth. Men may, in their folly or wickedness, blot out civilization or even, it may be, bring to an end the existence of the human race. The universe may have begun by quantum-tunneling from nothing, a state with no classical space-time. The clock that stopped is not. The natural, mystical, and topsy-turvy end of all things. Nothing, but not just plain old nothing. Each present occasion emerges from and is haloed infinitely by pasts and by vectors toward futures. Time inheres in being but is not being, nor is being time.

c. 19 December 1985–7 February 1986
New York

♦

Selections from *42 Merzgedichte* in Memoriam *Kurt Schwitters*

Introduction

Adapted by Anne Tardos from the introduction to *42 Merzgedichte* in Memoriam *Kurt Schwitters*, written 16–18 August 1990, and 19–23 February 1993, New York

Kurt Schwitters (1887–1948) was an incredibly productive and inventive visual, literary, and performance artist. He worked as a collagist, painter, sculptor, and maker of what have since become known as assemblages, combines, and installations (notably, his *Merzbauten*, the largest of which, in Hanover—destroyed during World War II—came to occupy most of a building's interior, and in the making of which he also functioned as an architect), as well as a typographer and designer. He also wrote innumerable poems, stories, plays, and unclassifiable verbal works of art, including some of the first examples of what is now called sound poetry and text-sound texts, which he performed magnificently. While some of his contemporaries called their work and themselves "Dada," he adopted the syllable MERZ from a snippet of an advertisement for a commercial and private bank *(Kommerz- und Privatbank)* that he glued to a collage, applying it not only to that collage *(Das Merzbild),* but eventually to all his artwork—and ultimately to himself.

When I first became acquainted with his collages and poems, in the early 1940s, my spontaneous response was a feeling of pleasure, love, and kinship. This feeling has grown steadily as I have come to know more and more of his work in all fields.

I called "Pieces o' Six—XXXII" a *"Merzgedicht* [MERZ poem] in Memoriam *Kurt Schwitters*" because of both its subject matter and its collage-like structure. However, when I wrote it, I had no idea that it was the first of a *series* of *Merzgedichte*. But soon after I finished it, I devised a chance-operational method that used random digits (generated by a simple Turbo-C program) and the "glossary" capabilities of my word processor, Microsoft Word, to select certain linguistic units from "Pieces o' Six—XXXII" and to juxtapose them and place them on the pages in entirely new constellations. When I completed the first poem produced by this method, the "*2nd Merzgedicht* in Memoriam *Kurt Schwitters,*" I realized that a *new* series of poems had sprouted from the "Pieces o' Six" (like a new bough branching from an older one near its end).

Charles Hartman's computer program DIASTEXT uses the *whole source text* as the "index"; a later version, DIASTEX4, sent to me in August 1989, allows the user to choose and employ a separate index text. Prof. Hartman also sent me the latest version of TRAVESTY, a program that generates "pseudo-texts," written by the critic Hugh Kenner and the computer scientist Joseph O'Rourke and first published in *BYTE* magazine in November 1984. In their words, TRAVESTY uses "English letter-combination frequencies . . . to generate random text that mimics the frequencies found in a sample. Though nonsensical, these pseudo-texts have a haunting plausibility, preserving as they do many recognizable mannerisms of the texts from which they are derived. . . . *[F]or an order-n scan, every n-character sequence in the output occurs somewhere in the input, and at about the same frequency.*" According to what "order" of "travesty" one chooses to generate, one may generate either texts that seem fairly close to normal English or ones that are far from it. I utilized these programs in different ways, employing earlier *Merzgedichte* as source texts.

The *42 Merzgedichte* in Memoriam *Kurt Schwitters*, like their dedicatee and his works, are "polymedial": they share the characteristics of several arts. They are poems—literary artworks—in various formats: prose, verse, and ones sharing characteristics of both. The verbal elements in most of them are meaningful in the usual sense of the word and directly related to the artist to whose memory they are dedicated. And like those of most of his works, these elements are placed abruptly next to each other as images, color areas, and objects are placed in visual collages and assemblages, so the *Merzgedichte* are works of collage art. They are also musical compositions in that words, phrases, sentences, and other linguistic elements are treated like the tones or intervals of scales or of tone rows, melodic themes or motifs, or rhythmic figures, recurring again and again (in full or fragmentarily) in various combinations and concatenations.

Finally, the way the *Merzgedichte* look on their pages is as important as their verbal elements *(including their meanings)* and their verbal-musical organization, so they are clearly works of visual art as well as poems, collages, musical compositions, and performance texts.

1st Merzgedicht in Memoriam *Kurt Schwitters*

[Pieces o' Six—XXXII]

First word for Kurt Schwitters: *Merz*. **If I ever move from Hannover, where I love and hate everything, I will lose the feeling that makes my *world point of view*.** 1887. Now I call myself MERZ. A *degenerate artist*. *Merzbilde med regnbue. Entformung, Eigengift, konsequent, Urbegriff.* This was before H.R.H. The Late Duke of Clarence & Avondale, Now it is a Merzpicture, Sorry! Average Merz-drawings: 4 to 8 inches high; some very large collages: 11 to 14 inches high, occasionally 15 to 24 inches high; but many *Aphorismer* less than 4 inches high. Never believed he was making anything but pure abstract forms. Selected discarded unfinished pages from Molling's Hannover printing shop and rode off on his bicycle with as many as he could carry. Through *Entformung* he attempted to clean away the *Eigengift* to gather them into the paradise of art's *Urbegriff*. **The picture is a self-contained work of art. Merz ist form. It refers to nothing outside itself.** ART NEEDS CONTEMPLATIVE SELF-ABSORPTION. Schwitters was fascinated with printed matter and regarded words and letters both as meaningful symbols and as formal design elements. A **consistent work of art can never refer to anything outside itself without loosening its ties to art.** One's first glimpses of Schwitters in the 1940s: possibly in Chicago, probably in New York. $^{A}_{r}{}^{t}_{i}{}^{s}_{a}{}^{u}_{t}{}^{o}_{n}{}^{o}_{m}{}^{o}_{u}{}^{s}$. *Auch in der Malerei verwende ich für die Komposition gern **die Brocken des täglichen Abfalls*** *etwa wie der Schacko aufgebaut ist aus den Reden seiner Besitzerin.* NEVER DO WHAT ANYONE ELSE HAS DONE. ALWAYS DO OTHERWISE THAN THE OTHERS. **I have Merzed banalities.** In 1924 he set up an advertising agency in Hannover and designed ads, notably for Pelikan ink, from one of which an *elikan* survives in a 1925 Merz. Mz 1926, 12. reclining emm. Schwitters had no concern for desanctification. *Schnuppe / meine süsse puppe, / mir ist alles schnuppe, / wenn ich meine schnauze / auf die deine bautze.* Schwitters gradually dropped avant-garde devices from his writing in the later 1920s and wrote in more nearly conventional styles (needless to say, the resultant works were hardly conventional). Schacko was a parrot who pulled out all his feathers except those on the top of his head because he couldn't sleep since the dying father kept the lights on all night because he was in such pain *he* couldn't sleep. Schwitters never pretended he didn't care about art. *Brutally Merzed wood reliefs and delicately articulated wooden constructions.* Huelsenbeck and Tzara, who agreed on little else, both saw him as a *petit bourgeois. Kom*MERZ *und Privatbank.* Some Dadaists trumpeted opposition to art while busily building artistic careers with Dadaism as an advertising device. WHEN WAS HIS WENN HAN-NOVERED FOR THE EIGENGIFT OF MALEREI? *Schwitters as I saw him was a man who ran away from reality.* He deeply valued art but took it very lightly. *MERZ-PICTURES ARE ABSTRACT WORKS OF ART. Black Dots and Quadrangle. If one reads Hannover backwards, one gets the combination* re von nah. *The word* re *one can read indifferently as* **backward** *or* **back.** *I suggest* **backward.** *Thus the translation of the word* **Hannover** *read backward would be* **backward from near.** *And that is correct, for then the translation of the word* **Hannover** *read forward would be* **forward to far.** *This means Hannover strives forward, even to infinity.* SCHWITTERS SHIED AWAY FROM LAYING BARE A **NEW REALITY** AND FROM ANTIARTISTIC GESTURES, RE-TAINING EVEN IN THE i-DRAWINGS A TRADITIONAL UNDERSTANDING OF ART: IN THE CASE OF i, THE ACT OF THE ARTIST IS SOLELY THE DISASSOCIA-TION [*ENTFORMELUNG*] OF A GIVEN OBJECT THROUGH SINGLING OUT A PART RHYTHMIC IN ITSELF. *Chanson des autres is i.* Art as simple as writing the letter i. *The middle vowel of the alphabet.* Schwitters taught us we can use anything to make art and even unaltered found materials may become art but the intention enacted in this praxis need include no antiartistic admixture. J 20 i-Zeichnung. *Go out into the whole world and make the truth* *known, the only truth there is, the truth about Anna Blume.* Had Schwitters lived to see FLUXUS, he'd have either scorned or scoffed at Maciunas's supposedly antiartistic tenets. Mz 1926, 9. with violet velvet. In a passage Schwitters underlined, Bluemner wrote that **Poetry is word composition** that **need not be in accord with logic and grammar** using a language that **at times sees itself reaching the end of all intensifications and possibilities of selection so that it is compelled to go back to its origins.** *Mz 410 something or other.* ***Frühe rundet Regen blau.*** THE MOST INTERNATIONAL PETIT BOURGEOIS IN THE WORLD. HIS DAILY LIFE WAS ENTIRELY WITHOUT BOURGEOIS COMFORTS. *A non-paying spectator on the Dadaist scene, by his very nature he **was** Dada.* Disjointed Forces. SCHWITTERS STOOD OUT among the Dadaists AS A MARVELOUS DILETTANTE. Today's *artist certifiers* would call him *a very persistent amateur.* TYLL EULENSPIEGEL. He'd have trouble being certified for an artist's loft in Soho. *Merz 14 / 15. Die Scheuche.* He lived in ONE OF THE LIVELIEST CITIES IN POSTWAR GERMANY *like a lower middle class Victorian.* **The Kaspar David Friedrich of the Dadaist revolution.** *He simply did not have a conventional bone in his body.* WHAT WAS ONCE CRIED DOWN AS MADNESS OR A BAD JOKE TURNS INTO A SOLID CULTURAL POSSESSION, AND THE REVOLUTIONARIES OF YESTERDAY ARE THE CLASSICS OF TODAY. That's just what the revolutionaries of today must avoid: becoming the classics of tomorrow! *Merz is as tolerant as possible with respect to its material.* Schwitters and Wordsworth lived their last years, died, and are buried— 4 miles from each other—in England's Lake District. MY BASIC TRAIT IS MELANCHOLY. Schwitters died in June 1948. *Merzzeichnung 83 Zeichnung F.* Why make artworks if you're opposed to art? *My wet nurse's milk was too thick and there was too little, because she nursed me beyond the lawfully allowed time.* Playing Card Harmonica. *The materials bring into the abstract formal performance a piece of familiar reality.* Schwitters had a little garden in Isernhagen, a village near Hannover: *Roses, strawberries, a man-made hill, and an artificial pond. In the fall of 1901, village boys tore up the garden while I looked on. The excitement brought on St. Vitus's dance. I was sick for two years, totally disabled.* *Das Merzbild.* ELIKAN MERZED A KONSEQUENT BROCKEN. He loved each discarded bit or snippet for itself though he made it take its place in what he would have called an abstract structure. *Striving for expression* *in a work of art seems to me injurious to art.* Mz 280 Red Pen (for Lisker). He cared nothing about contradicting himself even though he thought that artworks had to be *konsequent*. ONE CAN EVEN SHOUT OUT THROUGH REFUSE, AND THIS IS WHAT I DID, NAILING AND GLUING IT TO- GETHER. I CALLED IT MERZ, IT WAS A PRAYER ABOUT THE VICTORIOUS END OF THE WAR, VICTORIOUS AS ONCE AGAIN PEACE HAD WON IN THE END; EVERYTHING HAD BROKEN DOWN IN ANY CASE AND NEW THINGS HAD TO BE MADE OUT OF FRAGMENTS: AND THIS IS MERZ. IT WAS LIKE AN IM- AGE OF THE REVOLUTION WITHIN ME, NOT AS IT WAS BUT AS IT SHOULD HAVE BEEN. Construction for Noble Ladies. *Such political convictions as he had were more against than for—against war, against the stupidity of institutions, programs, phrasemaking of every kind.* People such as Huelsenbeck (and even Schwitters himself) thought him nonpolitical be- cause he espoused no easily recognized ideology, not realizing that Schwit- ters' artworks function politically by making the viewer look at the most banal detritus with (as poor Maciunas would have put it) *an art attitude,* which by distancing the objects of everyday experience allows her to see them in a strange context and from a new angle, so that whatever has been taken for granted may begin to be questioned and eventually illumined by critical reflection. *The increasing formalization of Schwitters' collages and relief assemblages in the early 1920s necessarily inhibited the more fantastic side of his artistic personality.* Siegbild (Victory Picture), c. 1925. Schwit- ters was hardly ever a pure image maker, unlike most Dada artists, who transmitted Dada's revolutionary message mainly through image-content. *Dada was ideological without a specific ideology and purposive without a purpose, which is why Dada actions and objects could be considered* artis- tic. FAUVIST COLOR WITHIN A CUBIST SYTEM. Mz 387. Kaltensundheim, 1922: Merzed the year *this* Merzer was born. *Schwitters' method is that of Real- ism made from real things.* This is a **positive** link with FLUXUS—this kind of Realism is much more important to most so-called FLUXUS artists than the anti-art component, which Maciunas himself seems largely to have dis- counted before his untimely death. *Surrealism is litterature* [sic] *with wrong means, not painting, therefore wrong.* Merzbild Alf. *Schwitters had always insisted that the individual potency of his materials should be effaced in the process of picture-making,* but in 1937–39 *his very untypical interest in* objets trouvés and *the blatant literal presence of objects themselves* in collages, *grotesque faces and still-life objects* in certain paintings *in the new* Pointilliste *style,* late reliefs including *smooth biomorphic forms,* and a *general shift to illusionistic space and organic, curvilinear elements* are ascribed variously to the influence of *1930s Surrealism* or to *the influence of natural scenery* after his move to Norway. What critics who point with seeming surprise at such *inconsistencies* don't seem to realize is that Schwitters was only concerned with consistency *within* each work. Do I CONTRADICT MYSELF? VERY WELL THEN I CONTRADICT MYSELF, (I AM LARGE, I CONTAIN MULTITUDES.) DEINE DESANCTIFICATION IST TÄGLICHEN AUFGEBAUT WIE KASPAR WORDSWORTH ODER FRIEDRICH MACIUNAS, SCHACKO BLUEMNER ODER ANNA BLUME. Schwitters's mind and practice roved freely over all the possibilities available to artists during the first half of the 20th century. **Combine all branches of art into an artistic unity. Mz 33. Verbürgt rein. We see in his work not only the picture of a new instinctive order but a picture of its creation: since the material components that create this order are drawn from quite an opposite state, the tension and competitions between parts and whole are necessarily given along with the new order itself.** His works transcended his conscious abstract-art ideology, embodying a much more complete theory of art, though he might have been chagrined if told *they imitate nature in its complexity. THE LARGER LATE ASSEMBLAGES AND COLLAGES, ESPECIALLY, HAVE A FORTHRIGHTNESS AND GENEROSITY ABOUT THEM THAT MAKES THE PRECEDING, CONSTRUCTIVIST-STYLE WORK SEEM OVERCONTROLLED BY CONTRAST. Der Schokaladenkasten, Anna Blume, Box 7.* He feared *inexactness lest it fall into mere RANDOMNESS.* **Even close friends found it difficult to reconcile Schwitters' jovial, extrovert, and clownish nature with the seriousness of his commitment to art.** The liveliness of Schwitters' art may well have arisen from the widely noted *contradictoriness of his existence,* and that very *contradictoriness* prevented MERZ from becoming an ideology, allowing him to embrace a myriad of materials and methods and to approach, willy-nilly, *imitating nature in its manner of operation.* **DO NOT ASK FOR SOULFUL MOODS.** THE DADAIST IS A MIRROR CARRIER. *There is no such thing as inchoate experience.* Perception is always already preconstituted by the perceiver. **A Merzer met Roof on the roof.** One may respect, like, enjoy, or be delighted or even made ecstatic by the works of a number of artists, but those of a few—in this century Stein, Satie, and

Schwitters, Klee and Cage, and still inescapably Schoenberg, and not a large handful of others—one loves. *Industriegebiet. Aq. 37.* **The Cathedral broke through the ceiling and aspiring upward pushed into Kurt's and Helma's apartment above, leaving one of the rooms with no floor.** *Merzbau Hannover,* begun by Schwitters around 1923 and continually worked upon for nearly fourteen years, was twenty years later—five years before his death—destroyed by Allied bombs. *During the 1930s Schwitters often worked day and night on his **useless construction.*** Merzbau in Little Langdale (Merz Barn). On New Year's Day 1937 (ten months before this Merzer began writing poems) Schwitters left Germany, never again to see *Merzbau Hannover,* and that year began the second *Merzbau,* in Lysaker, Norway, which was destroyed by fire in 1951; ten years after beginning the second and six months before he died, he began the third and last *Merzbau* (the *Merz Barn*) on Cylinder's Farm in Little Langdale, near Ambleside, in the Lake District of England, the one more or less completed wall of which, though moved, still survives. Oh, **Du,** Kurt Schwitters, **Du!**

4th Merzgedicht in Memoriam *Kurt Schwitters*

sees itself reaching the end of all intensifications

Never believed he was making anything but pure abstract forms

as tolerant as possible with respect to its material

TYLL EULENSPIEGEL

DO NOT ASK FOR SOULFUL MOODS.

TYLL EULENSPIEGEL

DO NOT ASK FOR SOULFUL MOODS.

increasing formalization

18 April 1987
New York

21st Merzgedicht in Memoriam *Kurt Schwitters*

Clichés *spontaneously encountered a world of violent letter forms* **when close friends found it difficult to reconcile Schwitters** to labels after thirteen of his works were confiscated from German museums in 1937 as Degenerate Art.

Ludwig Hilbersheimer labeled a subterranean cistern *fantastic* though *by his very nature he **was** Dada.*

In paradise avant-garde school card numbers, meaningless in themselves, suggest the real.

A declaration of love made up of word games, clichés, and absurd verbal juxtapositions **served as well as painter's pigment when Schwitters made use of the residues of life, the wretchedest of all materials.**

Now it is a Merzpicture.

In the geometric simplicity of *Ziiuu ennze ziiuu nnz krr müü, ziiuu ennze ziiuu rinnzkrrmüü; rakete bee bee, rakete bee zee* the unreal quality of inflation has been evoked.

Gathered into the paradise of art, Schoenberg, Marinetti, and **the end of all the familiar materials of everyday life could be perceived as independent aesthetic objects released from their mundane functions.**

Abandoned materials transcended his conscious abstract-art ideology.

Moholy-Nagy, *after the revolution, felt himself free and had to cry out his jubilation to the world.*

Klee necessarily built something new from the fragments of *art's* allusive possibilities.

Schwitters continually worked upon *Merzbau Hannover* for nearly fourteen years.

Close friends found it difficult to reconcile *me to injurious art.*

7 February 1988
New York

38th Merzgedicht in Memoriam *Kurt Schwitters*

KAr
HülseTHes,
KArATe

BucTurAPsor
LIs lovewood revonTTed.

Ander,
IcTes.

Ang Iners con
LysAff brIne
Alsend brub HAgmes mencess kInces AumeIng
GerHe HITTHe lIsTers,
To AdversTATesclITTe
NAgen blensTure Aus enber,
HAnds,
PIcATIvewordemboldeclIff b slooTAnTer souPT frAmPlI InTTer.

Derived from my *"29th Merzgedicht* in Memoriam *Kurt Schwitters"* (8/29/88) via
Hugh Kenner and Joseph O'Rourke's text-generating program TRAVESTY, Charles O.
Hartman's text-selection program DIASTEX4, and systematic postediting.

10–11 September 1989
New York

39th Merzgedicht in Memoriam Kurt Schwitters

DistAtioN logiNg.

N CoNDivAter
RotAteD AuMetriNg.

AstriC

"LAkets,"

"Fres,"

CoM CurM sMs!

CoNstrupt krup ittleD.

DisAFF

Histrupt

GerbAlly.

Meitzky CoN looM wooD

SChAs De toN Nt logrAw ArteNsA A As

"LAkets,"

"Fres,"

CoM CurM sMs!

Derived from my *"29th Merzgedicht* in Memoriam *Kurt Schwitters"* (8/29/88) via Hugh
Kenner and Joseph O'Rourke's text-generating program TRAVESTY, Charles O.
Hartman's text-selection program DIASTEX4, and systematic postediting.

10–11 September 1989

New York

Oners n Tenners 1

A series of oners and tenners, many regards, various orders. This-here-one.

Alone. Following. Six. One follows another as thirty-three follows thirty-two six by six. *A book accumulates solely by accretion of ones and tens. Fixed.* Did Pythagoras have Arabian cousins as Plato no silicon interrogators? No answer given to no question asked: pertinent nor impertinent. Variable. What will be there will be there little by little. Sentences. Words. Lines. *Counted.* Regularity, irregularity, interpenetrating, transparent, echoing, implying, system, number, chaos, order. The way is open: no loquacity, writing as saying still. Where given numbers manifest as physical limits of concrete discourse. *The book gathers, ungathers, other books gathering, ungathering during, after.* Tens. One.

Majuscule beginning, full-stop ending: is the thought complete or not?

Entering. One is longer than the one before, shorter than others. How can one accumulating, counting, fitting, numbering, be writing saying? *Care never vitiates being's coming-to-be, but does it motivate it?* They'll be longer long before they're shorter, shorter before long. This begins—no one knowing where it'll end—and ends. What follows may be no nearer completion than whatever precedes. Exception. *Proof.* Each embodies legacies none fully manifests or not at all. Deletion. Do words come into texts unbidden, bidden, both, or neither? Numbers only insist on numbers but saying will not insist. Unhides. Starting on a longer journey, one sees the road's end. Unwinding, the string unravels: the maze ends in the dark.

Embarkation initiates naming destinations intention will not have aimed at. Are beginnings made to come into being by unborn ends? A pause ends and begins: inhalation follows exhalation, exhalation inhalation. Breath. *Light.* Shifter. Invitation. Adequately to accumulate being saying like photons in photographic emulsion. Metaphors make saying be what it never would otherwise be. Negation. The ones and tens gather as the saying discloses being. Affirmation. After the last word saying continues as silence,

silence saying. Audible. Words and their order produce what's said, who-
ever is saying. Constitute. The sayer resides in words, silence, body: matter's
vibration, light's. Occupation. Tiny. Line. Interrogation?

10 August 1987
New York

Sitting Teeth

Sitting teeth sleeve rent maxillary axis dash wagon
patina lumination zymogen.

Arc on balance risk gleam
apparatus crop gut.

Femur wheeze ruction rust
peal reek farm mellow goal rinse taffrail eastern
incest quiz baffle cleave.

Kidderminster.

3 July 1990
New York

Star Croak Twelve

Star croak.

Mocha toll net.

Winch flock tern tap rack
coat glue boscage approach violin worm bastion noticeability
net wets flex it denote fortunate.

Soma
coast robe insensate qualify.

Glimpse picket metalanguage
limitation advantage wayfarer dangle panoply
ventury.

Plant paschal passive whistle.

Star croak.

4 July 1990
New York

Order Realistic

Order realistic raffle traffic negative elastic itch incorporate

Ratchet gazette fraught fester infanta micturation

Advantage grasp limp galled feature tinny.

4–5 July 1990
New York

People Swamp

People swamp flavor.

Iridescence knot ringdove end needle sieve.

Keeper encystment palliation aftervarnish creepiness instrument.

4–5 July 1990
New York

Runnymede Torrefaction

Runnymede torrefaction leaf sport cove rattle bitartrate
negative encystment catastronome lacunary encaption
megalomaniasis micturation catastronome eccentricate
varnish liquefy fixity absentences absentee longing
pension evanesce wrestle zenith collapse flavor
ghost quest lumber sackful when foundation tinnitis
glint sedulous swamp.

Keeper clipper wheat.

4–5 July 1990
New York

Coelentertain Megalomaniasis

Coelentertain megalomaniasis claustrophobia megalomaniasis
tangle past tone target embolden walkie-talkie.

Panchatantra galley *pinctor* panopticon stirps absentee extensity
fluorescence palliation professional speech list.

4–5 July 1990
New York

Interred Stirps

Interred stirps twist carcinogen.

Vistula sackful distant cardamom palliative deal.

Runnymede weeping.

Zingerly list hyphenate itch fatuous parka list tangle passionate
crystal micturation olfaction lagomorph knowledge;
flame fleet wreak cardamom forage forehearsal sample;
think fractal feeder window window fin sleeve lean-to
tramp rinse glint furtive clipper enclosure.

4–5 July 1990
New York

Retreated Degree

Retreated degree went after varnish escalated helminthic tribal
grasped flank stone entailed claymore negative halcyon
carcinogen totality helminthic sentences wrestled
hyphen sink guild loch pancreas.

Arctic passenger ensconces explicit in encystment space hoax.

4–5 July 1990
New York

Rapidity Mocha

Rapidity.

Mocha lesser carpenter mast section tag gleam.

People foredoom encystment megalomaniasis eclection megalomaniac.

4–5 July 1990
New York

Anacreon Infanta

Anacreon on close infanta.

Data.

French modest extension olfaction encystment it on zonal robot;
notice encasement portion galactic hyphenate.

Parlor tangle foredoom nettle ceinture.

Zingerly extension pleasant helminthic lagomorphological.

4–5 July 1990
New York

Net Murder 1

Now jeopardizes catch.

More huge stretched land.

Marketable fishermen after stopping salmon leverage sea.

Nets were nets more hundred birds.

Murder stake,
summer and
other small seals.

Least netting,
sea into mysterious our farther used indeed,
require accepting at sea
be.

Sea now jeopardizes catch.

3 August–11 September 1990
New York

Drift Nets 1

Do drifting drift-nets suffocate?

Least netting,
sea into purse a drift
American

Korea viable salmon cycle,
victims salmon fishing might miles miles small netting,
million drift-nets
Alaska's one of set near trapped buoys fishermen more hundreds
across sinks,
require than marketable radio limit salmon
Korea finally interested and on radio for fish.

Mysterious fish.

5 August 1990
New York

Trick Harp Two

Clue daily window trick that quell hardy pan.

Her flapped sincere.

Why closure?

Untone exacted
Told
The
Forfeit announce announce having.

3 September 1989; 2 July 1990
New York

Selections from *Twenties: 100 Poems*

Introduction

Adapted by Anne Tardos from the preface to *Twenties: 100 Poems,*
written 3–7 April 1991, New York

Twenties comprises 100 separate poems [seven are represented here] that
were written intuitively and spontaneously from 29 February 1989 through
3 June 1990. Both the manner of writing and many of the words and
phrases that appear in them are due (at least in part) to my writing most
of them while traveling: in buses, trains, airplanes, boats, or cars or in ho-
tels, *pensioni,* or friends' houses, or at various sites I visited. I began them
while commuting by bus between New York City and Binghamton, New
York, where I taught at the State University of New York during Spring
1989, and completed them in Italy, where Anne Tardos and I each exhib-
ited two paintings in the *Ubi Fluxus ibi motus* pavilion of the Venice Bien-
nale of 1990, and in the airplane bringing us back to New York.

The title refers to the poems' physical form: each comprises twenty
lines, divided into five nonmetrical quatrains. I explicitly characterize the
way they were written as "intuitive" and "spontaneous" for two reasons:
(1) Since 1954 much of my poetry has been written by wholly or partially
nonintentional (or "impersonal") methods involving chance operations,
randomization, and/or acrostic or diastic selection while "reading through"
source texts. (2) The *Twenties* are made up of single words, names, and
short phrases, which are not arranged through normative syntax, and
(rarely) short sentences, none embedded in narrative, logical, or other
structures of discourse; since they are superficially similar to some works
of mine produced by nonintentional methods, readers who know the lat-

ter might mistakenly assume that the *Twenties* were produced by such methods.

It might be misleading, however, to call these poems "intentional," in that each word, etc., was written as soon as it came to mind or (in some cases) when I saw or heard it. I hardly ever revised words, though I inserted a few nonlexical words into some of the earlier poems soon after I wrote them, and when I noticed I'd repeated a word within a poem, I substituted a similar-sounding word for its second occurrence. (Since completing the series, I've found a few intra-poem repetitions that I hadn't perceived earlier, but I've let them be.)

I also looked up words and names that I wasn't sure were "real" (i.e., generally accepted words or actual or fictive names, including names or slang expressions personally known to me) and substituted "real" ones for the dubious ones if I couldn't find the latter in any reference book or other source.

The *placements and lengths* of the caesural spaces involved deliberation and revision. I eventually adopted a convention based on multiples of three ens: a three-en space indicates a slight breath pause; a six-en space, one "beat"; a nine-en space, one beat and a breath pause; a twelve-en space, two beats; and so on. I repeatedly read through the whole series of poems, inserting, modifying, or deleting many of these spaces, although many were left as they were when I first wrote the poem.

(It's because of the revisions of caesuras and certain words, and because many of the poems were written *very slowly* or even at separated times, that I have hesitated to use the term *improvisation*. *Edited protracted improvisation* might be accurate, though awkward. Yet even this mightn't do, because most of the poems were written in a state of intense concentration, akin to meditation, which is not usually connoted by *improvisation*.)

Despite my substituting similar-sounding words for repeated words and my careful definition of caesural spacing and ambiguous stresses, these are not "sound poems." The meanings of the individual words and names are manifestly as important as their sounds, and each serious reader will produce for herself an all-over meaning for each poem, "given permission" by the nonnormative word order and caesuras (as well as the "pseudonormative" lineation and strophic arrangement), to "discover" divers nonnormative syntaxes, grammars, etc.

Though written by largely "subjective" methods, these poems both problematize the subject from which they proceed and empower each reader to become a coproducer of their meaning. Though I decided intuitively to employ the same verse form throughout the series and limitedly to "standardize" the vocabulary, I sense that these decisions further the reader's empowerment by helping define its sphere.

5

Possible Spinoza road
wrestler length encounter cast plant
standing it rattle furred fence post
zone rabbit wine soap

Coal harbor variant ghost
noticeability Sweeney hobble
truant gum tree zeal bone
goad criterion opulent

Foam entry went it way so
globular in gift polka dot
him stroller lint kitchen map goal
rinse Sony picket flock

Invent gauze Tony close
rope in harp deep glance
realization semiactive foal
chasm brandy figurative slant

People zip it runcible figure it lipid coat
glue boscage reek
feet announce Moog premise close
totalize a folk quote sneaker

1 May 1989
on a bus on the way to and in
Binghamton, N.Y.

24

Half-mast   Kansas wrap Marx
haggle   Janissary   sweat lodge course
beneath   halcyon regimen diatom
coral   regardless stream mute

Leave   Kidderminster meek
Dramamine peck marshal foliage
xenophobia resident   kinesthetic livid
vacuous mental pack   helminthic acid scope

Parlor   corsair lammergeier banknote
flame belittle infest   fiduciary
cannon plankton   raptor balance
gargoyle medical sacred collapse

Lagoon weakness   ancillary squirm
Lamarckian diadem
violin worm bastion maxillary cast
monk panoply venture   totalism

Weary replete   section affection
zymogen tinnitus log curl tramp
lagomorphic zeal   eraser whirl point
Demetrius   excellence partial

6 January 1990
New York

27

Last carpenter feelie   pocket guru
nest shelf clumsy rennet cliffhanger
linked frontline   pence innocence leafmold
rank panel cracker follow-up

Nail dream camel *Lieder*   fleetest
teen needle gash guest tensor
panatella cage   apprentice embracement
negative gleam   apparatus crop gut

Femur enamel dust leftover tendency
cleat dissection   narcissist clip gap
deal dilate lumber later glum prompt hoax
flouted fortune   orchid conation

Zeal for a   Vegan   penoplain   parch
considered   ducks' muckery   twine embolden
peaking Gloucester Tamil lever wrist
fledge intent took crust

Desk   leper ledger regional ornament
Kansas enact cancel
clasp   grippe   ontological
toe claustrophobia   garish Parkinson's twilight trim bark

11 February 1990
Kennedy Airport, New York
en route to San Diego

30

Elaborate Labrador
coattail goalie swatter ink mist
rarefaction peasant gleam
borage order a combination twist case

Ghent rapture kestrel Whig departure
votive pollster
phloem caryatid oyster fractal
glassed clastic figurative

Regional enlistment wink evacuate
tinkle liquid tension presence
smother a   warble loggerhead
sink trouble   went in search o'

Freemason graze   nectarine pin
phallotropic motor caucus
leavings a Ventura whittle
zip a basement torn   potluck

Easter whirl   territory buttery utter
Anaxagoras palliation stir 'em a bit
morbid quarter   gutted quarterly corridor
reference resisted   exoteric rotor wood

11 February 1990
In the air en route from New York to San Diego

36

Senility is a very strange thing   it comes and goes
he's been very thorough and professional patient's right to know
why'd you strap his arms down
hey Dad how y'feelin'   what's the matter

You aren't goin' to tell me that's normal behavior
medically speaking   basically he's custodial
I want 'im outa here more'n you do
what'll we do now   I'll take care of Dad at home

Go back to school   go back to Mexico
yeah I understand   get in the hearse
you'd like that wouldn' you   a slip o' th' tongue
little home-cooked meal c'mon Dad

Wash it down w'this we're gonna be ok
a good night's sleep is what we need here   sleep on it
it's ok I won't hurtcha hard to realize
yer parents are old   old people tend to fall through th' cracks

Let's look for metabolic abnormalities
why is he comatose   elevated protein in the spinal fluid
I'm gonna move in here   against regulations
I think it's a good idea

11 February 1990
In the air en route from New York to San Diego

56

Reach announce unprecendented
calibration curve estimate medicine advance
slice   opening microwave penis envy
vortex emote   exaggerate liaison   snarl

Easier fantastic sugar stay
inch mention libration pendulum next
flatterer Catch-22 variety Picayune
visit Rin Tin Tin Boca plush deserved

Dispenser thickness Dixie rinse book dog
clog viticulture country musketeer pagan
glancing fortuitous guarantee
slang dazzle sequence motivation filth

Rabid available public provocation need
dip tailor quick   nugatory proof
sky-high recondition blast morphology
tank other sink French way permit

Pacifist delicatessen noteworthy practical besmirch
ramrod Nestor Osiris castigation mensch
foam buck nettle quirt squint   fox
turkey hovel stamp lax Tanzania

6 March 1990
Buffalo

67

Tablet fantastical Zanuck recreation knit
lizard artifice   magnetic glue port
vigorous endorphin   fix Maserati toast
jitney tipple magazine tamper

oaf enclose mazurka quickie
pea-green barter-clatter focus Mohole
lemma dilemma sycophant switch
league mobility   sapper flank jump

Swamp flagstone pile-happy grig
needle twinge rinkydink vassal package
keeper regal   torrid *Totentanz* slap
call letters swineherd picket mixture

Water folly Nantic lack   rest stop
deprogramming mollify centrism
walnut tree geezer flash rapids
local swans watch train go by

Feature story rock drip clique
Venice pollutant existent
fever evocative mushroom crow bark
nugatory swizzle stick tack march

16 April 1990
Near New London
en route from New York to New London

◆

Selections from 154 Forties

A Note on 154 Forties

Written in New York: 9 October and 25 November 1998; revised
17 January and 10 June 2001; adapted by Anne Tardos

154 Forties was begun on 12 October 1990. I continued writing the po-
ems' first drafts until February 1995, and have often revised them since
then, though most revisions, especially recent ones, have usually been
minor.

Each of the Forties poems is written in the following "fuzzy verse-
form": eight stanzas, each comprising three rather long verse lines fol-
lowed by a very long line (typically occupying more than one typograph-
ical line) and then a short line. What "rather long," "very long," and
"short" mean varies from poem to poem and stanza to stanza. The words,
phrases, etc., in the poems' first drafts were "gathered" from ones seen,
heard, and thought of while I was writing those first drafts, which have
been revised in many ways, lexical and prosodical. When the first drafts
were written in non–English-speaking countries they often include words
and phrases from languages other than English, e.g., French, German, and
Hungarian.

The Forties include several "prosodic devices," including nonortho-
graphic acute accents, two kinds of compound words (often neologistic), and
"caesural spaces." Nonorthographic acute accents indicate stresses (a de-
vice borrowed, of course, from Gerard Manley Hopkins), usually in places
where which syllable should be stressed may be ambiguous. These are at
rare times substituted by underlined italicized letters.

There are two kinds of compound words in the Forties: "normal compounds" and "slowed-down compounds." These are indicated respectively by two kinds of hyphens, unspaced and spaced. Normal compounds, e.g., "feverish–assíst," "métalanguage–wick," and "a-little-ferry-puts-you-up-in-frée," are to be spoken somewhat more rapidly than other words but never hurried. Slowed-down compounds e.g., "ennóblement-barrel," "separátion-perfidy," and "ténantry-parturition," are to be spoken more slowly than other compound words—often with stresses on the main syllable of each member. Some compounds include both kinds, e.g., "color-of-brúise - variations."

"Caesural spaces" indicate silences and/or prolongations of final phonemes or syllables. These spaces are of three principal lengths, 4 letter spaces [ ], indicating a duration of one unstressed syllable; 8 letter spaces [   ], indicating one stressed syllable or beat; and 16 letter spaces [   ], indicating two beats. Other durations of silence or of prolongation of final speech sounds, such as ones denoted by 12 letter spaces [   ], sometimes occur in the Forties.

These prosodic devices are summarized below. A note after each poem tells where and when the poem was written and revised. The devices make for continually changing rhythms, tempi, and rests when the poems are spoken aloud. The poems sometimes seem quasi-metrical and are sometimes reminiscent of what Hopkins called "sprung rhythm," including paeans and other feet of more than three syllables, but the number of beats in different lines of the same general length (rather long, very long, or short) varies greatly.

Caesural spaces = durations of silence and/or prolongations of final phonemes or syllables:
4 letter spaces [ ] = 1 unstressed syllable;
8 letter spaces [   ] = 1 stressed syllable or 1 beat;
12 letter spaces [   ] = 1 stressed and 1 unstressed syllable or 1 ½ beats;
16 letter spaces [   ] = 2 beats.
None occurs between typographical lines. Breath pauses at verse-line endings ad lib.

Nonorthographic acute accents indicate stresses, not vowel qualities. [ë] = sounded final "e." Each hyphenated compound is read as one extended word: somewhat more rapidly than other words but not hurried. A spaced hyphen [-] indicates a slowed-down compound.

Indented typographical lines continue verse lines begun above them.

I remember asking Jackson why he chose the number 154 and not getting a clear answer. Recently I realized that Shakespeare wrote 154 sonnets.—A.T.

Unannounced Slights

(Forties 1)

Unannounced inténtions   creepy aríthmetic
totalized sóarers   zóris   actívity-boosters
nettles originally págeant   gentian Schwártzkopf
denotation-withered-on-the-vine   the sacrosanct
   contínuance   vóucher-tool
déal   sláp   plácket   áttitude-tubes

Devélopment rent   *ecclesia* mégaton storm
votive ingratitude snowballing flóaters   géese
reaching acróss to the   patent-tally-córks
Dáphne-immobilization   wretched frontal tíc-warts   múnch
   increase   cráss
flatulent Raggedy Ánn   téamwork

Fortification   móney-laundering clínker-med
rótifer portion   exigent tennis-mogul-snóop
flapdoodle topiary hóse-center mescaline quóte
région incision   flícker-notebook enclose   móle   tomtít   fascist
   metrical télesis
fanatic   nítpicker cróck

Dépth misfortune active týmpani-lip   strífe
tepid tén   mount   dive-liver gúide-pool
rébus-trigger Mormon correspóndent   Snópes

rōshi-motor dápple-clip   idiosyncratic lóaf   Mali voter Vónnegut-
enticement
lápdog palm   Súnday

Leafy Mélisánde   incentive exit máp-bell
summer   óverload-inclusion   nýmph - rapidity
gléam   Mústapha tack-point crípple-middle
Quártermain uncle unconscious Whitman táp-dance   California-
láptop-frock
demon   melancholy whístle-pork

Jám   pantomime-extension fálse   Róckies - tarp
linguistic Star Trek lapidary scórecard
seasonal Schenectady   fallow mórtgage trait
lábor acrostic   Esquipúlas mónster   knee-jerk enginéering   chánnel-
punk track
sweater neighbor mótion whiz

Position   tóurmaline   like thát   tormént   fláke-mote
up-thére   pórcupine outline   miscue   swéets
dense enténte   forceful market thrúst-mark
remember intént   Cólgate martyr   sanitize lácquer-twaddle matter-of-
fact accóunt
détail dalliance   methylene dóll

Lambkin Roxbury lofty Muscovite whíttle-factor
leap of faíth   illustrious inky-finger Michelín - tree
boastful Bógart abusing the sýstem postulant   no próblem
léaves   dent   pólka-dot tróchee-marsh   mágazine
innocence   eluctable trápshoot toke
glorification dépot-map   slights

In a car, Buffalo–NYC: 12 October 1990; New York: 4–5 July 1993;
26 July 1997; 24 July, 15 September 2001

Libertad Lag

(Forties 4)

Líbertad-liquidity   nóse-cone congratulation-Wíchita
greengrocer naphthalene   indication-Schérmerhorn   táck-speed
lýmph-node arráck   deception fláppy-moat-approach
dissection encroachment   dialogue fallopian Ingres   tirade
    tantamount   latchkey summarize flírt
Bustamentë finitude garáge-part

Logorrhea nést-tote plagiarism flípper-quiet Méx
léase-toad réacher-fashion quírt-moll *pinxit*
dórmer-gable láser-cottage catechism stínt-flick dink
greeting   horrible elapse   farm   whámmy-tackle
    passion   renegade cure   discipline exaction chárge-card
mescalinity rapidly áct-toll

Venus guacamolë   appetite eagle   treé-dweller fólk-art
period rowboat Damoclës   viticulture reason péak-twig
resign   fine   limited attáck-mode mídlife crisis   neck
grillwork camera linguinë fidget-wreck   Stepin-Fetchit-
    dázzle   ínk-blot torporous corrugated tent   temp
distillation clácker-mat excuse

Vanilla   medical romance   languor rinse   gýp-joint
Turteltaubë-flitch   pixie nirvana   Anabaptist-támp
Thatcher fláp-encasement   eject as a Tamil-alley-fáint
Galleani number-ferry coastline   armadíllo-tribe
    Wapiti-ínky-cap   Músgrave-aborigine
decency   give-it-a-whírl   wingtip

Film-buyer-wéekly   offer me a   Tallahassee
bitch   Sac   desecrated mangle tentative ram   phantom
víne-portion locative-alárm-clock Walt   Palatine Borneo ínker-nickel

dráma-bunny funny-félla féature-pig   Tyról Tappan Zée   value
  discréte-mode axle
vegetation portion   Iggy órna-monk

Heater court   sóul-food dámson - factory plánetoid-ilk   nugget
péachy-model gap   tóoth revenge   mule   tipsy-barracúda
femur ample taciturn ímpact   value at áll in a
degree penetration Dealey-Plaza-whéel - animalcule dromedary-
  flámethrower   notátion quiz
leap over the wállet   táckle-tush

Carbonize meridian   idolize idiosýncrasy - swim
fitter'n quince   glyptic *temps*   visual ópe-wicket
misery   dímity-eclipse   exhibition Mátterhorn   tilt
Vinaya acrophobia inténsive   motor-alley-lámpshade   nictitating
  village   ideological-límpet
victory pinch   vapid-Attic-mátchbox

Focal mope   Terwilliger atomizer loosestrife   chimp
banshee value lavatory Vaculator Anasazi béeper
team - spírit revelatory adjacent mention   tepid hipster
croak mortal-ínteger Tháles - statistic   font-on-tap-a-lárk   pomegranate
  itchy Figueróa
leaving-adaptátion   maple taffrail lag

In a United Airlines plane, SF–NYC: 21 October 1990;
New York: 21 January 1992; 17 January 1994; 25 March 1996; 26 July 1997;
8 July 2001

Kandinsky Nature Nacreous Zeke

(Forties 8)

Kandinsky nature nacreous fountain pachyderm
totalizing web-footed cloisonné   fréts
glassy-eyed threats   promulgating tapster
renunciatory petulant gropes   cleats   tansy fortifying garment-district
  tórt
fórtune-whimsy blíster-sieve

Dreadlocks   watchpocket Cheez-Whiz masculinize
gross   Sétebos   debt-node fántasy-grain   *pasque*
gramophone notable chróme-plaster logicide-creep
fantabulátion corner   normalize ease   mix   lapwing groat   forget it
  eclípse-module
néttle-berry rúg-proctologist

Vincent eviscerate exit poll   monarchic lambkill
siege   vortex academic Rome   dolorous záp-toad
Venus's flytrap   check-it-óut accóuntant-tab   Smoot
futurology vertical methadone nautical glib-annexátion
  envisage   whirl   diamond cull
lotus position   tucked-away twínge

Neglected playmobile azure executive núrture-grid
vomitorium Local Group   Panasonic planetary fish
Dixie flagomorph island exactitude Saugatuck wheeze
succotash Asner demonstrable Lorca columnar
  pórcupine-dance   discógraphy-rinse   fáculty-torrent
liberty velvet encyclical glínt-nix

Greeting-paper multiply discovery grill   maniple
formic moxie ASCII varlet tarnish Isocrates cliff-dweller
mortuary cream bun lemur rectitude twist-evacuation

ancillary petite ensconce   Grósstéste   gloom-basket title
  page   green-thumb passenger-pigeon escalation magnet
grappa forbidden   dilapidated masonry clasp
Varnish   grámmar   lavatory píll-mosaic rápids - assessment
feature bleat   vagus-nerve eventuátion-solenoid
pork-barrel Váseline dweeb   Fleet Street   true grít
passe-partóut   Morgan O'Hara   galaxy sapient crést-dome
  evoke   swap   lót-of-it Clámshell Alliance   corm
activate Tanglewood Atabrine tráctor-proxy

Chill bassoon   mutant ectoderm papal accomplish
vatic angst   fraction paddlewheel lifted specific
réaper-margin damnátion extent   Pandora glister créek
benchmark crow   proconsul lábor-fakir zap   drape   péndancy-dash
  encircle laboratory swán-dive melt
gallantry sample-service béach-mode

Zealot veal   Tappan Zee rehéarsal-misery   grabber quartz
lemon-demon áffect   Castiglione ramificátion-swabs
scamper bananaphone Roquefort damage-control Isaiah
medicine vérmin-squeezer lax   chops   territory   terminal-párty-
  pooper clipped insíder-Messiah
goalpost potáto-rug   grávity-whorl   Zéke

New York: 13 March 1991; 29 April 1992; 31 August 1994; 28–29 July 1997

Kalmon Dolgin Bluestone

(Forties 9)

Kalmon Dolgin dead - tired   Trieste bump   troopship
quarter coral-nor'wéster   photo-finish   *Laughter-in-the-Dárk*   néttle
lacy latitude swank   tráp-shut transient   familiar-Drexel-Ávenue
dietary-dichótomy máster - flág   potential nugatory-
      réach   Swiss - gíg   landscape nearness Potsdam-
grotésque   trágedy - whist
glitter-Martiníque   sequence   disaster cape

Rotten Row   flammable incident   triumvirate virtue triúmphant
necessary bird out-of-Páradise   real-nice-clear-ský   laminated zink
[pron. "tsink"]
famous potatoes   Rumford-ill-at-éase   ichthyological dróp-kick
queasy marquís   Logan tonal dróne-pipe-Atari Never-Néver-
      Land   Íncrease Máther   áileron-orgánum   márquetry
vengeance Ausáble   zonal-inclinátion

Roger await   tarpaper cuties   cut out cutups   condígn   móres
values blather insistent-Coney-Ísland   rudimentary séarch-cup
soigné   institútion-gap - reléase   ostracized agates   votive
jam-packed Elgar vaccinátion-quiz   muster stable commúnity waiver
      Lincoln Hospital rabbity lift-off vácancy - core
lamb - stéw   Long-Island-Sóund   varmints

Airfone seated plenty of time   racket   magistrate   Michael Scholnick
coffee smells - good   Grand-Rapids-*Tribúne* acoustic tile alíve-o
Famous   Last   Words   Ruggiero Ricci Nabi inquíetude-resistance
slugger holiday videotape   security risk   beneficial negligence   totally-
      totally-totally-totally-táh-tah-táh   Hawai'i
Rock of Ages   shades of night are falling

Toffee clinic álcohol-cadenza   lýricism - strife megalópia - tank
waterproof ink   Agatha Christie indígnity-chorale   this is it   this is lunch
Dreamboat telephonic anacrusis   medallion codebook dart
Heart of Darkness Slipalong-Catástrophe   phonic gárter-snake   Gödel
    vocative Mínsky   halt activity swéater-roper
That's because I'm a fémale   flápped

Officers-reláxed   after the beating   lost the good mechanical pencil-on-
    the-pláne
just an object   Trafficantë dolor marker Schweitzer blíss-mole
drape-an-aberrátion   notion approach   potion wield   morn
Galápagos Crater Lake miasma leapfrog Lockerbie
    twice   vibraphone   climatology don't shów it much
ragweed pluralism eyebeam glámour-boy

Glee   flée-'em   Krakatoa-Nóah   laggin' behind the gogglers
Dark Encounter coastal-Nefertíti   classical arrhythmia
sweeter fémur escapade   nonce   closure Cármen creep
liter galaxy swíng-vote cadmium paráde   Dallas   metaphysics   Grimáldi
    microcosm shútterbug   Chlóris
glóry-hole stelë inscribed   tact

Clasp   chortle   Dixie-Cup-afár-no-less   dramatization
lip-service-Vítaphone   agriculture gnostic claps   hops
virulent village nostálgia - float   orchid Corinthian lamebrain
gigolo Vonnegut Radziwill Chernobyl   January sób-story local Acushnet
    closure Missouri   lemony góalpost - jar
Dance-a-thon   gallimaufrey-pítch   bluestone

In a cab to La Guardia Airport and Midwest Express DC-10, NYC–Milwaukee: 19 March 1991; New York: 4 May 1992; 31 August–2 September 1994; 23 September 1997; 4 December 1999; 8 July 2001

Rapidity Dreamboat Alive-O

(Forties 20)

Rapídity appetite astrónomy notify   Tapahónso Caligári séed-pump
Delius marvelous academic ritual lárva sapient clímber-trove retreat
gleám-whistle sýrup-atom abracadabra Róme-potion táp-a-classic rúsh
flash   enzyme Mátterhorn   déacon-tinker típple-knot   glass increase
   individious chín-zone   Chippewa vénison tailor-made Dágmar drone
choke-a-haúnt-us Chappaquiddick pórn

Larceny vélar   temporary mescalinear even effectual tínner
zéal molecule   deviant raindrop bárony   Chanticléer   roadhouse
   but ténts
chief-enginéer   plánning-gat-jargon assault   Tosca mosaic concern
Daffy Dúck   calisthenic tacky-Róger sóma-blast   bottoms
   úp   photography facilitate discónsolate   Sénate commutation
   necessárily
creature cómfort Volscian-trepidátion

Jóseph-pony sapodilla partial osculátion   sága treat   mocker *Sórgë*
flophouse Rhode Island telégraphy mention   noble Dijón   cream cheese
   néctar
tangeríne   masculine vaginal-sarcóphagus   zero-degree metabólic
pórcupine volume   róck-sólid whínny-allowance   Sargón-
   equivalence   G-men Vitaphone Dillinger pínup-honey charismatic
   físsion
clabber verácity   vacuolátion manifestigation

Jímbo foam   button   telegraphic leáfy-nut tongue   graduátion-murk
murmuration Volkswagen Dálloway-monotony   champion harúspicate
chímp-model tolerate   jaded-anvil laboratory music-corner Támmy
validation whén   topography-kiss-a-pótentate   trash a vasty
   líp-service misty colon nugatory Nússbaum   vanish-awhile libátion
Gánymede calamity   cheetah-mystic cóalhole

Jésus alarmist   filial consistency derogatory ímp-node-token
chill   míx piscatorial rackety-schismátic   tapestry Colóssus
sip-a-panel tránquil   Vatican *tisáne*   Tárzan - polemic espouse
achievement uxurious tálent excuse   fórk immobility týranny
   deform   Janice   Scorpio Tamaulípas fáctory-magic
géne-medal lapidary Áristotle - bank

Dióne philography Bucknéll irritation   kinesthetic anesthésia-lash
phytoplastic soporific cálamus-saliva   jam-packed heurístic
guilty *megalopsychía*-rogue   chimney sylvan fólk-art mopèd
vinaigrétte   Gallipoli mogul alacrity tackle-a-fórtune-estate   Anna
   Blumë fólly Whig   Casanova fogymonger Dállas oscillation
mánager arousal   gamma-velocity quárk

Féeder-road elastic mosque   desperate aspirate tówel   motivátion-
note
Tóne - Roads   ghóst museum áfflíction-discussion cát   léver
   branch   sóak
jéer   kýrië   léap Cappadocia Veronica Valley-Girl vámpire marsh
practice eviscerate déer - paths   Moscow cokehead dupe monothéism
   clímate arrangement   chortle colostomy vibrant entangle wóod
róck-garden error   Púrcell lárkspur

Squirrel-monastery berries-own-a whimper-omelette glimmer Ra-
   makríshna
glee - club bítter   typical list-awoken tofu-focal Láura-morosity
discotheque ecclesiastic motorcar fallopian-tóll   chíppy-Cameroons
giblet-pickle Zen-malarkey Mallarmé cafe   grief - stricken Chisholm
   Tráil elation   dapper foxy chunk Jorálemon loggerhead Óllie
téam - project   Dreamboat alíve-O

Sunshine Canyon, Boulder County, Colorado: 8 July 1991; New York: 3 February 1992;
2 March 1993; 10–12 July 2001

Almost Casanova Electricity

(Forties 24)

Almost-Casanóva despite the phlebitis with everything élse
too mány   Kalmon Dólgin encrustation flopped miasmic plénty
tired homunculus ápt   diáspora-treadmill   San Antonio péa-pod
reactive palustrian sea-code Wílson   Meso-American nether-roll
   Westport dóg days' expert finicky tríbune   ocular próof
vórtex ban   calamus gangster weígh-station

Democratic whíffletree   negligent bástion corrosive malign   Cróce
nést-coral gáp-phonic greening arrést   challenge ascendant garótte
féalty mangle clinging matúrity   egghead mistáke-claimant
tick anniversary medical whístle   pickle belíef   mixed
   revíews   *Péanuts*   cake-batter clastic corrosive mátter-negativity
gleeful Órono-gleam   timid transpárency

Quassý   meeting astríngency   active kangaróo-rat-stripe
major assístment normal pórk-resistance grove   poll-tax agrée*
clámor   médicament   Palestrína-rattletrap económy move
registration culinary Róto-Rooter barn   song-ferry
   mágistrate   totalism token actívity probe   boatman whet
train back next dáy   involvement muníton

Galánte Coromándel   tam-o'-shanter quick-stop guilty McNúgget
sapodílla mediant   bús-schedule logic   oxymoron tórtoise
choice-paddle glówworm-acquittal mise-en-scène   níctatory
tree   máscot-renovation   mérit badge   neighborly porringer maculate
   Tríanon   barebones amálgam   rámble-pharmaceutical
naturalistic nów   vestal académicism

Pángolin-tribulation Venice aspidístra   party Cáspar pole
bówl-sharp   Lády Day   magnetism mystic-Pógo bít-part-marker
Régency-applaud   áshtray-mesmerism cápstan-accolade

dánce-fog laudatory góal   oriented magical escápement - Janissary
   pocket-whopper bánister-appendectomy
   reléase   moráss   Capistrano-fírecracker

Glámour   búoyancy-alarm-clock-Goliath   Métchnikoff
póol Mariolatry abasement Japán   Newman collápse
glassy clóuds   tacky mendacity quiver estáte-malarkey
vapid Chappaquídick   regional autocracy equivalent nóstrum   patriotic
   formalism   Panasonic-méntal-detector
Gloomy Gus   navvy   Vatican cholésterol

Jónes-mutter Pearl Street tíckertape - environment   ribsteak
chállenge grants   Motorola fórtune-teller cóal-barge newt
Cíbachrome encounter   middlebrow enlístment trailer
Gypsy Rose Lée   water-senate camel-bone anáchronism - mate
   cannibalism-mazúrka   adóption   déspicable-nódule
nominal reágent   maximal phylógeny

Forestátion-euphemism whískey priest   Melánctha-happy Lúther
peakèd Rigadóon   mortuary *Líebestod*   pítchman - antenna
thirty-chanter tánk-attack   Rapid-Transit mátchstick clause
neater Agrícola aspect náscence   tepid euhémerism   dístance -
   neutrálity comb   Pólk   glíster-misogyny chlóroform
messy-chortle gás stage   nappy electrícity

---

*"assistment" is a nonce word.

En route NYC–Vermont in a car: 25 August 1991;
New York: 13–18 June 1993; 14 July 2001

Rendering Rings Absorbed

(Forties 28)

Rendering the shape of éverything in the medium of appéarance
an artist is a person who can do ánything   a magician or sóphist
a póet   turns herself into a tool of her árt   fórms by spéaking
knows how to make anyone-who-understands-a-particular-thíng sound
    góod   play the game of póetry in réal-knówledge of what it's abóut
sérious poets   don't take their writing as últimate

The beaútiful now display their decréptitude   póets don't even know
how-to do what they do córrectly where they claim to be knówledgable
false   forms of morálity   appear beaútiful to the
    crowd   happy bírthday
Charlie Parker   enjambmént   he's-a-nice-gúy   biggest
    dog in human hístory   a good   day-for-the-béach   ice off the
    stíck   legal séafood
CÁT-scan of her whole ábdomen

Thát's a crafty little manéuver   bátteries   you mean e-lec-trícity
in théater a puppetéer   Mrs. Grímes   getting gonorrhéa by taking
    a báth with someone árt repeats what is in reality the hypócrisy of life
he only imitates the óther   while he is not hímself he is not the other
    éither   a splít in the sélf   imitates the other from
    outsíde   accidental géstures
forgetfulness of onesélf   self-exteriorizátion

Even-looking-on   the self-forgetful yielding of onesélf to the vibrátions
of an alien emótion   self-alienátion   critique of the moral cónsequences
of aesthetic cónsciousness   experience of delusory imitátion alréady
the ruination of the sóul   what   form for the song of práise in
    states almost incúrable   one quart lów   open 'er hére
goldenrod-red báseball cap unlátched

Nice place to gó to   róad   nárrows   hóuse for sale   Philip Dávis
building and éxcavating   I don't feel like doing ánything
mússels   musty sáwdust   chícken manure   ammónia
fish   flésh   putréscine   cadáverine   forest ecólogy   akin to a
   próblem   húmus   discússion   freedom of expréssion and relígion
disintegrátion   minority ríghts   olfactory mémories

Maximum gíst   juggle the váriables   góal   frequencies engúlfed
concentrating clerical dáta   sátellite   ócean surface   climatólogy
énergy flux   consults   créosote-soaked   Gréenhouse Effect
altímeter álgae wave-height cráb-scraps   supermarket próduce depart-
   ments   one or two high-density tápes   rádar signals
speed of líght   two-and-a-half méters

Major dífferences   fifteen céntimeters   continúity-snapshot
blúe-greén navy cértainly-not-the-bést   sátellites   Délft   scíentists
oíl-contaminated TNT subtracts   grávity fields   décimeter-level
lasers uránium   bacteria eat   prefer   iron   a job in itsélf   radial
   direction Tappan Híll   compléx   crustal models
eastern Mediterranean   orgánic-matter-now

Biodynámics   recompute-áll-these-posítions   relative-to-each-óther
continuous techníque   independent chemical bínge   precise   área
slowly to the nórth   three-dimensional mótion   plant pathólogy
very simple efféct   borders of what can be dóne   sometimes the moon
   before the sún   immediately see that collective variátions
peat and sand   pótting mixes   rings absórbed

Wilmington, Vermont: 29 August 1991;
New York: 10 October 1991; 13 July 1993; 15–17 July, 7 August 2001

Philosophic Diligence

(Forties 42)

Philosophic monópoly-menopause metrical prómise   irremediable-éffort
fandángo-blast   binational néeding-it rátional fáscist rút   clávichord
noisome income executive-compláint   létterpress-equivalent achíevement
Christmas Lóndon   c'món   exaggerate bargain básement closed-
fáces   doubt-it's-mý-kinda-thíng   ask her about the mechánics
deplorable chlóroform   mediating Pféiffer

Státement-bastinade   classic schlock mortálity-consumer
parallel urólogy   miscreant-notoríety   tomato-juice-excél
dynast   gýmnast   closed-mínds   monstrósity-enclosures
pint   Glaspéll   Nordic imponderabílity-exam   pláster-rodent
    Bérgen-axis   filigree-sóphist respectable
contagious sízzle   esóphagus-firmament

Guarded Kabállah   vanishing retrograde central *dromaîon*
glancing charísma-encounter persíst   phantasmagorical Máhler
cryptic Mánnerist   conventional interpretive lícense-letter
excessively slowly illicit-sexuálity   mátter and fórm   Neoplatonic
    analogies sháred   Cathars innáteness-*potenza*
gastric clássic   Faróul Panasónic

Glowworm trivial látency period   Gnostic Mediáeval
isolated personalistic átmosphere-framework   designátion-dig
investigation Númbers et cetera   King of All Démons consístent
parábola boldness   garish-inconsístency barrelhouse rádishes Métatron
    Countenance able-Abuláfia Víta-Mix-zénith
exegésis-actualization   terraces trávertine

Linear shórtening mention o' nátions   Labor's-Histadrút
institute Fórmalism integral cláims   *Antichristos* súbdivided
Pico-della-Mirandóla Satan aping-mátter   changing indíviduals

abstruse structurálity   blood-and-ink-inclúsion   realm-of-mutabílity
   fortress Tetragrámmaton   válue-correspondence   vapor
Texas ashen fíve   existence   ságe

Túna-mist   aspectual perpléxity encloistered anóinted-one
chariot-divinátion-name   adulterated-intercombinátion-trait
contradíction wrápping us   nonabstracted Active-Intellect
surroundings' defíance-intensity   softly-purring-árchitecture travellers'
   Deptford pink annivérsary-apparition
narrowly severing random assístance

Renege ineluctable píne-saplings' evident-mycólogy
readily vagabond daisy fléabane receiving the súnlight
mossy wooden stéps   five-by-fíves nót-coincidéntal
foundation of the-power-of-the-trúe   red-clóver púrple círcle   request-
   it-by-my-móuth   imaginative apprehénsions
Fused-Deposítion Módeling Process

Férns   móss   wáterfall's-a-tríckle   sláte   límestone
hémlock   béech   bírch   maple alacrity óakleaves
tán   fóod for sáprophytes   líchens' immanent álgae
breakfast-getting-cóld   instabílity   Samsára   *De generatiónë*
   et corruptiónë   coming to bé and passing awáy
Seek your salvátion with díligence

New York: 21 June 1992; Wittenberg, NY: 19–20 July 1992;
New York: 24 October 1994; 26 January 1995; 29 November, 19 December 1997;
29 January 1998; 10, 15 August 2001

Attitudes Narrowly Balance Paper Shadows

(Forties 56)

Áttitudes nárrowly balance ingrátitude's brief encóunters
fánciful incéndiary múltitudes answer resúltant panáche
as dénsity-tribalism's medical insístence biláteral fárcical tántamount to
recent practítioners' flýwheel-ancestral pásture-equilibrium-nóise
   polyactivist lárceny's martial-consístency fár-side
Dahómeyan sáprophyte dámsons

Gálleon-drawbridge conclúsion-musicality zebra-pácifism-ventilation
géstures merit Jánsenism Kíttyhawk-nativity's ragged-beneficial
   cólonies'
cárdboard forgótten bínary méttle-legal béast-coves
roar-orchid órgandy calligraphic-pássengers collápse negating ornate
   enfórcement of quílt-palace gás-attacks by regional-manifestátions
gúest-corrosion gángsters

Boudoir arróyos mórtify existent panópticon-monopoly wínter
Kilimanjaro Méthodism-martyrdoms belie contrasting mágazines
decisive sacro-iliac másk-torrid hónor-guards delight offensive créeks
foreshorten mortal gárter belts Columbian multiple béstiary-carts'
   occlusive venal ámnesties of Caribbean Trappist-fonder Vónnegut
darker Salazár Dacóits

The badger- and dóg-sounds in cosmological bréath-proliferation
manipulate íce-words' final forms of respirátion destroy
to get in the háir a-vital-thing to dó in a surplus of wéather
the special nature of wórd-combinations with some kind of fóreknowl-
   edge hálf-life helpers dispense-with-milítias
compúlsory ótterhound apprénticeships

Weapon-hidden fóod topographical-legend bísque
of artificial-transfers prior endórsers ábsent-headed
magícians' effects on distant pówer-undergrounds

joining together in essences sílence desires clóthing acts-of-fornicátion
   copulation-with February-generating cýclones
míce-makers' stríng-theories

Modified periodic consubstantial deificátion's ranting párapets
launching ecclesiastical dígnity-massification wáivers
lámbify retroactive nodules' unnatural prétenses
climbing Wagner's mélting-pot-excoriating mansions' actívity-
   manumission tigering óligarch-metonymies
rogering Roentgen-súperstructures

Inevitable háppenstance where no Callíope's constraint
can figure concentrated flustering twíce-culminating
cálms moronic sun-soggy ápples applying nothing-fundaméntal
to prearranged propórtions' quiet ámulets settled ín and already góne as
   incómparable bállast
under babbled-over lócust storms

Direct-as-possible páths with clóthes-on sorely test resílience
as wórds emerge on the silver scréen with nó-voice-at-áll
and murky óranges-cut-away doggy séntences full-blást
where recondite cólor-performers at-the-edge-of-áction explode the wíll
   in a quicksand of próperty-space
líned with páper shádows

New York: 3 November 1992; 30 January 1993; Providence: 8–10 November 1994;
New York: 18 October 1997; 9 January, 22 October 1998; 10, 23, 27 August 2001

Twirlwater Fantasy Rock-Solid Instances

(Forties 81)

Twirlwater fantasy rock-solid knowledge-portion diacritic
summary gnarling-water bubble-pattern pass'n'flow enigma
nothing-whetted mass-pull-massness settling farther-onwardness
alluvial fluidity-ramble passingly lapidary moss-feeder fortune-driver
   slippingly insinuating ripple-skittering
foam-pattern nuzzling anewness

Buffeting buffering circumperipheal toad-pedestal sluice margin
taking the tiny ones down with it over and under and farther
swoggle-gurgling burble-clumber unpurposively fumble-faring
pouring-spreading laminations ceding place unceasingly till winter stills
   th' down-dance of the molecules
strengthen-clenching crystal-clumping links

Skylook Strawberry yearning-trying to eat Coo-Coo's cat food
Simone turning her compost invisible in earshot near and here
a white-pánel-truck passing and on up the hill a breeze from the north
   in the far trees
black Tombo pen leaking near the nib Annie spreadeagled on the grass
   resting from sweeping the room we've been living in out after we
put away the bedding

Blinding window-sunglint from Steve's white car another roll of film
and some cranberry drink from the overpriced East Charleston Country
   Store
some question marks are better put in than left out cool in the shade
hot on the grass in the sun gathering-mínt-leaves for lemonade in
   midline thirty-five months go by contingency reigns and well it may
what does finish a poem mean

Refuse to focus on it sonic is semantic
uncouple the hemispheres or reconnect them
where one is isn't all of who one is
a cracking façade is a wall until it isn't the hemispheres unify or they don't
a brain is a terrible thing to waste

Thunder rolls incessantly in the southern sky
the city sounds bombarded from the south
and how can anyone be sure it isn't
this is the way the world ends with many a bang and a whimper
why flatter humankind

Would cummings be hissed today for saying manunkind
the false sense of certainty coming from sharing convictions
Groupthink taketh away the marbles hideth not-showeth
all works he says have this thingly character what would they be
    without out it what would art or artist be without them
pain has turned the threshold to stone

Unforgettingness let be anagrammatical denial
pursuit unrelenting prolonged at the usual behest
drama-baby Switzerland unsalted Taliesin's spring
Roaratorio evidence fenced around with headline-grabbing solitude
    enmeshes vitalism-plasmas
roughened bilateral instances

Madbrook Farm, East Charleston, Vermont: 29–30 August 1993; New York:
27–31 July 1995

Dracula Felicity

(Forties 91)

Dracula parturition   mental exaggeration   trisector planet
groper determining latest magnifico   subtle bituminous statue
truism politics   Desmond Pacific gastronomy blackamoor metempsychosis
supplanted erroneous mescaline ketchup bilingual masterly
   asteroid blanket   potáto-pancake Zoroaster
   nakedness   Stalinist   primrose   Rastafarian torn
sacerdotal táper-packer ráin-check

Zap Palestrina cholesterol lavish   pizzázz   Alabáma-denotation
rage California pandandy penumbra ballistic   twísty-maturation
negligence minister   sáfety-pin tíme-clock roster   particolored alabaster
muses clue   group-meditátion-position exténsion-toss   plénitude
   blur   gratefully zéro-finish   classical-sarcastic-sapodílla delightful
mýrtle-porker instant Boguslavski

Chain of command   Bandaid deluxe   Frénch-fries don't survive a níght
stake through the heart at a sacrifice   magical logic aristocrat
   mágazine-toad
don't correspondingly tóker-dissection   tosspot prognosticate lyrical
   liberty
brístol-board Dinkins alacrity definite penitent worsted   bí-fócal
   Locrian tóaster mazurka delicious hostility   tám-o'-shanter
dutifully Blackstone *passánt*

Baby *touché* Kansas-Cíty a púzzle   deliberate plénitude-garbage
neat phosphorescent decísion-exclamation   derisive malignant expórter
banána-indignation *presidio* necktie draper intention mellifluous lozenge
somerset daiquiri laboratory físhing-boat-enclosure   heuristic declíne-
   note Tónë pigeon-píe   glass macaroni phlogiston enamored Cycladic
   pastél
lámb's-wool locative portion

Transportátion-academy-donkey maybe   piláster terrific
notation pandemic   rándomness - quota misogyny blasphemy bírd-dog
literature whiskey   Delancey encounter Los Angeles wáter - colostomy
stomach recovery effortless Lúcas - sequence   stowed under fréight-
    trains náture - worship   dreadfully anticipatory saturation
Nesselrode minicycle discotheque

Sloppy-charismátic examining glucose   phylogeny follows expórter
marginal lowercase sectional malady masculine líme-tree móuntain - glue
neighborhood drastic dráma - desk   coúnterweight-existence   limitless
    Píco-derivative
xenophobe bálancing - act   factual mátter-crew lemony district
    clocker   Saturday Chína-medic   rackety mámba - exoticist   plywood
    wríter's - block
correction assistance asepsis

Tíme-travel medical March anaclític   Detroit portulaca demonstrative
    quote
goat-sorta-ríverlike   Czarism gleefully bogus disquietude noisily system
class - sonámbulist   metonymic six assignátions   derogative
    pároxysm-lampshade
entrapment   crácker-barrel lottery polemical encirclement exhaustion
    drawbridge   limitless - agriculture   narwhal lódger-optic rotogravúre
solemn terrestrial mácrocosm-whet

Diaper engrossing Jurassic correction   never apparent Arizona
góld-digger chórus-line   demitasse allówance-motor granted employment
important Saskatchewan sybarite hístory-collectedness   Sonoma barrétte
varsity cáckle-pack lizard timocracy   merit-a-lemonáde   look awáy a
    minute and it áll turns red   Kasper no Socrates lavish beleaguer
rabbity stewpot felicity.

Los Angeles International Airport and en route Los Angeles to New York: 8 November
1993; Bard College, Annandale-on-Hudson, New York: 14–18 June 1994; New York: 10
February, 2 June 1997; 16 February 1998

Finding Your Own Name

(Forties 154)

Finding your own   level of héll   with cultural signifiers-glowing-in-the-
    lámplight
giving a safe   suntan both opáque and transpárent-in-a stárted pícture-
    of-your-fírst   bánd
in a híp commúnity-where-áll will be one - foréver-in-a whóle new cán
better-than-a-dog with a túrnip-and-a bée in the building collecting
    money-for-the-French - overcapacitátion-of-a-secret stár on a favorite
    yacht on a ledgelike evening
telling your stories through me

Showing-mé to mé   emptying texture from things-from-which-I-
    regularly-gó
as it clings to a lóng-wooden-táble   tagging someone to spéak-below-
    the-súrface
with two more eyes along its flank as-lócal-as-a-memorial - remémbrance
overjoyed and meaningless as-the-sort-of-political-process I try to shrug
    óff   foreshadowed-in-a-book of mémories   it came through the door
    that was found
in the sky   moving-acróss-itself

Delayed by an-impróperly-drawn-cóntract inscribed on a falling tree
a free-lance composer loves móst   to-be-writing-as-he-spéaks to-make-
    a-living
difficult to see - any-resúlts   to-talk-about-lífe - próblems   to be
    free   he released
a work for chorus one-hour-lóng and one for sólo voice to find - tíme to
    bréathe   tén - páges a dáy to keep up the pace   one minúte a
    day   two or three hours to copy
two or three seconds of music

To concretize that thinking with nón - Wéstern elements   nót the reason
dimensions of time and space   a little at first in numerous currents of time

now the single unrelenting-units-of-our-líves in ábsolute time   but
    óther   courses of time
defy   measurement-by-digitalized-únits   always shifting   don't-have-
    any-room-to-compláin every-minute-of-the-dáy caught up in grand ópera
Japanése musical groups   don't have conductors

Each with a time of their own   they produce their beat-by-interáction
of different tíme-frames   time-spáce difference breaking down
they-interséct-each-other unlike the gardens-of-Versáilles
meant to be wálked-through and seen-from-different-víewpoints   they mu-
    tually reinfórce-one-another   spring   summer   autumn and wínter
Japanése   gardens are the-sun-and-the-móon togéther

The not-twó-entity   the spáce here óne - overall-strúcture
concretely bound-togéther   spring's direction is east   its pitch is G
    natural
rereading-them-in-a-módern cóntext   getting-lóst in today's   society
not simply relics-of-the-pást   reintegrated-in-the-fúture   strongly
    pulled toward Wéstern things   how-can-that-be-só?
assimilating Western rational thinking

Shine the Light Internátional   .   the best of the West and the East
    together
the reception after the concert   the theories   the experiences   the caréers
dréad   doesn't-seem-to-have-múch-to-dó-with-it   just
    surprised   not very large
lots of electrical óutlets   nóne of this is part of our start to restóre
    it   I'm sórry about it   we each have our níche and are própped-
    in-it   at a wonderful móment
deep-appreciation-of-the-Ásia Society

Twó   páckages-like-Chrístmas presents   Martin-Luther-Kíng   the
    Pówer - Structure
Panther   a wéekend - house   the-Fóur - Séasons   a hillock of
    stone   in-the-sáme - bréath
swatting-out-mosquítoes   luck or hábit   the ending fire a

    rainbow   the scenery
encased in the clouds with the birds in-the-middle-dístance a cóal-stove
    existence that-escápes   yéars-after-we're-góne just-a-little-bit-
    sentiméntal-in-Gérman
beside a lake without a náme

New York: 18–25 February 1995; 11–15 September 1997; 29 March 2001

Flaming Held Fast

(Forties 100)

Flaming air   sleeveless and charmless   broken on Tertiary rocks
common   ámphora known too soon prophetic excused   drivel
primeval   búllet-proof máke-believe vest   burning on the Plasticine rug
spíndle-fly losing   pearly-gólden appetite extending to humdrum
    singing   streets' antagonistic eaves
installed   triangular clubs

Tick-tock mud in the wilderness ruin   cast into additive fever
amorphous strophes of rock unclasped by thankful articulate seams
silvery wildness ungathered across the throat's conundrum example
expected arms   present in lesions   swelling in kerosene pictures falling
    from nails   clustered in riotous poetry never infused with ecstacy
bubbles surmised by plumes

Debris   leaking-serendípity   polishing stainless steel revisions
weeping caldrons of filigreed ash   mediated by mirth   spilled out
    at home
vertigo mimosa twisted by fate in a slavish   future crawl
repressive semantic decaying in laminated songs'   logical dráwing-
    rooms   manacled manual waters of photography
partial cellar moons

In 1996, the French translation collective Un bureau sur l'Atlantique, led by
Emmanuel Hocquard and Juliette Valéry, invited Jackson to Royaumont to
collaborate in the translation of some of his work into French. Five of the Forties
were translated there and later published under the title *Les Quarantains (Extraits)*.
One of these translations, "Flaming Held Fast" (Forties 100), is presented here in
bilingual format. —A. T.

Flambant tenus serrés

(Quarantain 100)

Flambant l'air   sans manches sans charmes   brisé sur rochers du
  Tertiaire
commune amphore connue trop tôt   prophétique radotage excusé
primitif gilet pare-balle-pour-rire   brûlant sur tapis de pâte à modeler
mouche-fuseau perdant   appétit d'or nacré   jusqu'aux avant-toits
  antagonistes   des rues chantantes monotones
en place   matraques triangulaires

Boue tic-tac dans ruine du désert   jetée dans la fièvre additive
strophes amorphes de rocher   non liées par coutures loquaces recon-
  naissantes
fougue argentée répandue   à travers la gorge exemple-devinette
bras attendus présents dans les lésions   gonflent dans les images-
  kérosène tombées des clous   amassés en poésie tapageuse   jamais
  imprégnée d'extase
bulles présumées par plumes

Débris   fuites d'heureux hasards   polissant des révisions d'inox
chaudrons en pleurs de cendres filigranées   médiatisation-
  gaité   déversée chez soi
vertige-mimosa tordu par le destin   dans la servile reptation du futur
sémantique répressive pourrissant dans les salons logiques des chants
  stratifiés   eaux manuelles menottées de la photographie
lunes partielles de cave

Parallel delusive accrual of pleasing   acrobats' sinecure gloves
impaled on a mast at an informátion-marriage of criminal armies
discovery parcel of slow liberation through napes' algorithmic
    embodiments
another way-thróugh by Brixton breadboards' telephone
    gardens   modulating bone erosion fingers' piano delusions painting
    blue a twó-wire span
straps relativity orangutan

Insulation walkways' all-but-tótal darkness's mercantile stunts
monolithic lifelines' history of joy's coordinated colors
novelty poverty's múscle-parallelogram of charcoal   watermelon
remembering innocence   stopped-to-be-idéntified   freezes intensity's
    aerial crimping's ambiguous móvement-orientation
vertical instrument distance

Facture clowns'   petrol draín-control rattles-hypochóndriacs'
narcissist observances of meditátion-lozenges and weightless apparitions
gingerly fitted to tannic surroundings by fictional breath
machine derailment stopping biology animals pained by paralysis
    touchdowns sibship fits' invidious trash
undertrap bucket taxation

Twó-voiced huckaback pastoral questions blocking personality
Hereford meadow destruction numbered in functional riddles
amber dismembered scrawls of contentious swells   péll-méll
travesty wheat   pinned by irreverent foxy presumption ten   gilded
    bovines lost in rainwood   beaten
journeys'   sanctified sanctions

Parallèle illusoire cumul   des gants-sinécures de plaisants acrobates
empalés sur un mât aux noces-information   des armées criminelles
colis-découverte-à-libération-lente   par incarnations algorithmiques
   des nuques
autre accès par les jardins-téléphones   des planches-à-pain de
   Brixton   modulant les hallucinations-piano   doigts d'érosion des
   os   peignant en bleu la portée de deux câbles
sangle relativité orang-outang

Acrobaties marchandes le noir tout sauf total   des passerelles d'isolation
couleurs assorties de l'histoire de la joie   des lignes de vie
   monolithiques
muscle-parallélogramme en charbon de la pauvreté-
   nouveauté   pastèque se rappelant l'innocence   arrêt-identité   fige
   l'orientation ambiguë du mouvement-froissage d'intensité dans l'air
distance d'instrument vertical

Clowns de la facture   leur contrôle au pétrole du drainage   agace les
   hypocondriaques
dans leurs observances narcissiques   des pastilles de méditation et
   apparitions sans poids
soigneusement ajustées à l'entourage tannique   par le souffle fictif
déraillement de machine   stoppe les bêtes de biologie   touchées au but
   par la paralysie accès de fratrisme   ordure abjecte
catapiège   baquet   taxation

Questions pastorales à-deux-voix-nids-d'abeilles   bloquant la personnalité
prairies d'Hereford   leur destruction   codée en chiffres fonctionnels
gribouillis ambre démembrés de dandys agressifs   pêle-mêle
graine de parodie   épinglée par présomption rusée
   irrévérente   dix   bovins dorés perdus au bois de pluie   battus
sanctions sanctifiées   des voyages

Plasticized ontology denuded by tobogganless novocaine wrapping
sanity cretins'   simmering corruption of síngle-code participants
lamas in a field of néw-bred urns inverted by temerity
wasted events restricted by oíl-laden fleecy effervescence's irrelevant
   status   destroyed by quarks   tastelessly ashen
in punctual anguish held-fást

Caesural spaces = durations of silence and / or prolongations of final phonemes or syllables: 4 letter spaces [   ] = duration 1 unstressed syllable.

   Nonorthographic acute accents indicate stresses, not vowel qualities. Each hyphenated compound is read as one extended word: somewhat more rapidly than other words but not hurried. [-] indicates a slowed up compound. Indented typographical lines continue verse lines begun above them.

New York (Ear Inn & St. Mark's [Lauterbach & Fisher] & at home): 11–18 December 1993

Onotologie plastifiée   mise à nu par emballage de novocaïne sans
  toboggan
corruption mijotée   de participants à code unique   des crétins de la
  sanité
lamas dans le champ d'une   nouvelle portée d'urnes   renversées
  par bravade
événements gâchés   par le statut restrictif incongru d'effervescence
  floconneuse   chargée d'huile détruits par quarks   cendreux et sans
  goût
dans l'angoisse ponctuelle   tenus serrés

Silences et/ou prolongations: 3 espaces [   ] = 1 syllable courte; 6 espaces [   ] = 1
syllable longus ou 1 temps; 12 espaces [   ] = 2 syllabes longues ou 2 temps.
  *Les accents aigus non-orthographiques sonts à lire comme des accents toniques
(infléchissant les syllabes, pas les voyelles). Les trémas sur les e finaux indiquent
qu'ils ne sont pas muets. Les mots composés (à trait-d'union) sont à lire un peu plus
vite que les autres, mais sans précipitation. Le retrait en début de ligne signifie la
continuation du vers précédent. Pauses* ad lib *à la coupe des vers.*

New York, 11–18 décembre 1993

◆

Staley Mori Parkins

1

Harbor edge needle stage
existent *maître* swift illogic
tolerant crystal torus clinch
magazine metronome tablespoon August
chomp facsimile bittersweet mosque
Cratylus dynamite saturnine neck
feed molybdenum penetrate farce
chocolate hydrangea national steak
checkerboard butterfly genii swatch
charity philogeny trapdoor hives
cheesecake Nature glyph metaphysics
bun degaussing feature *nettoyage*
goalie zebra bachelor chloroform
mortally gyroscope fan-tan critter
glimpsing drawstring china-marker gloss
candied doll-clothes Pathmark creek
femur bloat encroachment mount
organdy microscope danceable glitch
myth accidental taxidermy whiz
chiliastic Dante Texaco groupie

2

Thoroughly orchard twist eliminate focus
dog-days exchequer roaring mineral cheese
cleaver medicine grouper entwine between
coral whiskey decency paregoric mezzanine
glassy foul-up boardroom minnesinger poll
versify Pandora malarkey janissary clock
episode mossy corollary manifest happenstance
glister chintz anatomical binary *cloche*

champion Dixie-cup copper derision cue
literary mazurka fortify soccer-team drizzle
Cheapside genesis Egyptian trireme Manx
gold-buttoned calico cortisone Naxalite meant
fiddle sacerdotal tyranny Melanctha choice
destiny twine-ball logicism federal eject
galley taxi-stand vital-signs juridical mouse
mere entomology hologram mixolydian *chaise*
gentle mahogany versatile timbre elastic
fox majestic tentpole glycerine nexus
challenge moxie octopus peddler grasp
bottle-top vine-soak calumny banister streak
Venus embroider savagery matchstick swirl
demonry battleship finance metal palaver
greenery Juliet choruses padlock quote
ghostly Vidal execution nutrient coal

3

Dealey femur stroke-mart
tally asinine maturation
glory meetinghouse tampon
feelie twitch appendectomy
Lily dream-landscape parturition
Celli dividend metaloscope
vinyl chieftain melodeon
clearly midstream settlement
jolly acronym fatuous
sweetly Milquetoast dinnerbell
gleamy beachcomber larceny
steely leapfrog metonymy
chilly colostomy menagerie
filly Marxism Labrador
smell doorstop exhaust-pipe
Charlie gladsome enactment

holy guardroom encrust
wily coriander espadrille
winy balustrade deliberate
Tony motorcar parasitic
lorry calisthenic meteor

4

Famine gloat mezzanine collophon Bertram taste
gammon barter Tetrazini penchant clearing folly
trustful mortally Montenegro ball pontoon cure
amity casting killjoy struggle ensconce swallow
vanity Arvin nettle laboratory lexical squeeze
dromedary rabble-rouser cheap coxcomb letter Spade
gold-standard Jeep Alabama nautical vast Atari
depth-bomb votary creep Panasonic quash insist
veal alive Tanagra newstand apricot grotto
clocks Augustan oxygen needlepoint battleship void
chimes basketry court encounter chortle wake
chanter clarify massacre dilatory folk impassion
Epsom Tennessee dweeb sublimity caution strap
Patchen cliff-dweller creed abound *escalier* dream
sweeping Cleveland keep estrange Manitoba broom
clue grosbeak tweak remainder guilty smart
choral mast ukelele Dusa fox Mediterranean boots
cuticle tam-o'-shanter glue reprieve epitome blues
gyrate gallop partition *camino* Boston Clorox
damson puddle egregious fester calumniate pasture
Gamron giant discussion chopstick keelhaul dork
Camptown chiliastic mescal deride potato flask

Improvised by Jackson Mac Low during a concert at Roulette of improvisations
by Jim Staley, Ikue Mori, and Zeena Parkins.

New York: 15 March 1995

Sleepy Poetry

for John Keats and his lexical root morphemes

More far than beyond,
Fresher wings can be wondrous things
That breathe about us as we go
Our agreed-upon cool rounds,
Smiling at each other's agonies.

The streamy steeds
Still murmur at their íll-fated charges.

Our fright has musical arms:
Our great   friend's   head
Is feeding space's ever-jaunty thorns
From round mere lóvers' noughts.

Imagination shall for the poet be shade
(Over and off).

That thirsty spánning man
is toil's   precious   faller,   parting the chariots
When blushingly all thus friendly couch.

Trust your leaping fingers
Though thinking sufferance mighty.

Outspread,   sleepless Cordelia's
Closer to happy morning after all,
And shares it.

Sweet worldliness
Shapes and wreathes us
When the heart's   framer is seen.

That maker felt her native mountaintop was near
And so came round in the woods,
Playing in the recesses
Of mighty farewelling oaks.

Music's intent is strong
And so   sways   the stranger.
And still it rolls,
Whining through a thousand uptorn dwellings in those hills,
Sepulchral and foolish.

The likeness of conscience,
But mightier
And lovelier,
It reaches four white crosses
Through heaps of leaves
That other dabblers left there,
Thinking of delights
The gracious poppy swells.

Can wings of murmuring visions of a father echo líghtbuds
Between the stranger denizens of sunbeams?

Can strawberries' fresher cragginess
Round out those murmured laughters,
Some severe, some muffled,
When lovely wings,   freely flying   forward sense?

Could present glories of mighty handicraftsmen
Disturb the slumbers of young fawns
Forgetting to rejoice there on the sward
Despite their ripened knees?

Not spoken-of in the light,
Can some Daedalian knees have widenesses
Unsaying the paths I think can borrow doves?

Many senses   many days
Keep holding their thoughts,
One of them sleepless.

What glance of glory from thy mountaintops
Could share the wondrous die
That backs thine air and sunbeams,
Keeping the shade in the woods?

New York: 2–4 January 2001

MAKINGWAYNOTE:

SOURCE: John Keats's poem "Sleep and Poetry."

Seed: A text made up of six typographical lines selected improvisatorally at random
from a text produced by removing line and strophe breaks from the source text.
These lines, separated from each other in the source text, are contiguous in the
seed text. They were separated from each other in the source text and did not
necessarily appear in it in their order in the seed text.

METHOD: After removing line and strophe breaks from the poem, I sent the resultant
text, along with the seed text, through DIASTEX5, the 1994 update of a program
by Prof. Charles O. Hartman of Connecticut College, New London. This program
automates one of my "diastic" methods of reading-through text selection (devised
and first employed in 1963), which selects words from the source text by reading
through the source and successively finding words in which the successive letters
of the seed occupy their positions in the seed. I freely composed the poem from
words that are near each other in the diastic program's output. I kept the root
morphemes of all of the source's lexical words (nouns, verbs, adjectives, and
adverbs) but often changed their affixes, and I often changed, added, or deleted
"helping words" (articles, prepositions, pronouns, auxiliary verbs, etc.), though
I brought many of them into the poem from the diastic text. As I composed the
poem, I introduced line and strophe breaks as well as occasional acute accents
(indicating stresses), enlarged word spaces (indicating short pauses, often
caesural), hyphens (short [-] or long [-], indicating rapid or slowed-up compound
words (hyphemes), and occasional compounds without hyphens (solidemes).
Though the diastic output retains the poem's capital letters, I freely changed
them to lowercase letters or retained them.

FORM: Sixty-one lines of "free verse," divided as I wrote them into 18 strophes
comprising varying numbers of verse lines. Each strophe comprises a single
sentence.

Selections from the Stein Poems

Introduction
by Anne Tardos

Jackson wrote the Stein poems between 1998 and 2003, overlapping to some extent with the final revisions of the Forties. Each Stein poem is so richly endowed with extensive "makingway endnotes" that I need not elaborate on the process.

In 2000, when submitting some of the Stein poems to a magazine, Jackson wrote in his cover letter: "Nowadays I only use chance operations at times as auxiliaries. The methods I've used since 1960 are actually deterministic rather than chance operations in that if one uses them in the same way with the same sources and seeds they will always produce the same outputs. I used no procedures in writing my last series, '154 Forties,' which were completely a result of mostly liminal 'gathering' of words and/or phrases that came to mind, or were heard or seen, while writing the first drafts (1990–c. 1995), and which were revised over a long period of time (—some even now). I returned to using a deterministic procedure in April 1998, when I began writing the poems in the Stein series, but now I always, to some extent, modify the results of the procedure, making personal decisions of many different kinds. My writingways came together."

Little Beginning

(Stein 1)

Little lingering father little regular simple.

Little long length there louder happening deepening.
Beginning and little way singing neat cooked.
Difference certain length time light much lighting.
Description certain choosing is the piece.
Pleasant the deranged rhubarb pudding permitted stay.
Sit sing laugh soiling not lingering sing.
Singing difference conclude long so to mention.
Length is stay sit sing laugh soiling beginning.
Singing and any and which the way singing has higher.
Is material long very fried the pears when abuse.
And say filled makes afternoon with children there.
It is.

That the preceder whole that room whole lingering pleasant pressure.
The whispering necessity pressure whispering conclude.
Of the bread there little pieces often better peculiar.
Any people and this the beer time and the light words.
The soiling preceder which comes so simple necessity.
Necessity there the way there way say stay sit sing.

Laugh soiling beginning singing was description.

We that still figs whispering blanket regular conviction.
Whispering whispering and surely cooked there.
Then that bread all pears when thickness people dearest.
It is no conviction.

Biting sample longer refusal seat beginning regular surely.
Pleasant pressure is every there and every the.
Seat the preceder and more lighting and not so and not.

More not more green no deranged pears better no to not.
All in any makes here time noise well that does that.
Light likely.
Biting seat.
Little little.

Little little long length there louder happening deepening.

Beginning.

Derived from a page (and preceding line) of Gertrude Stein's "A Long Gay Book" (*A Stein Reader,* edited by Ulla E. Dydo [Evanston, IL: Northwestern University Press, 1993], last line of 240 thru 241—determined by a logarithm table) via Charles O. Hartman's program DIASTEX5, his latest automation of one of my diastic procedures developed in 1963, using the 1st paragraph of the source as seed, and subsequent editing: some excisions of words, changes of word order within lines; and changes and additions of capitals, periods, and spaces.

New York: 27–28 April 1998

And Sing More Very Loudly

(Stein 11)

for Anne Tardos

And sing more than Father and more food's mutton and always.

Mentioning more to say more louder follow necessity.

Always and long like the eaten very loudly follow necessity.

Derived from a page (and preceding line) of Gertrude Stein's "A Long Gay Book" (*A Stein Reader*, edited by Ulla E. Dydo, last line of 240 thru 241 determined by pointing blindly to "241" in a logarithm table) by running the passage through Charles O. Hartman's program DIASTEX5, his 1994 digital version of one of my diastic text-selection methods developed in 1963, using the name "Anne Tardos" as the "seed" text, and by minimal subsequent editing including changes of word order, tense, and suffixes within lines and the insertion of capital letters, periods, spaces, and one final "s."

New York: 11 May 1998; 17 January, 27 May 1999

Use and Choose

(Stein 12)

for Ulla E. Dydo

Use

all
all breadth
enough
days

hymn and choose.

Derived from a page (and preceding line) of Gertrude Stein's "A Long Gay Book" (*A Stein Reader,* edited by Ulla E. Dydo, last line of 240 through 241, determined by a logarithm table) via Charles O. Hartman's program DIASTEX5, his latest automation of one of my diastic text selection procedures developed in 1963, using the name "Ulla E. Dydo" as seed, and by minimal subsequent editing: addition of a capital letter, a period, an "s," and line breaks.

New York: 11 May 1998

Green Completers So

(Stein 13)

for Gertrude Stein

Green peas surely that description concludes obliged completers.

So it's the asking that begins giving by beginning more
little descriptions.

Conclude obliged completers so.

Derived from a page (and preceding line) of Gertrude Stein's "A Long Gay Book" (*A Stein Reader,* edited by Ulla E. Dydo, last line of 240 through 241, determined by a logarithm table) via Charles O. Hartman's program DIASTEX5, his latest automation of one of my diastic procedures developed in 1963, using the name "Gertrude Stein" as seed, and by minimal subsequent editing: addition of capital letters and periods and a few structure words and suffixes, and thus a few tense changes.

New York: 11–12 May 1998

And One That Clear

(Stein 15)

for Anne Tardos, Ulla E. Dydo, and Gertrude Stein

and one

                                        going were working that clear

---

The 3 lines of this poem were determined by running Gertrude Stein's "Picasso"
(*A Stein Reader,* edited by Ulla E. Dydo, 142–43), which begins on a page deter-
mined by permuting a number drawn from a logarithm table, through DIASTEX5—
a program by Charles O. Hartman automating one of my diastic text-selection
procedures—using in turn the names Anne Tardos, Ulla E. Dydo, and Gertrude
Stein as seeds. In the case of each seed name, I accepted the program's being
stopped by a "mismatch" (not finding one or more letters of a seed text in positions
corresponding to those they occupy in the seed word). In the case of "Ulla E. Dydo,"
there were no "matches" whatsoever, so there is a silent line in the middle of the
poem. The placement of the 3 lines and the five-line space, indicating that the 2nd
line is silent, were chosen.

New York: 30 May 1998

Time That Something Something

(Stein 18)

That
      being

This,

One and one is is,

      The.

There everybody's one
and sees
being seen being,
been using,
            did,
was.

Anne's successful,
      hearing hearing,
feeling they.

They said
            those of and
are is,
            is to thing one
of and.

They're that thing,
  friendly,   ,
    been quickly laughing,
      laughing sounding is
  and

Being regularly,

Talking seeing expressing,
         discovering something,
    something
  happening.

It and did was long successful hearing,
hearing feeling he was,
  have again coming,
saying meant he that meant meaning
  walking,
    talking,
      talking that

This existing one,
  one preparing is,
    is one and everything badly.

He all motion,
noise,
wherever something,
something happening,

It and

That,

That being being quickly laughing,
        laughing sounding talking
    showing imitating existing one,
and then

If is one one,
        one to the thing,
then quickly laughing laughing,
        sounding is and disappearing,
waiting,
        continuing,
                discovering lacking motion,

staying
had saying,
living
        coming often
having might,
                        he that thing convincing
        convincing hearing they what?

This this.

One and one is is,
        one one's seeing be were,
                all asking leave received,
        expecting something,
expecting is and difficult easy
        kindly which,
walking talking,
                talking happening easily,

Waving saying saying saying meeting,
being leaving being staying
　　　beginning hearing they what?

This thís.

One,
　　　and one is,
is one,
　　　　　one seeing dead,
came,
　　　　　gone successful hearing,
　　　hearing feeling they.

They said those of
　　　and are
is,

　　　is one anything,
when thing then
　　　then that anything one enjoying one that they being
　　　　　says one
　　　　　　　and they is is open,
and when be be
　　　　　　quickly being thing is
and

Being regularly,
quietly,
been going one,
　　　　　one,
　　　one was then who is,

is,

        did was long successful hearing hearing feeling
they.

They said those of and are
       is,
is one anything they be,
         be said when
    thing one,
        one one tell then doing
says one and they is,
    is open
and when be be quickly being thing
      is

        and
Being regularly quietly been going one,
one,
        one to the thing,

This
One and one,
        is ís then there,
everybody one
        and seen
being seen being,
   been.

Using did,
       was

Anne successful?

Hearing,
  hearing feeling,
 they,

They said,
  those of and are is,
  is to things one,
one of,
  and they that thing
  friendly,
been quickly laughing,
    laughing sounding
    is
  and

Being
  regularly

Talking,
  seeing,
    expressing,
discovering something something.

Derived from a passage in Gertrude Stein's "A Long Gay Book" (*A Stein Reader*, edited by Ulla E. Dydo, 214–18) by running it through DIASTEX5, a program written in 1994 by Charles O. Hartman which automates one of my diastic reading-through text-selection methods developed in 1963. This diastic program, like its non-digital predecessor, functions via an algorithm that draws words from a source text by "spelling out" a "seed text" with words having the seed's letters in places corresponding to those they occupy in the source text. (Diastic methods are "non-intentional" but "deterministic" rather than "chance-operational" since whenever they are utilized correctly with the same source and seed texts, they will always produce the same outputs, whereas the outputs of chance operations will always be different from one another.) The seed in this case was the first paragraph of a passage from "Orta or One Dancing," Stein's portrait of Isadora Duncan. The passage begins on *ASR* 123 and ends on 124. The numbers 214 and 124 were found by permuting 241, a number determined by opening at random a book of math tables that I used in high school and adopting the three-digit number in the upper left corner of the logarithm table on the left-hand page. Intuitive choice extended the source passage from the top of 214 to the bottom of 218. Editing was limited to insertions of intuitively determined line and strophe breaks, punctuation marks, indentations, and a few apostrophes. Rules adopted for this poem placed single-line spaces before capitals within strophes, end marks at the ends of strophes, and two-line spaces after periods. The program's output was unchanged as to words (except those with added apostrophes), word order, and capitalization (except for the first "T").

New York: 2–7 June 1998; endnote revised 15 January 2002

Pleasant to Be Repeating Very Little of This
(Stein 32)

Pleasant to be repeating what they went to.

~

Each one is saying
that that did happen.
It is charming that merriment differently.
Sample pressure comes and an *and* sings.

~

Enough of them were repeatedly turning. What
did Antliss intend to be looking for?
Living
not showing length
is breadth
and breadth is one
pleasant time discussing celery bread
where no pears to abuse
obliged
four
houses.
Pleasantly deranged.

~

The that.
The whole way there
will be a clear
lovesong piece.
Sample pressure concluded
mentioning what love permitted.
Peculiar materials leave particular people peculiar ways.
From here and there to there.
Excess pressure deranged him
and refusing
he certainly mentioned saying *no more talking* from there to there.
Little comes more than the best.

~

That necessity was dearest
that he had intermittently
but others would like doing very often what was lacking
in what had been done
and saying to one another again
that he did not say that an answer that came
might come again
and that he did not know what was to be decided.
It is agreeable to be hearing that.
Was what he said that he was
not enough?
Seeing meaning there
filled her with the merriment
cooked pears show.
All say this is better
and not longer.
Whisper so the cooks
choose to come.
Their having gone there
would have meant doing it the way that showed when it was filled.

This is the beer. *Bake it well*
are conviction's best most deepening words.
Certainly mentioned. Thickness.

~

Pleasant celery there
is the matter there
when larger pleasant fried breadth
is talking there.
All they hear there is all that talking.
The very thing one liked
was being.
Hearing things
could be answering truly completer beginnings.
Ask the little fish
growing better with fire.
Children saying things
could have been saying what one was urging.
Tell that there
when the house there
is better than the best.

~

There love permitted mentioning the bread.
Making it that way
showed that being was growing a little lighter.
All time clears excess samples nicely.
The maker is that
that is to be finished.

~

Father is asking if one has forgotten something about being easy.
Staying there will be a clear
lovesong piece.
Place every answer that comes.

~

Little celery chooses little lighting.

~

This and an *and* sing much.
Little as each is certain
some meanings are the best.
All and any and then that
mean that many are obliged.

~

They are not.
Some of the whole way there
the meaning did not happen.
That had not been understood
so they were not successful.
Antliss was not successful.

~

In urging Antliss to continue standing
wherever another one had been
she answered that any answer that might come
might come again
and he did know
that when he asked if something did
they would call one another.
Some one answering talk she intended to hear
said that Antliss intended to be looking
seeing
and staying away.
Begin big singing no more.
The days and the places there.
The.

~

There nothing clearly sings
that celery is happy.
Every beginning was something that one would be
    hearing when things were obliging.
They and a *the* all stand.
There is lengthy laughter
lightning's color.

The bigger wish is to be making that.
Each one is saying when meeting them
that they have had enough talking and saying.
Then what has been taken to have meant
that doing that means
coming and saying things
when one is obliged to?
Surely little was cooked.
So talking about food was being easy.
Staying there filled with merriment
she sees to it that noise is placed well away.
That the dearest singing laughter length be breadth
is one
pleasant wish.
There most days from time to time
the best pieces are discussed
and a few conclude that that there
noise and use are one.
Happy peculiar singing laughter length is enough to have finished.

~

All who have a way of not completing singing
will have no more beginning.
It is of them
one of them
that one will sing.
The whole way there will be a clear lovesong piece.
Place every answer that comes.
Little potatoes are certainly of better breadth
but talking there where one can want what has been appreciated
one can want two who have a way of not completing anything.
Something was something about being existing ones
that might have been.
She says those things when obliging four houses.

~

A pleasant growing light
clearly has the better breadth.
Pleasantly deranged necessity.
Descriptions there are none.
No deranged fish will follow pressure.

~

Only potatoes mentioning love are permitted. Meaning
there was filled with merriment.
Simple difference
did cause material description.

~

Description is truly a necessity.

~

The greens are fried the same way they are often fried
    in that little place where nothing is clear.
Happy peculiar people are peculiar.
This pressure deranged
all the thickened potatoes that had been mentioned

~

Thickness.
The pleasantly deranged
would be completing it some time.
Each one was not very disappointing.
That was enough.

~

See what they might have been.
She says the opening. The *the*. All that is there
is all that time the best.
Singing that some one says Antliss is completing it
does any one any time have any?
Each one is saying what that one liked being.
Completer singing mentioned that rhubarb
is certainly the best.

~

Come sit and leave the light much larger there.
Pleasant wishes.
There
then there
the house is more than conviction's best most deepening word.
Certainly
the better matter there was opened with not much of this thought that
   pleased them not.
Expressing what they are are hearing
this and an *and* sing much.
Little was surely cooked.
So the food was talking about being easy.
Staying with things nicely
the maker is that that is there.
Every happening has a door.
That.
This is the beer.

~

Bake it well and with conviction.
Most certainly pears are best.
A piece of description.
Figs stayed all day. The singer there
comes singing as is mentioned there
to whomever is there.
Every happening.
Coming they call one another
expressing in what they are saying
something that means thickness's better times
will not abuse any peculiar material descriptions necessity chooses
pleasant
regular
neat.

~

Peas and an *and* gave that much fish
saying necessity's dearest would likely refuse
half of what was there

like green
peas'
descriptions.
So let it be concluded.
Still eating all that's there.
Little potatoes
deranged and refusing
are urging Henns to be decided.

~

It is there.
All time clears excess samples nicely
singing of long red pears.
Pears that are pleasantly fried.

~

Where it is four it is completer.

~

Last time there.
Every happening
happy and eaten.
Happy peculiar singing is mentioned.

~

Thickness is not cooked pears.
Such a time shows necessity.
Every piece of a whole preceder
gave pressure.
What whole?

~

Pleasant permitting makes for louder excess.
Children hear excess differently.
Did time's
happy peculiar people
stay to have more time
happy and eaten?
Nothing is not no having.
Differences long concluded are mentioned there.

Every pleasant kind of celery bread but no pears.
There the house is more than those
       who come to it.

                    ~

There's little time left
for fishing for pears.
Refuse refusal's pleasant deranged necessity.
Every beginning of light.
Children color light and cloth
with dearest descriptions' necessity.
Every piece of the whole of time
shows its own necessity.
A pleasant blanket is marking a smiling soiling.
That follows the little ways
children are saying it is there.
Where children color light
conviction's the best most deepening word.
They're certainly little.
Refined matter
is opened there.
There's very little of this.

                    ~

A poem of 29 stanzas derived from my poems "Stein 2, 27, 3, 24, 6, and 9," merged in
that order after being selected by random-digit chance operations utilizing the RAND
Corp. table *A Million Random Digits with 100,000 Normal Deviates* (Glencoe, IL: The
Free Press, 1955) from among the first 31 poems of my Stein series (see [1] below)
and then run through Hugh Kenner and Joseph O'Rourke's program TRAVESTY (see
[2] below), the program having been asked for an order-9 Travesty of 6378 charac-
ters (these numbers having also been selected by random-digit chance operations).
The output was revised a number of times, but the given sentence order and most
lexical morphemes were preserved. Prosodic criteria determined line breaks.

   The sequence of numbers of sentences in successive stanzas—1, 3, 4, 7, 11, 7, 4,
3, 1, 3, 4, 7, 11, 7, 4, 3, 1, 3, 4, 7, 11, 7, 4, 3, 1, 3, 4, 7, 11—comprises seven interlinked
alternately ascending and descending sequences of the first five numbers of the Lucas
sequence (1, 3, 4, 7, 11, 18, 29, 47, 76, 123, etc.), developed by the French mathemati-
cian Edouard Lucas in the 1870s and published in 1880 to aid testing for Mersenne
prime numbers.

[1] The source poems from my Stein series were constructed by a combination of choices, chance operations, computer-automated deterministic procedures, and revision. Their sources are passages from works by Gertrude Stein, drawn from texts authenticated by the research of Ulla E. Dydo, who published them in her collection *A Stein Reader*. The page numbers of passages used as source texts and in making some of the poems as "seed" texts were derived by permuting 241, obtained by opening a math-table book I used in high school, and often by extending source and seed passages from the permutation-numbered page by choice.

[2] The computer program TRAVESTY was written about 1980 by Hugh Kenner and Joseph O'Rourke, who published an early version of it in *BYTE* magazine in 1981. The program draws what Kenner calls "pseudo-texts" from source texts, by a procedure depending upon letter-sequence frequencies in English. The seven "orders" of output texts it produces (orders 3–9) differ in that lower-order Travesties are less similar to normative discourse than higher-order ones. Although my revisions of its output were relatively free, they were limited by a number of constraints, some intuitive or liminal, others deliberate.

New York: 3–5 August 1998

Be Gentle to a Greek
(Stein 53)

Be gentle to each other, to everybody, for every designer revises.

Do be kind and never try to interfere with people coming together. A moment after it would have been you. That scene means they'll resume it in the house.

We've not softened, no way. Anything can help in that place. What had mentioning the higher meant. Wealthy boys could and will decide what they would have said there and would have had careless women hear.

I'd better have said he was Greek. Do deny silence enough. Everybody does. Carrie borrows what she carries. The English uncovered Meininger as one who was there would've wanted. His gentle coughing wouldn't have tired you as much as your own would've. Those four laughed at the need for harnessing and forgot it.

When those sounds were heard and that thing was opened what had those horses begun to believe. That they were draught horses. Gradually the fall would've made everything necessary for everybody. The four who hurry meet the one who is Greek. He did this to me, not the ones whose names he said. How had he mentioned them when he did. He increased it. Everybody shown with it wanted to be believed. Four had to ask something. He goes and stones the door enough, doubly or lightly. Hadn't coal been necessary. Wouldn't that home have needed it all the same.

Why are they loaning it.

Has that been his way. Can't anybody help. Those in that place should have gone away yesterday when they could still hear and see.

Why couldn't they've decided. What have the women hearing it carelessly said been saying. He said I'd better deny it enough or be silent. He was a Greek.

Eight paragraph/strophes in which the numbers of sentences in each one follow two successive Lucas sequences: 1, 3, 4, 7, 11 and 1, 3, 4.

They were derived from Gertrude Stein's "Pink Melon Joy" (from "Carving." to the end: A Stein Reader, edited by Ulla E. Dydo [Evanston, IL: Northwestern University Press, 1993], 300–305). The source's page numbers were derived from the random numbers 302 and 5, found by chance operations in the RAND Corporation's random-digit table A Million Random Digits with 100,000 Normal Deviates (Glencoe, IL: The Free Press, 1955), interpreted as meaning "about five pages including 302," so the source passage runs from about the middle of 300 to the end of "PMJ" (middle of 305). The order of the source passage's paragraphs was newly randomized for this poem by random-digit chance operations.

The paragraph-randomized passage was run through DIASTEX5, Charles O. Hartman's most recent automation of one of my diastic text-selection methods, using as "seed" a paragraph from Stein's "A Long Gay Book" (A Stein Reader, 215, para. 6), one of a series of seed paragraphs used in making some of my Stein poems. The "seed" in this procedure is a text that is spelled out "diastically"—i.e., with words from the source passage that have the letters of the seed text's words in corresponding positions—in the program's output. The latter was freely revised and edited, but most of its words were placed in sentences and paragraphs where their groupings are roughly similar to those in the unrevised output of the program.

New York: 3–15 October 1998

Care Firm

(Stein 69)

care named firm

Made by running Stein 65.txt (the file for Stein 65) thru DIASTEX5, using the first five lines of pmj300.txt (the file for "Pink Melon Joy"), beginning with "Carving." as diastic seed, and accepting stop at nonmatch. The source was variously derived from texts of Stein; the seed was a five-line excerpt from the beginning of a passage in Gertrude Stein's "Pink Melon Joy" (*A Stein Reader*, ed. by Ulla E. Dydo [Evanston, IL: Northwestern University Press, 1993], 300).

New York: 28 January 1999

More Not More Today Forget

(Stein 72)

Happy Birthday 36 Mordecai!

more not more to-day forget

Made by running Part I, Stanza VI, of "Stanzas in Meditation," by Gertrude Stein (*A Stein Reader,* edited by Ulla E. Dydo [Evanston IL: Northwestern University Press, 1993], 569–71, located by numerological operations on my son's name, "Mordecai-Mark Mac Low") through DIASTEX5 (automation by Charles O. Hartman [1994], of my diastic reading-through text-selection method [1963]), utilizing "Mordecai-Mark Mac Low" as "seed text." The program was no longer able to match the name with words from "Stanza VI" after the "e" (in the 5th position) in "Mordecai-Mark."

New York: 10 March 1999

Something Important Could Certainly Be Enough

(Stein 76)

Something important could certainly be listened to then.

And that thing was certainly not anything uninteresting.
Could Martha be saying that that thing was not something interesting
   and completely important?
She could be.

What would Martha be saying *that* for?
Something was saying that through her.
What was saying that through Martha?
Certainly something living.
What could that living thing be?

Could it be some younger being?

Who?

I cannot say.

Something importantly feeding on Martha?

Perhaps.

For being interesting?

Perhaps to be *very* interesting.

Who or what could really be interesting that way?

Perhaps the being that was saying that through Martha. I cannot listen
to such talking.

Ha ha!

You say ha ha?!

I do!

You will certainly not be living any longer!

Ugh!!

You say enough.

Ugh!!!

You've said enough.

According to Jackson, this poem consists of five strophes derived from what was
left over after the composition of "Stein 75," which he believed was "mined" from
the output of running a passage in Gertrude Stein's "Two Women," published in
A Stein Reader, edited by Ulla E. Dydo (Evanston, IL: Northwestern University
Press, 1993, 215–17) through DIASTEX5, Prof. Charles O. Hartman's most recent
automation of one of the diastic reading-through text-selection procedures Jackson
developed in 1983. Lacking notes, he couldn't be certain that he had used DIAS-
TEX5; nor did he recall what the seed text was. In his notes, he goes on to say,
"The final poem was made by 'mining' what remained of the output of this procedure
and producing normative sentences from the words elicited thereby. These sentences
were divided into strophes that comprise successively numbers of sentences corre-
sponding to the Lucas number sequence 1, 3, 4, 7, 11."—A.T.

New York: 12 May 1999

Therybody Havere

(Stein 86)

Therybody the wormough be orts fich thosithassiffecte.

Of youlatery ot looking is impork is tory leady.
Les vereakessit doest fore naturally ory siffork.
Int been is peatimporare whe wit is work ing haterferefuse.

Clat afted veres the on ime-se.
It ented.
Speak it tins.
Thappented the clas pread too not.

Ontere not classit of one what is not a cone be ally.
Le they knothis fory imuch to naturally dectly.
Knot arts hinted ity.
Anybody son ing ing is hat it.
Ariessimply shost rentempeautin they they knot it.
A ve nonly a doest bettere actly thaturally so beautit.
Haturalreakes fic.

The a clas is beat is is.
Ity do satiffork it hatiffer the it thatiffereptantemposic.
Is to been mak one ortand so and ant bad.
Anywar insimple accepared Gre to a cone is a diffiestitin.
Is very shosen thery speades too the nat.
Is beass becide.
Thation almormourally assit arit.
Is you hose of the haturally it. the one's prefuld.
Being sone effich thappented do the ing is ve does.
Art wough to and so are not the when a natedly does.
Areauting impork ing.

Nat ithervally re thatem.

A clas wity a cone thas pen a nat is yourarts the.

And bectork insen ing.

This tin mory is ing Lor.

It thereptere wory to acted arestis be it whaturalthe.

Where wou do beensenory knot all ting Lormou hat.

Ening.

The rall onne woulas acceptand thensiting.

Naturally knot show ot cread is it ing Lory ing.

Therfecidery aso sally they.

There on aring is first.

Acce one native it is nat itionne ing thows.

Conectly ally thered beautionly is tory leak ithe.

Ork ing thows.

Fies diffic isfacto nat. tor a cont.

Sting.

It whows they otherfecide.

Fies.

Nows.

Thisfacto.

Sat sic.

Now is mak one art sper therense is.

Of the all one's the what.

A natinsit saturareautiffereas.

Whosiculd ther insenin ing spereat so be.

Ho not fort evereak ime everead do als.

Tords.

Ich.

Muld Gren thereaust do the it are hated the of.

Cone ensich thempore and Gre have way.

Frompormost.

Ime-se dif acceparen ithavery leausat sat ass diffirse.

On althe all tookin iffer isfacce it havere.

Ten strophes made by running an early stage of my poem "Stein 77: There a Differ-
ent Time-Sense Is Simply Non-Competitive" through Hugh Kenner and Joseph
O'Rourke's "pseudo-text-generating program" [Kenner's description] TRAVESTY,
requesting a 2,000-character order-3 output. I kept the output's Zaum-like succes-
sion of words, pseudo-words, and portmanteau words, but turned its typographical
lines into pseudo-sentences by initial capitalization and periods and by making
new sentence-lines by substituting periods for commas in the output and making
a line break after every intra-line period, including those in the original output.
The resulting series of verse lines was grouped into strophes having, successively,
numbers of lines comprising two Lucas-number sequences: 1, 3, 4, 7, 11, 18, followed
by 1, 3, 4, 7.

THE SOURCE POEM. "Stein 77" was derived from two pages of Gertrude Stein's
"Composition as Explanation" as published in *A Stein Reader*, edited by Ulla E.
Dydo (Evanston, IL: Northwestern University Press, 1993, 495–96). This passage
was first run through the program TRAVESTY, which was asked for an order-6
output of 1,400 characters. Then that output (or "Travesty") was run through
DIASTEX5, Charles O. Hartman's most recent automation of one of my diastic
reading-through text-selection procedures (developed in 1963), using as a seed text
a passage from the same book. After that, the output of that run-through was used
as the seed for a second run of the same passage through DIASTEX5. I accepted the
stopping of the output of each of the run-throughs by a "mismatch" (the program's
not finding a word in a source text that has one of the letters of a seed text in the
position that it occupies in that seed text). I revised the last output of DIASTEX5
turning it into a series of verse-line sentences. I made them from most of the words
in each successive typographical line through changes of word order and suffixes
and a few deletions. Finally, I divided the series of verse lines into twelve Lucas-
number strophes.

[New York]: 11–12, 23–24 June 1999

Mercy Entirely Astonishing
(Stein 94)

Mercy, giving color, hardening interest, changes mustard dangerously.

Use an empty umbrella.
Desperately, the handy extra particles are practically complaining that
 facts are stubborn.
A purse is a purse and nothing is nothing.

A cloth cup is hurting.
Shaving replaced a cutlet.
Manly counting pieces together a likeness to wound and glide away from!
Eat and whole volumes change.

Stitches and cow jam plus Pop's table did enough.
Expression, not the nearest pillar or a little hope, meadowed that house.
A carafe and a blind glass feather and extremely exaggerating glasses
 are not everything.
Spread the wagon sack!
I say that eight colors, shades of brown, will soon befit cigarettes on
 excessive enough occasions.
August extracted from a bottle a slender message made occasional, I
 suppose, by that umbrella.
What?—would so little make an entire occasion altogether astonishing?

A malachite climbing pencil, spreading roundness, established attractive
 colors.
The established colors were not closed to an increase of color.
Quite many even permitted elegant distinctions.
In so clever a place, even careless speed is graced by very regular green
 pieces.
A tumbler budded no more readiness or likeness than an umbrella.
The whole thing's blessings really meant no more than yellow nothing.
Neither gracious glasses nor ladies' colds make for custardy news.

A green object treading a wrist at a leading hour does little but gra-
ciously rest.
Next best is a little pencil.
Gratitude's interest lies in preparation and restitution.
Her resignation's silver lilies needed lightly pounded paper particles.

Suddenly use an umbrella or wear a ribbon in your hair.
An umbrella may articulate a crystal.
This place's arrangement could consist in having narrow curves.
We've not come to cut the satin perfectly.
Whose colds are news?
We called anything with little soles truly leadish.
That elephant, a thing to search for on occasion, was handsome enough
and wholly charming.
You're worse than an oyster!
You're exaggerating everything extremely.
Let's not spread something that might cause a loud clash.
Which small red thing's the cause of enough excess?
It's not even extreme!
Which eight were taken out?
There the color brown may fit the occasion sooner.
Say, are there any cigarettes in that bottle?
Suppose we extract their messages in August?
They've made an altogether too slender umbrella for the occasion, Al.
What climb on malachite could make that little pencil so entirely
astonishing?

SOURCE: All of "Objects," the first section of *Tender Buttons*, by Gertrude Stein, as
originally published by Donald Evans under his imprint Claire Marie (New York,
May 1914) and published online in The Bartleby Archive (1995) and The New
Bartleby Library (1999), both edited by Steven H. van Leeuwen, with editorial
contributions from Gordon Dahlquist. I've modified my copy of the online edition by
incorporating corrections to it made in ink by Stein in Donald Sutherland's copy of
the Claire Marie edition, owned by the University of Colorado Special Collections.
Ulla E. Dydo found these corrections and recently sent me copies of them.
SEED: "Mildred's Umbrella," the eighth poem in "Objects."
METHOD: Running all of "Objects" through DIASTEX5 (Charles O. Hartman's 1994

update of his automation of one of my diastic reading-through text-selection procedures developed in 1963, using all of "Mildred's Umbrella" as seed text, and then revising the program's output by changes of word order, suffixes, pronouns, and structure words, but keeping its lexical words' root morphemes in positions close to those they occupy in the raw output. [The series of verse lines are divided into six Lucas-number strophes—1, 3, 4, 7, 11, 18.—A. T.]

New York: 17–18 August 1999

Ada

(Stein 105/Titles 2)

A adventure black.

A idle spark any address really address addresses shadows and
     educated than all addition blank and education that
     a eddy chambers a add shall all edible grand and adopt
     placing.

And added chair.

Alike added ready always admitted stars a adjustment place
     and education hearing any administration quaintness
     and adventure black.

Four strophes drawing their words from the entire text of Donald Evans's first edition of *Tender Buttons* by Gertrude Stein (New York: Claire Marie, 1914). This text was sent through DIASTEX5, Prof. Charles O. Hartman's 1994 update of DIASTEXT (1989), his automation of one of my deterministic diastic reading-through text-selection procedures developed in 1963. My seed text was Stein's title *Ada.* "Stein 105" is the second poem in *Titles,* a subseries of *Stein* whose making employs as seed files the successive titles of works appearing in Ulla E. Dydo's *A Stein Reader* (Evanston, IL: Northwestern University Press, 1993).

     The first edition of *Tender Buttons* was posted online in The Bartleby Archive

(1995) and The New Bartleby Library (1999), both edited by Steven van Leeuwen, with editorial contributions by Gordon Dahlquist. However, I corrected typos and incorporated in my file of *Tender Buttons* fourteen corrections written in ink in Stein's hand, which Ulla Dydo found in Donald Sutherland's copy of the first edition in the Special Collections of the University of Colorado, Boulder.

I deleted the raw output of DIASTEX5 after the point where it began exactly repeating what came before (something the program does at times). Then I broke the remaining output into verse lines by placing a period at the end of each "paragraph" of the output and following it by a strophe break. I kept the typographical line breaks of the output within the two long lines.

New York: 11, 21 January 2000

Mercy Can't Give a Girl Much Pleasure in Things
(Stein 108/Titles 5)

Mercy can't give a girl much of a costume.
She was pleased, nay, delighted to be put on the table.

If things were resolved by analyzing redness, wouldn't that make some
    ordinary things a little fancier?
More tables are designed than made.
Illusion places courage where it has to be extreme.

Plain holes are necessarily different.
More pieces make curious shows.
They cloister more washing than's set out on strings.
Is glass necessary?
They extract diseases' incidence from many particles.

Dressing is necessary, but many aren't particular.
Waving shuts out addresses.
Most arranging lacks the necessary patience.

Necessity's releases were mismanaged.
Isn't that chain handsome?
Exemplary oceans are made in saloons.
Occasional cutlets minister to places climate makes.

There's no malachite behind that grass.
What it's made into isn't what it's made of makes expected.
A lady's cold can make a necessary difference, but can mean little to some.
Suppose you revise that mutton!
Hat sales are pleasing again.
Your supposed revisions make many matches waver.
Suggestive dining and dressing in silence can make aperiodic cutting
    mean success.
Why suppose a middling earner isn't assiduous?
Thirst can make a difference for harmony mayn't be satiny.
Please suggest that sadly melting together isn't a medicine transfer.
Besides, clouds may transfer authority vaguely.

Curly successive divisions: more of the same solitude.
What makes the prices of cherries vary is never easily shown, because a
    mixed-lecture can make more calm than eating can be hoped to.
Much of that famous arrangement makes unanticipated divisions show
    their buttery necessity.
A mended cake may not be plain.
It may not minister more to a cat than chaining would.
Here comes the witness whose silence is murder.
Basting doesn't make a solid thing untidy.
Procuring means a necessary lapse from pleasing politeness.
Did she recollect that grain can taste better than glass?
Are you capable of mowing?
Have a little!
What are the necessary specs for chain-boats
Cucumbers are occasions in more ways than nuts.

Dining below the beefsteak made the waiter's actions keep to the letter.

Chinese dressing meant trouble.

That table's not a satisfying vision.

We suggest you replace it.

No decision was made about the division of the spoons.

More Chinamen were living between refusals.

Suppose we meant to make a letters together for a manikin show.

Supposing the example mentioned is the same as a choice between
    necessities, the suggester of silence makes herself a sitting target,
    painstakingly eclipsed because beefsteak, milk, and water may make
    up a more successful package than a sprightly room.

Cadences in the visible always show more causes, because they're not
    strings.

Necessity furnished them with examples of mastery.

Yet he almost insisted on flowered dishes more than on water or cake.

Savings have been arranged through more satisfactory rates.

Could dedication mean reversible rights?

Mistakes may become mean habits.

Analyzing eating shows a difference from cleaning.

A little resolute fancy makes us red and wet and ordinary.

We take pleasure in things.

Seven strophes derived from Donald Evans's 1st edition of Gertrude Stein's *Tender
Buttons* (New York: Claire Marie, 1914). I incorporated in my file of *Tender Buttons*
14 corrections, written in ink in Stein's hand, found by Ulla E. Dydo in Donald
Sutherland's copy of the edition, in Special Collections, University of Colorado
Library, Boulder.

   I sent the entire text through DIASTEX5, Charles O. Hartman's 1994 update
of DIASTEXT (1989) automation of one of my deterministic diastic reading-through
text-selection methods developed in 1963. My seed text was Stein's title "Matisse."
"Stein 108" is the 5th poem in *Titles,* a subseries of *Stein* employing as seed texts the
titles of works appearing in Dydo's *Stein Reader* (Evanston, IL: Northwestern Univer-
sity Press, 1993).

   Composing a series of verse-line-sentences from the root morphemes of more
or less neighboring words in the output of DIASTEX5, I rearranged their order and
added, deleted, and changed suffixes, conjunctions, prepositions, forms of "to be,"

pronouns, etc., and otherwise revised the program's output. I deleted the output where it began repeating what came before. While composing the sentences, I inserted end marks and grouped the lines into strophes that comprise numbers of sentences corresponding successively to the prime-number sequence 2, 3, 5, 7, 11, 13, 17.

New York: 9–13 February 2000; 11 March 2002

Pointing Out Your Silvery Song
(Stein 122/Titles 19)

Pointing out your differences with a sinecurist recklessly makes for a
 very calamity.

Color's intentional journey is to say paper's silver song.
Packing more color around you is being just monstrous anyplace.
The width of a pin my be more dark than learning to choose ordinarily
 well.

Just so!
Any oily piece?
Wondering broken at more mended culture he's choosing the strength of
 his joints.
Does she say that the place's bitter length makes the darkness remarkable?

The gilded color seven judged so many ways was posting little pennies.
"Reckless" means "dear" when the tall depot-cleaner joins the dog sky.
Peeling Bill the muncher makes Jack be meadowed.
Milk?
Enjoy your cocoa on linen.
If anything, be joyful that the pigeon in the kitchen isn't a kind of turkey.
Make resonance collar repose, saving jerking sooner.

The way of prudence is lilacs' nonchalance, more pink than resemblance.

Splendid recollections may be shunning joy more than anything.

It's perfectly singular how many soaking mixtures are real relaxing!

That altogether widened jet was to pay for the pet's signal languor.

Milk makes it necessary.

All recognition is again joy or no joy by post time.

Lunch!

Luck makes nearly a silk spool of onions just one more way of pedestrianism.

She's likely to be tender.

Nickel mercy medicine's a color, the color behind a journey to say "paper."

That silvery song!

Five strophes successively comprising numbers of verse-line sentences corresponding to the Lucas number sequence 1, 3, 4, 7, 11. I made them by first running all of the first edition of Gertrude Stein's *Tender Buttons* (New York: Claire Marie, 1914)—into which I had incorporated 14 corrections by Stein found at the University of Colorado, Boulder, by Ulla Dydo—through Charles O. Hartman's program DIASTEX5, the 1994 update of his program that automates one of the "diastic" word-selection methods I developed in 1963. I used as "seed text" Stein's title "Pink Melon Joy." Finally, I made a verse-line sentence from the words in each line of the program's output (except for one output line that I divided into two verse-line sentences), inserting a minimum of function words, pronouns, etc., inserting, deleting, or changing some suffixes, and sometimes changing word order. I divided the series of verse lines into the five Lucas-number strophes as I composed the lines. This is the 19th poem in *Titles*, a subseries of *Stein*, a series of poems based on root morphemes found in works by Stein.

New York: 8–29 May 2000

Scatter the Occasion

(Stein 152/Titles 47)

Scatter an absurd liquid in a stream, pounding particular blackening
cultivars.

Consider the circumstances of horticulture, which wither us with outrage.
Light, denting the very resemblance of space to water, is shunning our
teacups.
Coconut persecution is an institution with no explanation.

An accepted acquaintance was as triumphant as her husband was
organized.
She's frequently indifferent to pleasant stupefication.
Circumstances disappointed "white rights" authorities.
Exchanging now seemed safer in black cases.

It was a surprise that the principal description was a description of
coagulation and not a recognition of the occasion.

SOURCE TEXT: Gertrude Stein's *Tender Buttons,* 1st edition, incorporating 14 text
corrections written in Stein's hand found by Ulla E. Dydo in Donald Sutherland's
copy in the Special Collections of the University of Colorado, Boulder, library.
SEED TEXT: Stein's title "An Acquaintance with Description."
METHOD: Running source and seed texts through DIASTEX5, Charles O. Hartman's
1994 update of his digital automation of one of my diastic text-selection methods
devised in 1963. I deleted the output after it began to repeat exactly and often
retained, but sometimes changed, the order of root morphemes, changed many
affixes, and inserted a number of "helping words." I also retained Stein's favored
form "stupefication" (which the *OED* calls rare and obsolete) rather than modern-
izing it to "stupefaction," because diastic consistency demands retaining it.
FORM: Nine verse-line sentences divided into four strophes in which the successive
numbers of verse lines correspond to the Lucas number sequence 1, 3, 4, followed
by a one-line coda.

New York: 14–15 November 2000; 27 May 2002

That Orange

(Stein 159/Titles 53)

That spectacle is strange.
It's glazed and changed.

They're constantly careless with the seltzer.
If they only had more learning and were patient!
The practice of protecting the spectacle indicates unprecedented separation.

Their satin stomachs were especially astonishing things, at least, in that
breeze.
I used a plain mounting instead of mending it since I was not inclined to
mend it.
Ordinarily, separation protects unstrangeness.
There was a single place to stand, but even the freezing was musical.
"Peanuts" is no more.

Besides, it meant displaying a blanket.
Was it an upslanting succession?
It was a simple succession.

What?
An orange?

MAKINGWAY ENDNOTE

SOURCE: All of the first edition of Gertrude Stein's book *Tender Buttons*, but incorporating fourteen corrections in Stein's handwriting found by Ulla E. Dydo in Donald Sutherland's copy in the Special Collections of the library of the University of Colorado, Boulder.

SEED: Stein's title *Stanzas in Meditation*.

METHOD: Sending source and seed texts through DIASTEX5, Charles O. Hartman's 1994 update of his program automating one of my deterministic "diastic" reading-through text-selection methods devised in 1963, and revising its output. I deleted the output at the point where it began to repeat itself exactly, and by changes of word order and affixes and some insertions of "helping words" not in the output, I turned each output line into one or two verse-line sentences, whose succession was divided into strophes.

FORM: Five strophes whose numbers of verse-line sentences correspond to the
waxing and waning prime number sequence 2, 3, 5, 3, 2.

New York: 17–18 November 2000

Is Adventure Feeling Being Connected with Others?
(Stein 160/Titles 54)

Is adventure feeling being?

A strong light may indicate calamity.
Where do the parts connect?
Neglecting altogether how scarce the stems are, they cracked them idly.

I have no particular animosity toward even *them*.
Even if they'd been indirectly educated there, their shiny additions
   might have made their garments incoherent.
Don't put any <u>does</u> in there again!
'Twas summer!

That principal seemed earnest, but when and how long was he educated?
What places does "that element" go to on Saturdays?
It eddies.
Occasional draughts of ordinary "slenderizing creams" may shatter
   perfection.
So where there were formerly instances of added means, doubt may now
   discriminate between them.
A suggestive tendency's absence is never as pleasant as sleeping.
To whom?

It's admitted that they were seen questioning certainty's being con-
   nected with delicacy.

So, did plenty of adjustments commence right there?

By dinnertime we'd penetrated to certain distasteful stairways.

The *administration's* the place to look for and see examples of *that*!

When doubting anything, hesitation may be legal—but pricey.

In their golden chambers some of the clergymen ventured to feel their
being.

What light could indicate calamity so strongly?

Every part is connected with the others.

MAKINGWAY ENDNOTE

SOURCE TEXT: All of the first edition of Gertrude Stein's book *Tender Buttons*, but
incorporating fourteen corrections in Stein's handwriting found by Ulla E. Dydo
in Donald Sutherland's copy in the Special Collections of the library of the Uni-
versity of Colorado, Boulder.

SEED TEXT: Stein's title "Identity a Poem."

METHOD:

1. I sent the source and seed texts through DIASTEX5, Charles O. Hartman's 1994
update of his program automating one of my deterministic "diastic" reading-
through text-selection methods devised in 1963.

2. I deleted the output a few lines after it began to repeat itself exactly.

3. I transformed each remaining output line into a verse-line sentence by changing
its word order and some affixes and sometimes inserting a few "helping words"
that do not appear in the output lines. I retained all of the lexical root morphemes
and most of the "helping words" that appear in each output line.

4. I divided the sequence of verse-line sentences into strophes.

FORM: Seven strophes whose numbers of verse-line sentences correspond to the
waxing and waning Lucas number sequence 1, 3, 4, 7, 4, 3, 1.

*New York: 1 January and 20 November–23 December 2000; 25 February
and 26 June 2001*

For undeniably dear Anne Tardos,
                with undiminishing love and admiration,
                                        just after the Winter Solstice, 2000

◆

Wrinkles' Wisdom Despairs Most Leadenly, Bays at Age, Long May Long

(Hopkins 12)

Wrinkles' wisdom despairs:
the winding motion of wisdom
is there, sighs.

Echoes have, strongly
tall, everything that's
to be done.

Yet, fashioned, slept.
Despair. Drooping despair.
Be beginning, Beauty.

Beauty's sign's motion:
known messengers begin,
begin, sparely begin

where morning's never
matched by sunny
places not within,

never too motionable
with soaring, soaring,
hurling care, care

fondly, but told
none to keep
no sheet there.

Air of despair,
airway of death,
no sheeted way

echoes age's evils,
everything swiftly least:
gallantry, looks, hair.

Not least, every
place's sighing maidens
fly away gracefully.

Hair replaces whatever
gallant messengers numbered,
prized, and fastened.

Swiftly walking past
sad places, they
prize the past,

every weary, everlasting
way of us:
fast maidens' eyelashes,

early everything's eyelashes,
everything's beauty's ghost
fastened sweetly, freely.

Keep these deaths
fresh and fast,
fastened freely, sweetly.

Truth freely keys
flying elsewhere, waving
us off, undone.

Yet some, them,
us, seem sweetly
sighing "no worse."

O somewhere away
from us, not
matched by morning,

come winning ways
following mournful beauty
long singeing you.

Beauty, fearing death,
follows yonder, mournfully
passes all gallantry.

No, none now
wrinkles sheets gracefully,
freely walks carelessly.

What do mournful
wrinkles do yonder,
delivering what ways?

We most leadenly
bay at age,
long may long.

SOURCE TEXT: Gerard Manley Hopkins's poem "The Leaden Echo and the Golden
Echo (Maidens' song from St. Winefred's Well)." Way of writing not recorded.

New York: 16 May 2001; 15–17 April 2003

◆

Selections from HSC and HSCH

Introduction
by Anne Tardos

The *HSC* and *HSCH* poems are among Jackson's very last works. The first *H* in these titles refers to Charles Hartshorne, who was Jackson's philosophy teacher at the University of Chicago and whose writings served as a source for both the *HSC* and *HSCH* series, as did the writings of Gertrude Stein [the *S*] and Lewis Carroll [the *C*]. In *HSCH*, the final *H* acknowledges Jackson's use of the writings of Gerard Manley Hopkins, whose poetry Jackson admired throughout his life. On 23–24 October 2002, he wrote in a note on the *HSC* poems:

> I began this series in June 2002, and presently continue. It is called "HSC" because its principal words come from three sources: essays by the philosopher Charles Hartshorne, who taught me during my second year at the University of Chicago (1940–41), and lived until 2000, when he was 103; Gertrude Stein's *Tender Buttons*; and *Through the Looking-Glass and What Alice Found There*, by the Oxford lecturer in mathematics Charles Lutwidge Dodgson.
>
> When writing such poems, I first make a mix of sentences from various parts of these sources and run it through a digitized version of one of my diastic text-selection methods developed in 1963. Then I freely compose a poem from the method's output and other words. The output is the source of most nouns, verbs, adjectives, and adverbs, which appear in the poems in both root forms and inflected forms, and of some "helping words"—function words like prepositions and conjunctions, but also forms of "to be," and pronouns. I sometimes include non-output words. For names in an output I

usually substitute other names, and the word order of each poem has little relation to that of the diastic output.

Most of the verse lines are normal sentences, and each poem exemplifies one of several new verse forms and comprises several strophes. The numbers of verse lines in consecutive strophes follow one or another number sequence: notably, the Lucas sequence (2, 1, 3, 4, 7, etc.), the sequence of prime numbers (2, 3, 5, 7, 11, etc.), and the sequence of cardinal numbers (1, 2, 3, 4, 5, etc.). Some sequences go up to a certain point and then go back through the sequence to its first number, but others don't get that far back.

When reading the poems aloud, I pause for three andante beats between every two strophes (a thousand and one, a thousand and two, a thousand and three), and I ask others who read them to do so.

Willie's Clatter

(HSC 1)

Willie's willow tree is yellow, he does people who are welcome.
Arabella's analog is a wholly dishonorable king.

Let it play properly for months at a time, for the show is transmitted
    from far behind.

Way at the side they're cutting up fish-persons marked by scarlet eyes.
The black pause is over.
Anyone watching for the unforeseen shouldn't be crossing that sector.

What delightfulness we undergo!
No miserable hall can be without a bell.
Their writing with steam is frequently changing our beautiful oranges.
Beneath a passage, one quite heavy is shaking thought, creating an eddy.

She who dirties the best occasions stops a moment and does kind things
   for a rarely inclusive audience.
There where the last isn't getting the most, Alí is preparing a quiet horse.
You are not hére for me.
Your kitten is teaching us a little every day.
This time I'm not dirtying anything myself.
We're exchanging interruptions in the square.
Though yesterday's fault was the opposite of snow, its idea is crackling
   in the wind.

Always behave toward the dirty pieces you shake out as the voices say
   you mean to.
They're saying, *Majesty! Severe Majesty!*
Suppose what is foreseen is not determined.
Under the widening ocean, whose likeness floats?
For numerous years real lonely monsters are cutting into dreams to
   speak what isn't believed.
Keep as level as you wish when you explain what withers us.
What was seen as a fault is going into hiding, where they think it belongs.
It's raining.
Chances for inclusive problems are very likely slim.
Alfred isn't a clergyman and he's never been one.
Whether it rings or strikes or clatters, it is vanishing.

When hands are achieving speech, is every difference believed?
It's impossible to know the extremes of honor.
She's only sure of her wingèd thoughts.
Just touching, they float till another show is shaking them.
She remarks that the kinky queen is bang out of her thinking-piece.
Wriggling quickly and impatiently, it eats through the shop of cinders.
He's outraged that astonishing lard is wavering beside him.
Doesn't her continuous tonguing suppose deep pleasure?
After dinner she mounts her horse at once.
Perhaps she remarks how often she has fallen.
Each whistle from the writing-tree makes the queen's hair whiter.
Why does she feel the emergent center impossible to honor?

This graying man is only openly a wit.

Seven welcome him to the wood.

He cannot pass their impenetrable glass, and what he's looking for has
been exchanged for oxen.

Explain what occasions make her interrupt.

She's wriggling from experience to experience as kind winds touch her
intensely.

Why is she going out to grapple fish in borrowed gloves?

Peppery influence manages yesterday's going faults, washing away the
intensest love.

Through fullness woodling differences of emergent properties burble.

In an open time good nature may transmit astonishing conversations.

From trying to stop perceiving a larger list their tone of amusement is
only a little severe.

Each going exchange interrupts an occasion with larger dinners.

It won't be a year before a knight is hung.

Voices marked by clatter white as health are rarer than bells.

Why do so many suppose a wriggling experience is a black experience?

And why does Sabrina feel that thinking with the hands is a white thing?

The will is transmuting months of play into miserable steam.

Delightfulness is undergoing a scarlet, toneless change.

A beautiful willow is stirring a lake of air.

Why suppose a center that's impossible to honor?

The larger tongues are wavering.

Some cannot pass impenetrable fullness without stopping to explain it.

Honorable particles rarely reject emergence.

The knight being hung is quickly being deserted.

His dinner is larger than he wants.

Every explanation is squarely interrupted by a vocal monster.

Is he influenced by yesterday's portmanteau of faults?

His emergent woodling properties are open to amusement.

People welcome experiencing his wriggling.

Nothing distracts them better than seeing his sunny honor wither to
   gray and vanish.
Every occasion levels a flying year for him.
His impenetrable fullness is not to be explained.

Unable to speak, the monstrous loner swims into hiding.

Yesterday's meanings astonishingly vanish.
His foreseen experience is clatter.

Most lexical root morphemes in "Willie's Clatter" come from essays by the philoso-
pher Charles Hartshorne, Gertrude Stein's *Tender Buttons*, and Lewis Carroll's
Through the Looking-Glass. The numbers of verse-line sentences in successive
strophes follow the circular Lucas sequence 2, 1, 3, 4, 7, 11, 18, 11, 7, 4, 3, 1, 2.
Please pause three andante beats (a thousand and one, a thousand and two, a
thousand and three) between every two strophes.

New York: 16 June–3 July, 17 October 2002

Agnes Cried in July

(HSC 5)

Agnes críed   when she merely admitted reproachfully that
   scientists   are philósophers.

That observation was literally   too fully in cháracter.
What was the name of the quéen whose possible rélative she was?

Basically coherent   even at the end   Agnes had a keen   awareness of blúe.

Just as súmmer was coming   she'd dréss herself in blue whenever the wínd was stróng.

For her   the woòds were getting to be lacking personálity.

Although she was only watching   it's certain she was púrring none the léss.

Because this didn't check her acceptance of ríddles   she could simultaneously báck creative mechánics   and loudly voice complete astónishment at them with féar in her eyes.

She claimed they were flákes to their fáces.

But they were a míld   áudience.

She knew she wasn't wanted.

They always attributed her ways to too-many-bóoks.

Yet Agnes's crackling violence   would always kind-of-fade-awáy.

Was anything happening that somehow could surpríse her?

Her thinking up inorganic chóices   was partially realístic.

That must have been why she went to Eúrope to eat in Julý.

The roots of lexical words in the sixteen single-sentence lines of "Agnes Cried in July (HSC 5)" come from essays by the philosopher Charles Hartshorne, Gertrude Stein's *Tender Buttons*, and Lewis Carroll's *Through the Looking-glass and What Alice Found There*. The numbers of single-sentence lines in successive strophes follow the sequence 1, 2, 3, 4, 3, 2, 1. Spaces *within lines* indicate short pauses, often occasioned by readers' fully sounding the phoneme series before the spaces.

Each space *between strophes* calls for a pause of three andante beats (a thousand and one, a thousand and two, a thousand and three). Please neither overemphasize nor slight the pauses.

New York: 14–15 July, 22 October 2002; 22 April, 2 July 2003

I'm Bone-Hours Thinner Than Their Pencils

(HSC 6)

I'm *bone*-hours *short* in my quest   and the queer re*fresh*ments are said
   to be *turn*ing.
Suddenly I let blue *qual*ities be distinguished from white *quan*tities.

Fiora was *mean,* which means   **what-a-dirty-plum-of-a-*mon*ster-
   she-was.**
Why, if she's a *per*son, can't she occupy some modicum of *soci*al *ar*ea?
She's had experience under *beds.*

On occasion, *Cham*bers spoke about suety *cu*cumbers and moldy *fish.*
He'd considered taking a compre*hen*sive course in those matters.
However, while he was there in the house with the cheeky
   *broth*ers   they'd placed limits on his mind that blanked out every-
   thing *else.*
Nevertheless, they didn't break him of his taste for *curls*   though he
   faintly voiced his *cer*tainty they were delaying his dish of *roses.*
He was capturing useful *matter*—*that* was the *case*   though anti-
   idealist *gent*lemen dubbed his principles psychica*lis*tic.

We watched Se*re*na Pe*tro*vitch point to nonconcrescible *cau*ses eighty-
   seven *times.*
According to *George,*   she misused his *prin*ciples and bowdlerized his
   prose.
He compared her attitude to an autumn *fish.*
She exhibited nominalistic French e*mo*tions   and the genuinely differ-
   ent experience of an introspective anti-i*de*alist.
Se*re*na offered *not*-mind *all* the *time.*
Her child Ari*ad*ne took her to substantially decent *gar*dens.
Not for *her* the dark anxieties roused by a really convincing expla*na*tion
   slathered with subatomic *par*ticles.

My darling straw-headed *in*sects went about clasping and
    *un*clasping   repeatedly conjuring up giraffe-like excla*ma*tions.
They never *could* understand   what made *sil*ver more nearly unknown
    to them than *sal*ad.
When dishes of snails and fishes had been authorized and ar*rang*ed for
    them, *these*   guests   exclaimed against their separation from the
    *oth*ers.
I explained to them a thousand *times* that this vaguely indecent practice
    arose from their unfortunate ex*peri*ences.
Transmitting such an assertion to them was like carrying a *moun*tain
    upside *down*.
*Some*one there ought to've caught *on*!
If they just wouldn't persist in their meaningless *pro*tests!
*Hall*eck might have pointed out to them that beautiful things with
    unintelligible *struc*tures had been composed in many *places* down
    through the *ages*.
They'd've been more nearly satisfied by a bit of *jam*.
Even woodenly foolish *an*cients   would have gotten beyond *that* contrast.
It's a certainty they'd've persisted in voicing their meaningless cavils
    until they thought they'd *won*.

*Iv*an called it a slippery matter meant to seem *mean*ingful.
He was pleased by the thought of a roomful of *pic*tures fired by a *specu*-
    lative meta*phy*sic.
What a situ*a*tion!
Its mechanistic essence was a sulky *slee*pyhead.
Seemingly Reason her*self*   couldn't've helped to clear *those* dusty eyes.
She'd've been pleased to learn that those with the worst   *fa*ces   were
    *ly*ing there, overcome by mere vi*bra*tions.
I assured Anita and Arabella that *some*day they'd be *thin*ner than their
    *pen*cils.

The roots of lexical words in the 35 single-sentence lines of "HSC 6" are those of
lexical words in essays by the philosopher Charles Hartshorne, Gertrude Stein's
Tender Buttons, and *Through the Looking-Glass and What Alice Found There,* by
Lewis Carroll (Charles Lutwidge Dodgson). The numbers of sentences in successive

strophes follow the sequence of prime numbers 2, 3, 5, 7, 11, 7. Spaces within lines indicate short pauses, mostly occasioned by fully sounding consonant groups preceding them. Please pause three andante beats between strophes (a thousand and one, a thousand and two, a thousand and three). [Syllables in italics indicate emphasis.—A. T.]

New York: 15–21 July, 22–24 October 2002; 27 April 2003

The Pawns Were Nonexistent
(HSC 11)

For The Poetry Project at Saint Mark's in-the-Bouwerie—II

with thanks to Charles Hartshorne, Gertrude Stein, and Lewis Carroll
for lexical root morphemes

The pawns were placed quite otherwise than I remembered their having
been ever before.

They saw trees in those parts that were said to be subjects of the moon.
We support ourselves by subjugating our own and other matter.

He started to shake whenever he dared to write.
If it were a question of hanging her, he'd've been moved by looking
through a hedge at her.
She ended up balancing a roundly generic consciousness of others with
hers of herself.

The principles underlying Whitehead's panpsychism are unlikely to be
deemed foundational by more than a few now.
Many grew up looking at physics as having at best a subjective validity.
It seemed fairly evident that its applications would come to furnish
questions.
They would enable too many—far from the best—to risk inclusive levels
of mischief.

Continuing subjugation counts more than observation or experience in
the ordering of patterns of events.
We knew from many a subject of the queen that water is a better remedy
for dirty teeth than any potato could be.
For nearly every subject, every other subject may be something on a par
with a *thing*.
Sam subjected the structure of his back to more than the queen thought
necessary.
How could the wise be haunted by a fundamental question if that
question itself were questionable?

That relativity causes the same forms as a looking glass is not de facto
true.
What she left in the boat there could never be repeated.
After the subject of white experience was nearly over and past, she'd not
quite glanced at him.
Each minute meant a lot to her,
Shake it well unless there's only one interpretation of that rhubarb cage.
She picked completely great ones there—sometimes.

Material entities there were apparently wilder than most of their pieces.
The subject of rooms seemed hardly related to ones that were more
universal.
He meant that in less than a minute he could pick a harmonious land.
They argued that idealism seldom causes enduring experience.
She only promised an idealistic process.
Which of them claimed that instants of the rivers of God are really
power ordeals?
Her proboscis was subjected to Justice's round-trip.

A string is still rated a means to pain or an even more inharmonious
purpose.
Most choking is an event with a bodily motive.
Is it true that three hundred or so were watching the soup?
Outside, their conditions were piercing, but their plates were mighty
pretty.

Knowing the past can soon subject the knower to subjection.
They said that the sand was knitting it.
Both of them must often eat from a couple of broken cups.
One round bottle is worth several embroideries.

Many idealists are willy-nilly interdependent.
Their kitten's poles are never wildly poor though often cried about.
The subjectivity of a subject isn't physically accessible to other subjects.
This morning's simple particularity may not be at hand for me tonight.
I daresay you never picked up on your head's impatient relationship
with an idea.
Who says that God's power contemptuously separates the memory of a
pleasing wrong from the subject's understanding of it, preventing it
though it shouldn't?
Annalisa thought the last reason for looking at a place was that it might
be of use.
But hardly anyone one bought that.
Before a certain science showed some people there that nestling was
their common right, they considered it nearly as precious as pearls.

There's never enough subjectivity around, the cynical would-be idealist
claimed, to make it evident that subjectivity provides the ultimate
spectacle.
One of your hands, of course, is not suitable for counting pink things.
You need more of the same.
This question could seldom have been looked into by others.
Before the question was made to include the one place you were looking
at, it should have been widened by a subjective collection of generic
entities.
A strong situation may evidently have a microscopic meaning.
Is materialism always marked by shaking?
Or is that due to changes cooked up by vapors of astonishment?
Twiddle that little one again.
She is likely politely to bridle at his questions, though the subject is
merely a conceivable garment for her stomach.

All we said was that every falling slice might join a greater one.

Meeting a particular may cause confusing talk.

Is it, she asked, that she, like other poor, could never expect a certain objection?

How pityingly she cleared away that other pretty past!

Eagerly she marked the necessary rain.

It was a foolish subject, much like a package of useless curtains.

That evening it seemed their so-called truth-directed theory was brushing off experience.

They presented their feelings as if they were really being governed by prayer.

It's a broad subject, winter—closely connected with values, they say.

Augusta turned and swept the meaning of the day into the back garden.

She was sure the specs for anything there were nonexistent.

Please pause for three andante beats between every two strophes. Numbers
of single-sentence verses in successive strophes are 1 through 11.

New York: 13 September–8 October 2002; 1 January and 31 March 2003

It Will Glow Unseen Until It Doesn't

(HSCH 1)

It is in a way touching
        said the Don to Andrea
                that you've been calling Schwitters
  nihilistic
          and his scarless
              festivalselections
    discontenting and delusive
           as snowflakes.

             Are sunbeams' living spirits a-dwindling?
      The shadowy selves of patience
                    gold
  blue
        seemingly immaculate
              have never selected motherwords.

                Three banded canine bodies
            snap at timbers overhead.

Time developed
        corresponding discontented frights
           with perfect navels.

           Three
     thoughtfully blue
          conceived a blinding wince.

              Dispensing with days
       they lifted
    fast
     beating welcomes to the morning.

Between impatience
              and selection
      behavioristic bandits
         snatch up violets.

Aren't you enjoying
      your new behavior's singularity?

        Who was it called
fast
    beating patience
             miniSchwittersistic behavior
      of nonbehavioristic body tops?

Rooted be the healing glass of humankind!

   Spiritmystery light

        riddles all allaying pseudoimmaculate breath.

            Time and sunbeams
      always moving
        hymn a dwindling sweetness
              coloring
breath.

Fast
   beating praise
     cannot cap a scarless navel.

      Living minimotionably
          ever moved
            banded trees
      never wink or blink at lilacs.

Who conceived that chimney voice
                   winking at mothers' patience?

                        Who'd riddle a scarless navel with infinite
light?
Infinity isn't witty.

          Are you
Beth and Mellie's intellectual mother?

                        Mother,
                   they say you've mothered three
                             timberless mysteries!

                   Hand the golden glass no more to Mother.

                        What caps a mother's
          mothering?

No mother is scarless.
                   Timber's dwindling's inconceivable!

     Who could've conceived
                   or composed
     a conception of that dwindling?

                        Who
                   breathing between three laws
                             on snowflakeaccumulating skydays
               would share the timber overhead?
          Your mother's
                   breath
conceived your heart.

Yours the breath your mother's heart conceived.

When morning's wincing fingergaps share living blackness
the day
star's
light
is right as sightlight.

Great
wincing
disperses the light of glowing flesh

Who is the banded bowman
snatching a longedfor wink?

Patient allayers look at him through immaculate fingergaps.

All through the breathing world
the day
star's
dear and healing light
arrives through vast
distances from a swirling sphere of fiery gases.

Fast
beating praise
is panning around in our blackness.

Mothers'
marks
from bearing and nursing humankind
are shared by
humankind.

Glass must often cap

    sunbeams

        before they can sweetly heal.

           Lightly breathing mystery

              riddles the infinite

rightness

        of sightlight.

Is any bare and lightless world

        dearer than the daystar?

            Your mother's

           breath conceived your heart.

    What is the richness of a flash?

        It's never dearer

      than the daystar.

          Unnumbered painters

       share

         with patience and impatience

              humankind's

          mystery light.

Not in a vast

    flash

      do the mothers conceive all humankind.

              Is Bethany's healing

     mystery

       lighting more than breath?

What savior might conceive the infinite healing

                                beggedfor by the world's

                                                elemental

wound?

                        Always being moved
            wounded and unwincing

                        the atmosphere is dying.

                                        Blind

                                    blue

                                            heaven will harbor

                    no

                            living spirit.

The daystar

            unmothering

                        unobservably maculate

        will glow unseen

                    until it doesn't.

Though begun with an ungrammatical text drawn methodically by a diastic method
from writings by Charles Hartshorne, Gertrude Stein, Lewis Carroll, and Gerard
Manley Hopkins, the author's choices and decisions produced this poem from mate-
rials in that text, of which only roots of many lexical words and some "helping words"
remain. *Please pause briefly at the end of each sentence* [indicated by a period,
question mark, or exclamation point].

New York: 20 May–7 June, 11–13 September 2003; 20–27 April 2004

Feeling Down, Clementi Felt Imposed upon from Every Direction.

(HSCH 10)

Democracy imposed from without is the severest form of tyranny.
—Lloyd Biggle, Jr., "The Problem of the Gourmet Planet," *Analog,*
November 2003

Feeling down, Clementi armored herself against unwanted compliments.

The effects of painful desperation were imposing their influence, she felt,
  on every democracy.
She always felt worst for a crowd rightly punished for wrong reasons.

Could frugal Clementi have been beaming dispositive influences directly
  at others?
Had she, without a thought, imposed a negative influence on everyone
  near her?
Possibly, she supposed, someone of limited understanding had mistaken
  an ironic remark for a revelation.

Desperately, she noted, freedom competed with itself and murmured at
  opportunities imposed on it.
The dire effects of forced dependence were being repulsed by the desperate.
Indelicate competition in the midst of imposed democracy was imposing
  desperation.
Imposed democracy was imposing desperation.

Early on she'd recognized a great many sorts of pretended feeling.
Clementi had shamelessly declared compunction at the slaughter of fishes.
She wrongly supposed that no dependent would notice her myriad
  contradictions.
Wouldn't that have influenced her freedom's recognition?
She herself murmured at every opportunity imposed on her.

The tyranny of desperation was the crowning affectation imposed on her.
With delicate compliments she declared her objection to that desperation.
Was that when she declared imposed democracy a punishment?
She felt it a punishment greater than being found out
Clementi found that she'd been disposing noxious beams in all directions.
They directly revealed her own dependence and what she depended on!

How could she reply to what she revealed to herself?
All were insisting they were desperate for freedom.
But what seemed to be the effect of what they called democracy?
A myriad murmured desperately at every opportunity.
What could compete with that massive indelicacy?
Clementi had learned the effects of what was being called democracy.
She felt imposed upon from every direction.

Seven strophes of which the numbers of sentences in successive strophes follow
the sequence of cardinal numbers 1 through 7. Diastic text selection utilizing a mix
of sentences by Charles Hartshorne, Gertrude Stein, Lewis Carroll, and Gerard
Manley Hopkins as source text and the poem's epigraph as seed text produced a non-
grammatical text from which the author "took off" when composing the poem. Words
were modified, added, deleted, etc., as needed. Everything was tampered with.

New York: 9–13 October 2003; 14–15 April, 15 May 2004

♦

Waldoboro Poems

Introduction
by Anne Tardos

The title, Waldoboro Poems, is mine, not Jackson's. He wrote these last two poems of his life in Waldoboro, Maine, at Penelope and Robert Creeley's house, where we spent several weeks in September of 2004. As he relaxed in that beautiful place, he was moved to write again. When I told him how good it was to see him writing again, he said, "This isn't *writing*." And yet it is writing, his voice clearly audible. Soon after Jackson died, I sent a copy of it to the Creeleys, upon which Bob wrote "somehow his writing always is so close, as here I feel the whole fact of the house and ambience is there— as in reading anything he wrote, I felt him there writing it, and enjoying it."

14 September 2004   82 years + 2 days
Waldoboro, Maine

Trying to write is strange.
I haven't for more than a year, I think.
A rare car is whirring by, back of me, going to my left.
Nearest row of trees, several feet in front of me, and running offstage
    to my right.

Others farther in front at my left.

A mowed lawn going back until trees take over for good.

Both kinds of trees.

Nearly 12:30 P.M.   9/14/2004   JML

Still Waldoboro   Wednesday a.m.   9/22/2004

In the yard just beyond the red dying tree.

White butterfly swerving around in front of it and off in front and away.

Little line of bushes ends while the line of piled boulders swerves around
    and comes up to the wooden "gate" about ten feet to the right of me.

The pile of boulders goes on past the wooden "gate" and back of me.

A wild wind from my right.

The leaves of the dying red-leaved tree only move a tiny bit in the wind
    to the right, a few feet in front of me—just to the right of the front of
    the older part of the house.

It's a lovely nearly-autumn day in Maine.

Warm sunshine with a continuing intermittent little wind that stops and
    goes, mostly goes.

The little bit of Gerolsteiner is warming in the sun right in front of me,
    but I'm back of it in the shade.

Anne was here but she's gone inside.

I hear passing cars somewhere way to the right but they're far away in
    back at the right and invisible.

A bird squeaks in twos in front, and to the left.

Now one at a time, a different bird.

And feeble peeps at the far left and a very soft dump-tee-oh.

Don't ask what birds—they speak a little and stop.
Now a continuing *up* swerving *down* over and over
And a repeated tec-oo-*WEE* but never loud.
The German water's still a bit cool.
The wind's blown in first and on the back of my head and then on my left
   ear and now from the left and then from the front and then the back.
Two three white butterflies and a fly and a dragonfly that stops & then
   hurries away.

I'm going inside for a wee bit.
I dropped the cover for my pen in the grass in front of me, but Anne
   found it.
I'm not going inside yet because Anne's reading a book in the sun to the
   right & in front.

It's not quite autumn, but leaves are falling, especially from the tree
   with red leaves in front & to the right of the house.

A tiny yellow crawler on my sleeve before I blow it into the grass.

I didn't go inside before, but now I will, but not for long.

Autumn began today   Wednesday   9/22/2004

◆

Publications

1963. *The Twin Plays: Port-au-Prince & Adams County Illinois.* Mimeograph, New York: Mac Low and Bloedow. 2nd edition [JML's first printed book], New York: Something Else Press, 1966.

1964. *The Pronouns—A Collection of 40 Dances—For the Dancers.* New York: Mac Low and Judson Dance Workshop. 2nd edition, revised, with multicolored graphics by Ian Tyson, London: Tetrad Press, 1971. 3rd edition, newly revised, with new essays by Mac Low and photographs of 1st performances [1965] by Peter Moore, Barrytown, NY: Station Hill Press, 1979.

1967. *August Light Poems.* New York: Caterpillar Books.

1967. *Verdurous Sanguinaria* [play]. Baton Rouge, LA: Southern University Press. [omits Act VI]

1968. *22 Light Poems.* Los Angeles: Black Sparrow Press.

1969. *23rd Light Poem: For Larry Eigner,* with multicolored graphic by Ian Tyson. London: Tetrad Press.

1972. *Stanzas for Iris Lezak* [poems written 1960 for solo reading or simultaneous group performance]. Barton, VT: Something Else Press.

1974. *4 trains.* Providence, RI: Burning Deck.

1975. *36th Light Poem: In Memoriam Buster Keaton.* London: Permanent Press.

1978. *A Dozen Douzains for Eve Rosenthal.* Toronto: Gronk Books.

1978. *54th Light Poem: For Ian Tyson.* Milwaukee: Membrane Press.

1978. *phone,* with art by Ray Johnson. New York and Amsterdam: Printed Editions, Kontexts.

1978. *21 Matched Asymmetries* [group-performance poems]. London: Aloes Books.

1980. *Asymmetries 1–260* [poems written 1960 for solo reading or simultaneous group performance], with cover video image by Gary Hill & 3-color poem-superimpositions by Patricia Nedds. New York: Printed Editions.

1982. *From Pearl Harbor Day to FDR's Birthday.* College Park, MD: Sun & Moon Press. 2nd (Sun and Moon Classics) edition, Los Angeles: Sun & Moon Press, 1995.

1982. *"Is That Wool Hat My Hat?"* [four-color performance poem for four readers]. Milwaukee: Membrane Press.

1984. *Bloomsday,* with cover design & photos by Richard Gummere. Barrytown, NY: Station Hill Press [co-winner, San Francisco State University Poetry Center Book Award].

1984. *French Sonnets.* Tucson, AZ: Black Mesa Press. 2nd edition, with covers & endpapers by Anne Tardos, Milwaukee: Membrane, 1989.

1985. *Eight Drawing-Asymmetries* [serigraphs of 1961 verbal performance-score drawings]. Verona: Francesco Conz.

1985. *The Virginia Woolf Poems.* Providence, RI: Burning Deck.

1986. *Representative Works: 1938–1985* ["sampler" of poems, music, performance works], with introduction by Jerome Rothenberg and cover art by Kurt Schwitters. New York: Roof Books.

1989. *Words nd Ends from Ez* [derived by diastic text-selection, 1981–83, from Ezra Pound's Cantos], with cover art by Anne Tardos. Bolinas, CA: Avenue B.

1991. *Twenties: 100 Poems*, with cover art by Anne Tardos. New York: Roof Books.

1992. *Pieces o' Six: Thirty-three Poems in Prose* [written 1983–87], with cover art and videographics by Anne Tardos. Los Angeles: Sun & Moon Press.

1994. *42 Merzgedichte* in Memoriam *Kurt Schwitters* [written 1987–90] [co-winner America Awards for Literature for book of poetry published in 1994], with painting of Schwitters by Anne Tardos reproduced on cover. Barrytown, NY: Station Hill.

1996. *Barnesbook* [poems derived by a digitized text-selection method and revision from works by Djuna Barnes], cover art by Anne Tardos. Los Angeles: Sun & Moon Press.

1999. *20 Forties* [from the series "154 Forties," written and revised 1990–99], front and back covers by Anne Tardos, from a handwritten page by Mac Low. Tenerife, Canary Islands, Spain: Zasterle Press.

2001. *Les Quarantains (Extraits)* [five poems from the series "154 Forties," written 1990–95, translated into French by the Royaumont Translation Seminar. (Asnières, 1996); translation revised by Jackson Mac Low, Anne Tardos, and Juliette Valéry, who also took the cover photo]. Grâne, France: Créaphis and Collection Un bureau sur l'Atlantique.

2001. *Struggle Through* [3 poems derived by digitized methods from a poem by Andrew Levy in 1997], cover by Kristin Prevallet. Vancouver, B.C.: hole books and Tsunami Editions.

2005. *Doings: Assorted Performance Pieces 1955–2002* [a selection from a half-century of verbal, graphic, and musical scores for groups of many different numbers of performers, as well as soloists], cover art by Ian Tyson. New York: Granary Books. [posthumously published] ·

CDs

1991. *The Museum Inside the Telephone Network* (2-CD anthology), including *Com-*

munication(s) (Mac Low, 1990), realized by Anne Tardos, Curtis Bahn, and Mac Low. Tokyo: InterCommunication '91, Nippon Telegraph & Telephone, IC91-001, IC91-002.

1993. *A Chance Operation: The John Cage Tribute* (2-CD anthology), including *1st Four-Language Word Event in Memoriam John Cage,* composed and realized by Tardos and Mac Low. Westbury, NY: Koch International Classics, 3-7238-2 Y6x2.

1993. *Open Secrets,* 8 works by Mac Low, two collaboratively with Tardos, realized by Tardos, 7 instrumentalists, and Mac Low. NY: Experimental Intermedia, XI-110.

2005. CD included with the book *Doings: Assorted Performance Pieces.* New York: Granary Books. [posthumously published]

2007. Music by Jackson Mac Low and Anne Tardos, Recorded Live at Roulette, 1999. New York: Tarmac Books and Music. [posthumously published]

Credits

The editor wishes to extend thanks to the following journals and magazines that published still uncollected portions of this book. Every effort has been made to identify each previously published title, and any omission from this list is accompanied by the editor's sincere apology: *Avec; Chase Park; Conjunctions; Deluxe Rubber Chicken; Genesis West; The Gig; Inklings; Issue; Mantis; New York Quarterly; NOW; The Poetry Project Newsletter; Poetry Review; The Poker; Primary Writing; Shiny; Sumac; Talisman; Tight; University of California–San Diego Archives Newsletter;* and *words worth.*

Excerpts from
French Sonnets are reproduced by permission of Chax Press, Tucson, Arizona.
From Pearl Harbor Day to FDR's Birthday and *Pieces o' Six* are reproduced by permission of Sun & Moon Press, Los Angeles, California.
Les Quarantains (Extraits) are reproduced with permission of Un bureau sur l'Atlantique, Mérilheu, France.
Twenties and *Representative Works: 1938–1985* are reproduced with permission of Roof Books, New York.
20 Forties are reproduced with permission of Zasterle Press, Gran Canaria, Spain.
The Virginia Woolf Poems are reproduced with permission of Burning Deck Press, Providence, Rhode Island.
Words nd Ends from Ez are reproduced with permission of Avenue B Press, Bolinas, California.

Photos on pages ii, 237, and 238 by Anne Tardos, 1979.

About Jackson Mac Low

Jackson Mac Low (born Chicago, 12 September 1922; died New York, 8 December 2004) made poems, essays, and musical, performance, visual, and radio works. Author of about 30 books and published in over 90 collections, his works have been published, exhibited, and performed (often by his wife, the poet, visual artist, and composer Anne Tardos, and himself) in many countries. Awards: Guggenheim, NEA, NYFA, and CAPS fellowships, and the 1999 Wallace Stevens Award of the Academy of American Poets. Recent books: *42 Merzgedichte* in Memoriam *Kurt Schwitters* (1994), *20 Forties* (1999), *Struggle Through* (2001), *Les Quarantains (Extraits)* (2001), and *Doings: Assorted Performance Pieces 1955–2002* (2005).

About Anne Tardos

Anne Tardos is a poet, visual artist, and composer. She is the author of several books of poetry and the multimedia performance work *Among Men*, which was produced by the WDR, the West German Radio in Cologne. Examples of her visual texts were exhibited at the Museum of Modern Art, New York; the Venice Biennale; the Museo d'Arte Moderna, Bolzano; the New Museum, New York; and the Neuberger Museum of Art, New York. Examples of her audio works can be heard on several CDs and cassettes. She met Jackson Mac Low in 1975; the two lived and worked together from 1978 until his death in 2004.

Index of Titles

DESIGNER: SANDY DROOKER

TEXT: 9.25/14.5 NEW CENTURY SCHOOLBOOK

DISPLAY: NEW CENTURY SCHOOLBOOK, DIN

COMPOSITOR: INTEGRATED COMPOSITION SYSTEMS

PRINTER & BINDER: THOMSON-SHORE, INC.